# Loved and Feared

# Loved and Feared

Buddy McLean,
Boss of The Notorious Winter Hill Gang
During Boston's Irish Mob War

Larry Leavitt

Strategic Book Publishing and Rights Co.

Strategic Book Publishing & Rights Co., LLC
USA | Singapore
www.sbpra.com

For information about special discounts for bulk purchases, please contact Strategic Book Publishing and Rights Co. Special Sales, at bookorder@sbpra.net.

ISBN: 978-1-950860-12-8

*Loved and Feared* is based, in part, on interviews conducted with persons either involved or with direct knowledge of the events presented. Places and names used are the actual names as related to the author and represent the best recollection of those reporting.

# Acknowledgements

My father provided the initial impetus for this book. When I first mentioned the possibility to him, his reaction was, "Absolutely, who better to write about?"

For the early research, I am indebted to members of Teamsters Union Local 25. In addition, I spent many hours listening to the family and friends of Buddy. Those conversations began after some groundwork done by Elaine Linehan that led to conversations with Charlie McLaughlin, whose father, Bernie, is a central figure to this story.

Much information was gleaned from conversations with Jean McLean, Michael McLean, Bobby and Lea Caggiano, Kellie McLean, Tommy Kelley, and Sean Canty.

Jean McLean's sisters Joan and Mary, along with Joan's husband, Jim, provided some fond memories.

Some Charlestown perspective was provided by Jackie Mansfield, Billy Coleman, and Mickey Murphy.

Much of the credit for completing this book must go to my editor, Joe Ross, of Rosstrum Publishing. The lessons I learned from him were of great help. His main advice throughout the project was, "Show me, don't tell me."

He was right. Thanks, Joe.

I also owe many thanks to my daughter, Jen. Her advice on "showing" a story was a big help. Her creativity in organizing the photos for the book helped bring it all together.

I love you, Jen.

Other people who agreed to be interviewed requested anonymity. I respect their wishes.

I sincerely offer my apologies to anyone I accidentally omitted.

Larry Leavitt

The words written in these pages are with reminders of all the fathers who taught and helped their sons to become good, strong, stand-up men. Therefore, this book is dedicated to the memory of James E. Leavitt.

I love you, Dad.

# Foreword

The odds are high that most people will experience at least one confrontation in their lifetime. When faced with an aggressive antagonist, a person will react in one of three ways:

The most common response is to do nothing or freeze up. This is being passive and brings out feelings of fear and cowardice.

The second and much less common response is to become verbally aggressive. The confronted person makes threatening remarks and belittles the antagonist. Posturing occurs, and occasionally sloppy, physical violence follows.

The least common reaction is assertion. The assertive person will stand up for himself and others. An assertive person can clearly state his or her position and intention without disrespecting or threatening the aggressor. Assertive people are rarely intimidated. They tend to not look for trouble, but when it comes their way they are prepared, and they respond. When a person this smart and this prepared is pushed too far, he/she can become dangerous.

The words and actions of Buddy McLean are the epitome of assertiveness.

# Somerville's Favorite Son

*July 9, 1949*

It was a sweltering hot morning at the Charlestown Navy Yard. The sun was just beginning to rise over Boston Harbor. An inexperienced New Hampshire native, Lieutenant Michael Ross, was the day's base officer. Sweat poured through his shirt, despite the early morning hour. He was irritated as he worked on the reports that ruined his plans to spend the day with his girlfriend at nearby Revere Beach. He continued to wipe the sweat from his brow between strokes of his pen.

*What a rotten place to be at six o'clock on a Sunday morning in July,* Ross thought as he grabbed his pen and clipboard and began the walk from his office to the infirmary. He had to interview four sailors recovering from the battering they had received the previous night at the Alibi Club in Charlestown. The Alibi was a hotspot nightclub located on Main Street, just outside Charlestown's action-packed City Square. The club and the square were within walking distance of the Navy Yard.

Ross entered the room where the four were lying in beds, side by side. Their injuries were extreme: two concussions, one broken nose and jaw, several bad facial and neck lacerations, the result of being launched through the passenger-side window of a parked Oldsmobile. In addition, there were a few fractured ribs, a broken clavicle, a sprained ankle, and numerous cuts and bruises.

The attending physician merely nodded when Ross asked permission to interview the victims. Ross woke the sailors and demanded to be informed. "Okay, tell me right now. What the hell happened to you guys?" The men tried to look at each other but remained mute. The superior warned, "You better speak up, and fast, or you'll never leave this yard for the rest of your days in the Navy."

With his chin resting on his chest, and eyes looking at his hands, one sailor spoke up and admitted, "Some guy in the bar beat the shit out of us."

The officer's jaw dropped as he asked, "One guy?" The pen and clipboard cluttered as they bounced off the floor.

The sailor tried to nod. "Yeah, Lieutenant. One guy, but I've never seen anyone like him. He was strong, and fast, and tough as a nickel steak."

It took Ross a moment to comprehend, then he asked, "Four against one, and you guys end up here. How the fuck was that possible?"

The sailor, apparently the spokesman of the group, replied meekly, "It started as a one-on-one fight outside the club. Sonny was totally overmatched, so we tried to break it up. Next thing you know, we're all fighting him, but he wouldn't go down. I never saw anyone so tough. Then he started getting some shots in, and it's going back and forth, and finally he wore us down. Then he keeps going, and we ended up here."

"Wore you down? What? Were you guys falling-down drunk?"

"Yes, sir, we were all drunk, but not that bad. This kid was unbelievable, I swear to Christ."

"Kid? Was he big? Did you get this fuckin' kid's name?" inquired the officer.

The sailor said, "No, sir. He's young, and he was hanging with some longshoremen. I think he's from Somerville. Someone might have called him Buddy."

\* \* \*

The sailor-slamming fireball who single-handedly put four men in hospital beds was James J. "Buddy" McLean. He was a longshoreman from Somerville, a blue-collar, hardscrabble municipality a bit north of Boston. At the time, Buddy McLean was becoming well-known throughout Greater Boston as a talented street fighter.

His hometown was the most densely populated city in New England. Somerville has a long history of great high school basketball teams, but it was also home to many dangerous street toughs who liked starting trouble and picking fights. People residing in Somerville were brought up to be competitive, assertive, and aggressive.

At nineteen years old, Buddy McLean had already proven himself to be the best puncher in Somerville, where even the strong influence of the heavily attended Catholic Church was barely able to contain the fierce, bloodthirsty spirit of the predominantly Irish and Italian parish. Now, even at that age, his reputation as a terrific street fighter was beginning to spread throughout the area. Without seeking recognition, the young, unassuming, physically fit, baby-faced Irishman began his ascension to the title, "toughest guy around." A product of his own hard-hitting East Somerville environment, he fought to get by in a location where violence was a common occurrence. As he became more celebrated, the challenges accelerated.

It was also at about this time that the young scrapper organized a few of his close friends into a makeshift crew to pilfer assorted goods from several Boston ship docks.

The cohorts not only respected, but they idolized McLean. On top of that, they had absolute trust and loyalty to him. Eventually, he built a larger following. Years later, a Boston newspaper writer would label them the "Winter Hill Gang."

## July 12, 1949

A rookie Somerville police officer named Ed Kelly and his veteran partner were having a slice of pizza at Raymond Grande's Regene Pizzeria on Winter Hill. The new cop began asking questions about the young street fighter.

"Bill, you know anything about this kid, Buddy McLean?"

"Sure. Everybody knows him. Why?"

"I heard he put four sailors in the hospital the other night, messed them up real bad."

"Yeah, I heard about that, too. What about it?"

"Is this guy for real? I heard he's a young kid and not all that big."

"All true. I hope you're not looking to fight him."

"No," the rookie replied, "I just want to find out who the hell he is and anything else I should know about him."

"He's a jaw breaker and a law breaker. But he's a great guy, and everybody around here loves him. Isn't that right, Ray?"

The shop's owner responded from behind the counter, "You got that right. He's a hell of a nice kid."

Bill continued, "He's always a complete gentleman; never says a cuss word. He's a little on the quiet side, but he's friendly and very generous, and I'm not lying when I tell you he'd give you the shirt right off his back. He fights a lot, and he has sailors down at the Navy Yard and tough guys coming from all over New England to try him. No one can take him. He never starts fights, but he doesn't avoid them either. And he ends most of them pretty damn quick. I think he likes pounding all those wiseass brawlers who want to take him on, but he won't talk about it. He never brags. Like I said, he's quiet, right, Ray?"

"Yup, great kid, and quiet, too."

"What about the law-breaking part?"

Bill nodded. "Him and his pals swipe goods off the docks over in Charlestown. That's where they work."

"Longshoremen?"

"Yup, unloading the ships coming into Boston. Then they sell it real cheap over here."

"Nobody bothers to arrest him for this?"

"Hell no!" Bill laughed. "In fact, most of the cops buy things from him. And he gets good stuff. I'll introduce you to him sometime."

*May 10, 2004*

Long retired and elderly, the former Somerville police officer, Ed Kelly, was sitting in Leone's Pizza, across the street from where Regene Pizzaria used to be. Over a thick slice of pepperoni pizza, he reminisced to a group of young Somerville cops about the city's once favorite son.

"McLean was unbelievably popular during the fifties and sixties. More than any athlete, movie star, or entertainer, he was the obsession around here. People by the carloads, from miles around Boston, driving up Broadway, right out there," he said, pointing in the general direction of the plate glass windows along the street beyond. "And all with high hopes of just getting a look at him. There were so many, I couldn't put a number to it. He had scars on his head and neck from all the fighting, but he was a real good-looking guy. Lord, he fought so much. And he was always in great shape. Not big, but he had all these muscles popping out. He had a washboard stomach, too. Hundreds of young women, hanging out their car windows, waving and screaming, 'Oh my God! There he is! Hi, Handsome; Hi, Buddy; Hey, Good-Looking; Marry me, Buddy!'"

The cops all had a good laugh. The old-timer continued, "He'd just smile at them and wave back, unless one might become a nuisance. Then he'd let her know, 'Sorry, darling; I'm already married.' He was no goody two-shoes. He did a lot of bad things. But he did a hell of a lot of good things, too. He had a few issues with the Somerville PD, but he got along well with most of the cops in this city. But, not all of them. I'd rather not talk about those assholes. I liked Buddy. He was always nice to me and to my family."

A young patrolman spoke up. "Ed, you make him sound like the best thing that ever happened in Somerville."

"He was the greatest man I ever met."

"He did some nasty shit, though."

"Yeah, he did. But the fighting was all brought on by people who made him angry. And believe me, Buddy McLean was the last guy you wanted to make angry. But, all that aside; he probably was the best thing that ever happened to this city. Crime rate was down when he walked the streets." Kelly smiled. "Except, of course, for the crimes Buddy and his pals were responsible for. But I tell you, the wiseass punks and the bad guys were leery of him."

One of the other young cops responded, "So he was popular and everybody loved him; but, at the same time; he was a crime boss, a killer, and he beat the shit out of hundreds of people. Is that right?"

"It's Somerville, for Christ's sake, the toughest city anywhere. The population was a hundred twenty thousand back then. A lot of crime and violence was happening here every day. He had to fight. They came looking for him. And for those who were living around here during the fifties and sixties, Buddy McLean was the most familiar name in this city."

"He could have been the mayor?"

"Easily. However, there was always that underlying fear—don't get him mad. Anyone who crossed Buddy McLean was going to see his dark side."

"I heard he wasn't that big and that he didn't look like a fighter," stated another cop.

"Like I said, he was a very handsome and well-groomed man. And no, he did not look like a fighter. But he had a long, lean build, five feet eleven inches tall, and one hundred seventy-five pounds with sixteen-inch arms, a forty-three-inch chest, and a thirty-inch waist. He worked out, all the time. And he had large, strong hands, made for fighting."

"So, he was in decent shape, but not that big."

"He was always in great shape, very fit, always ready to square off. And many men, with much more size than Buddy, either backed down or took the beating of their lives. He fought hundreds of times, and he never lost."

*July 12, 1949*

During that same evening, when Officer Bill Walsh was teaching rookie Ed Kelly about Buddy McLean, a group of men were a few blocks down the hill, toward Charlestown, sitting on a front porch drinking ice-cold bottles of Budweiser. The house they were drinking at was directly across the street from Foss Park. The men all worked in the Teamsters Union, Local 25, in nearby Sullivan Square, Charlestown. Dave Adams, the man who lived in the house, had invited his coworkers over to have a few beers and to show them something cool.

"All right, Dave. You got us all over here. Now what?"

"Hang on a minute. Drink your beer, it won't be much longer," responded Dave.

"This better be good. I'm gonna miss the first couple races down at Wonderland."

"Then I'm doing you a favor; too,' cause you fuckin' never win."

All the men had a good chuckle. Then Dave stood up as he looked out at the park. "Okay. Here we go, boys."

"What?"

"Here he comes, right on time."

All the men were looking across toward the park as a lone figure came closer.

"Hey, it's Buddy McLean. What's he doing here, and why's he wearing a sweat suit in this heat?"

"This is why I called you guys over. You all get to watch him work out."

The men became stone silent as they studied McLean beginning to go through his paces. He started with a quick set of jumping jacks, then ran a couple of laps around the park. On the first lap, he waved to the men on the porch as he trotted by. They all waved back and shouted, "Hi Buddy." Then he stopped and performed one hundred perfect push-ups and the same number of sit-ups. When he finished the sit-ups, Buddy jumped up and took off running at a quick pace.

"Jesus, look at him go. He's fuckin' fast," remarked the dog-track gambler.

"Like a bat out of hell. Where's he going?" asked another man.

"He runs all the way out to the Stone Zoo and back," replied Dave. "He'll be back in about an hour, and he'll get down for more push-ups and sit-ups. Can you believe all those push-ups? You got to see him on the jungle gym, over there. He does pull-ups like there's no tomorrow. If it's not snowing or raining, he's out there every day after work."

"How far is it to the zoo?"

"Five miles. Course, don't forget, if you run five miles out, you gotta run five miles back, too."

"Holy crap, that's unbelievable."

"Let's have a few more beers and wait for him to come back," suggested the greyhound gambler.

"I thought you were going to the track?"

"Nah, this is more fun."

"And less expensive," added Dave.

As the men were sipping their beers, a car full of young women pulled away from the curb next to the park.

One of the Teamsters remarked, "Those chickies are beautiful. I wonder what they were doing over there."

"Same thing we were just doing," replied Dave.

"What?"

"It happens all the time, people from all over come down here to watch him work out."

"You're shittin' me."

"Nope."

"And he's here every day?"

"No, he'll change it up sometimes. But wherever he trains, he goes at it real hard, and people stop and watch."

"Wow."

"Yeah, I asked him one time why he works out so hard. He told me, 'A fight might come my way anytime or anyplace. I have to be ready.'"

"He does fight more than anyone I know."

"Yup, every Friday night he's down at the Alibi. He stands at the front door so that if a fight is gonna happen, it's taken outside. He doesn't say much. He just waits there with his friends. Some brave or crazy bastard always comes by to try him. His reputation gets bigger every week. Navy Yard sailors, local boxers, huge, tough men from all over Boston, they come by, looking to make a name for themselves. Most of them get carried away or they are rushed to the hospital."

"Dave, have you ever seen him fight?"

"Yeah, I've seen him go a couple times—it's unbelievable."

"Why? What's he do?"

"It was the same thing both times, full speed ahead, no retreat. He punches fast, hard, and non-stop. He never gets tired, and he can take a punch, too. Someone told me that McLean does not mind getting hit and that he rather enjoys the contact. It brings out the best of his Irish temper and pushes him to fight harder."

# All Heart

*November 22, 1959*

As well-known as he was as a street fighter, Buddy also had a reputation for extreme generosity, especially with children.

On the Sunday afternoon before Thanksgiving, Buddy pulled his big box truck into the enormous Mystic Avenue projects. He had his son Jimmy with him. Buddy raised the back door to his truck, then lifted Jimmy into the back.

"Okay, Jim; you keep stacking the boxes at the edge while I deliver them."

"What if somebody grabs one when I'm not looking?"

"Look how many we have, Jim. They'd be helping us get rid of them."

Right away, the projects began buzzing with anticipation. Janice McKenzie answered a phone call from her neighbor, Doris Delaney.

"Hi Janice, it's Doris. Guess what?"

"I don't know. Tell me."

"Buddy McLean is going around handing out turkeys and pies."

"Oh shit! I better jump in the shower."

"There's no time, he'll be at your place in a few minutes. Just brush your hair and throw on some makeup and perfume."

"Damn it, my house is a disaster. I want to invite him in for coffee. What should I do?"

"I'll run over and help you get ready. That way, I get to see him again."

"All right, but hurry up."

## July 3, 1960

On a steamy hot Sunday afternoon, Buddy rounded up his children for a walk down to the projects. Once they arrived, the family was swarmed by hundreds of project kids. "Mr. McLean is here! Mr. McLean is here!" The children knew they were in for a treat—free ice cream.

"Let's get a line going right here, kids. Then everybody gets one."

"You've got a heart of gold, Buddy," said one of the project mothers.

"My pleasure, Doreen."

Buddy would have it set up so that two fully packed ice cream trucks met him at the playground in the projects. After every child was taken care of, Buddy gave the drivers a generous cash tip, along with footing the entire bill. "Here you go, fellas. I'll give you a call in a week or so, and we'll do it again."

"Anytime you want us, Buddy, we'll be there. You're the best guy around, Buddy. Thanks again."

"All right, fellas, I'll see you guys soon."

The drivers loved Buddy, not only for the gratuity, but also for the huge volume of ice cream they were able to sell in less than one hour.

## August 6, 1960

Alice McInnis was a hardworking Somerville woman who held down a full-time job as a waitress at Mike Khoury's State Spa on lower Broadway, along with taking care of her three-bedroom apartment in the Mystic Avenue projects that the widow and her nine children occupied.

Buddy and his wife, Jean, had been friendly with Alice for a few years and knew about her financial problems. Jean urged, "Buddy, why don't you stop by Alice's apartment and see if you can help her out?"

"That's a good idea."

"That poor woman has a tough life."

"All right, I'll take a ride over."

While he was there having a cup of coffee with Alice, Buddy took note of how clean the apartment was kept, but also noticed the old and worn furniture. At the same time, he wondered how she could organize the family's daily routine.

"Alice, I don't know how you do it."

"What's that hon?"

"How do you work full-time and keep this house so neat and organized?"

"The kids all have chores to do, with a schedule to keep, and everybody pitches in, even the little ones."

"Wow, that's great. You run a tight ship here, Alice."

"Yeah, well, that's the way it has to be. What other choice do I have?"

"You're right."

"Why do you want to know all this? You writing a damn book or something?"

"I'm not writing anything. I'd just like to help you out a little around here."

"What do you want to do? Sweep the floor?"

Buddy laughed, "No, I just want to buy a few things for the family."

"God knows, we could use a few things here and there, but you don't have to do that."

"But I want to."

"Well, we'd be grateful for anything you can do."

Buddy went out and bought all new furniture for the entire apartment: bunk beds, bureaus, chairs, sofas, a television set, a dining room set, a new refrigerator, vacuum cleaner, a new bedroom set for Alice, and much more. Buddy had it all bought and delivered to her apartment the same day.

When the huge furniture truck pulled away from the apartment building, and when all was said and done, each child had a separate bed and bureau, a seat at the new dining table, and enough seating for everyone to watch TV at the same time. The dwelling became known throughout the projects as "Alice's Palace."

And Alice McInnis was always quick to tell anyone who would listen, "He's the sweetest man I ever met."

# Growing Up in Somerville

Buddy was born out of wedlock in Boston, January 26, 1930. The mother abandoned the baby, and the father was unable to assume responsibility. He was raised by an East Somerville woman named Mary Rapoza.

20 Radcliffe Road

Bill McLean, a Boston longshoreman, would stop by the Rapoza home on Radcliffe Road once a week to drop off some money and spend a few minutes with his son.

"The kid looks like he's doing pretty good, Mary. I appreciate you taking him in."

"Don't mention it, Bill. I love this boy. You can come by anytime. You're his father. Someday, he's going to need your help."

"I will, Mary, thank you."

This went on for many years. Eventually, Buddy and his father developed a stronger relationship.

## January 3, 1951

Buddy met his birth mother, Dorothy Guider, shortly after he got married. She was looking to acquire some money from her hard-working son.

"You turned out okay, and you look like you're doing pretty well for yourself. What do you think? Can you help your ma out?"

"What do you want?"

"A couple hundred dollars. I fell behind on the rent."

"Yeah, I'll help you, but you are not my ma. You gave that job up a long time ago."

He never heard from his birth mother again. Mary Rapoza was the woman he loved as his mother. He always called her "Ma."

# Calling Him Buddy

During the toddler years, Buddy was routinely surrounded by Rapoza family members. The Earles and the Hendersons were either living at or often visiting the three-family apartment home.

It was Mary's nephew, Harold Earle, a young, rugged Somerville truck driver who took note of the way everyone shared a liking for the fine-looking, well-behaved lad. He anointed the young McLean with the nickname "Buddy." Of course, the tag stuck, and from then on that was how he was referred to.

Starting in kindergarten and lasting through his junior high school years, Buddy conducted himself as a gentleman, but he was never one to allow bullying toward himself or his friends. Buddy stood up to kids in the higher grades more than a few times. Bigger, older kids learned it was not worth the effort to pick on Buddy McLean, for the simple reason that he would not quit in a fight and that he could go all day. Years of learning from and competing with the elder, athletic, and tough Earle and Henderson children had provided Buddy with a head start to deal with the elementary school bullies and the hoodlums of East Somerville.

*October 3, 1941*

When Buddy was in the final year at Foster Elementary School, a teacher recommended him to the principal for duty as a crossing guard in front of the building.

17

"I need someone good out there. It's chaotic after school lets out."

"I think McLean is your guy. He's responsible, he's intelligent, and most of the kids are afraid of him."

Buddy, 1941

"Why is that?"

"He can beat the shit out of any one of them."

"Hmm, that might be what we need out there."

The principal agreed and gave the desirable assignment to young McLean. Buddy was also known as a serious individual, and he was stern with the other students when he performed his duties. However, sometimes he could be a bit rough around the edges.

During the first week of his assignment, Buddy was confronted with some disorderly behavior.

"Hey, Rizzo, I told you, you got to cross in the crosswalk."

"I ain't no kindy-gartener, McLean. So fuck off."

Rizzo and his friends were laughing hysterically when one of them warned, "Here he comes."

Buddy rushed up to Rizzo. "What'd you say to me?"

"I said, kiss my ass!"

As Rizzo turned to his friends for approval, he received a heavy slap on the back of his head. One of Rizzo's friends started toward Buddy and was met with a mind-jarring right cross to the face. Two sixth-grade punks were down and crying in less than three seconds.

When Rizzo and his friends complained about Buddy getting physical with them, the principal simply advised the lads, "McLean is in charge out there. Do what he tells you and quit your crying. Now get the hell out of my office."

\* \* \*

The sixth-grade Rizzo boy that Buddy slapped had an older brother who showed up in the schoolyard the next day at dismissal time. The fifteen-year-old and a few of his pals followed Buddy out to the front of the building, taunting him every step of the way.

The older brother asked Buddy, "You think you're tough, picking on these little kids, McLean?"

"They're my age, and I only straighten out the ones who got it coming."

"Yeah? Well now you're going to get fuckin' straightened out. What do you think about that, tough guy?"

"I'll fight every one of you guys, right after I finish my duty."

"No. Right now, you little shit."

The eleven-year-old McLean asked, "Who wants to go first?"

The older Rizzo said, "Me."

Buddy squared off with the teen, and as the boy threw a wide roundhouse right-hand punch, Buddy ducked and charged forward, driving his right shoulder into the teen's midsection while lifting his legs from behind the knees. Rizzo slammed his head on the pavement as he fell back. Buddy was on Rizzo before he had a chance to recover. Punches rained down on the boy's face. Rizzo whimpered and tried to cover up. One of the other teens attacked from a forty-five-degree angle behind Buddy and kicked him in the ribs.

"Hmmph," Buddy grunted as he absorbed the kick and wrapped his arm around the second teen's shin and rolled onto the leg, hyperextending the second teen's knee. As number two toppled back in a heap, Buddy continued forward in a somersault roll and ended up sitting on number two's chest. Two hellacious blows landed on number two's face before the third teen charged in and grabbed Buddy from behind by his hair and pulled back. As Buddy was being yanked away, he grabbed number two's ears. Teen number two screamed, "Ahh fuuuck. Let him go," to his friend, which the third teen did. In an instant, Buddy was standing and ready to go at it with the third teen, who raised his hands, palms facing Buddy, and started to back up. A swarm of over one hundred children gathered at the scene, cheering on their crossing guard and taunting the teen bullies.

"Get him, Buddy."

"Kick his ass."

"What's the matter? You guys scared of a sixth grader?"

"Yup, they're a bunch of cowards."

The first two boys made it to their feet and called to the third teen, "Eddie, let's go."

"Yeah, go home, you fuckin' mama's boys."

As the bullies were making their departure, Rizzo promised Buddy, "We're not going to forget this, McLean. Your days are numbered."

Without speaking, Buddy sprinted straight at him like an attack dog and hit the unsteady teen with an all-out body slam. Down hard for the second time in less than two minutes, the first teen was defenseless as Buddy sat on his chest, grabbed each side of his head and bounced it off the sidewalk.

"This fuckin' kid is tough," said one of the other two teens as they stayed back a few feet.

"What are you guys going to do to me?" asked McLean.

"Nothing, McLean. Stop, please. It's done. Let me up," sniveled the older boy.

As Buddy rose to his feet, the sixth-grade Rizzo boy, who had dispatched his older brother to beat up Buddy, yelled out from the crowd, "You're a dirty fighter, McLean."

"Who's calling me a dirty fighter?" a snarling McLean demanded.

The younger Rizzo brother ran for his life.

# The Formative Years

*April 6, 1943*

After school one day, Buddy was approached by his friend Martin "Pushka" Murphy.

"Buddy."

"Hey, Pushka. How are you?"

"Good. Hey, my cousin Vinny works over at Fay's Strapping, and he told me they're looking to hire some kids. What do you think?"

"Yeah, sounds good. Count me in. What about Howie and John?"

"Yeah, they can come, too. The company needs the help."

The two boys and their friends John Hurley and Howie Winter landed coveted jobs working at Fay's Strapping Company in Somerville. The employment consisted of strapping and loading boxes that were being prepared for shipment nationwide. It was Pushka's cousin, Vinny Murphy, who helped the youngsters start their careers in the workforce. Vinny was a well-respected mechanic at Fay's Transportation, owned by the same family that had the strapping business. When he observed how well the boys were doing at Fay's, he called a friend who worked in the Teamsters Union. "Artie, is Durago's still looking for dockworkers?"

"Yeah, they are; Vin. Do you have someone?"

"I have four young kids. They're about thirteen or fourteen, but they really hustle. You should bring them in."

"What are they doing now?"

"Working at Fay's Strapping, but we both know they can do better with the Teamsters."

"Thirteen, I don't know."

"They work as good as anybody you have down there, trust me. Plus, you guys need the help."

"If they're so good, why are you trying to get rid of them? Do they steal?"

"No, Art. Listen, one of them is my cousin. You will love these kids. I promise."

"All right, I'll tell the old man."

In 1943, most of the Boston men ages eighteen to twenty-five were away, serving in World War II. Thirteen-year-old Buddy McLean jumped at the opportunity to work for Teamsters Union Local 25 in Charlestown. A Somerville man named Arthur O'Rourke helped Buddy and his friends get started. Arthur was a valued Teamster truck driver who later became the secretary/treasurer for Local 25. John Hurley, Pushka Murphy, and Howie Winter stayed for a short time. They developed other interests and only filled in occasionally. But Buddy kept at it. He worked every time there was an opportunity.

The work schedule for young McLean was mostly late afternoon and sporadic weekends. The assignment consisted of loading, unloading, and sweeping out trailers at Durago's Trucking in Somerville. The labor was physically taxing, but it paid exceptionally well—twenty dollars per trailer to unload and sweep. Another twenty for loading outgoing freight capped off the young Highlander's workday. (The nickname for Somerville High School's athletic teams is the Highlanders.) Moving steadily and with a sense of urgency, Buddy completed his daily assignment in less than four hours, almost an hour ahead of the older men doing the same work.

## February 4, 1944

One afternoon, the dock supervisor watched as his crew was unloading trailers: *That young kid is the best one here. He's faster and more careful than anyone else, always the first one done. And none of his freight is ever missing.*

"I wish I had ten more workers like you," said the supervisor to Buddy later in the afternoon and in front of the other employees, who were taking a break, "then this place would really be humming."

After the boss had walked away and was out of earshot, one of the men loading trailers with Buddy walked up to him and threatened young McLean. "You're making us all look bad. You better slow it down."

"I think you should work faster, or else you might be out of a job," responded Buddy.

The other men laughed. The man who threatened Buddy grabbed him by the shirt, balled his other hand into a fist by his shoulder, and warned, "Either you do what I tell you, or I'm going to knock your fuckin' teeth out."

Buddy instantly and violently shoved the man back. "Let's go, right now." The recently turned fourteen-year-old McLean was ready to duke it out with a man ten years older, six inches taller, and fifty pounds heavier.

Another man watching the confrontation stepped in front of Buddy and spoke starkly to the dockworker. "You're not going to touch this kid again. If you do, I'm going to knock you out. And that's a good thing, 'cause it saves you the embarrassment of him knocking you out."

"That little shit ain't gonna fuckin' knock me out. I'll kill the little cocksucker."

"You already know he can outwork you. That makes him stronger and faster than you. And the kid has heart, something you'll never have. He won't quit in a fight until you're down and out. You leave him alone and go do your job, or, I promise, you'll be leaving here a lot uglier than you already are."

The laborer sneered at Buddy for a moment, then walked away. He never bothered Buddy again. The man who stepped in on Buddy's behalf was Billy McCarthy, a tough, hard-working Somerville resident who was twelve years older. Billy was a Teamster truck driver who would stand up against any injustice without hesitation.

Afterward, Buddy mentioned to Billy, "I appreciate what you said, Billy, but I can handle that guy myself."

"I know you can, kid. I was saving that asshole from you beatin' the shit out of him."

They both had a good laugh; and they became great friends from that day forward.

## April 7, 1944

On a cold evening, Buddy was just finishing a trailer when Harold Earle happened to walk by him.

"How's it going, kid?"

"Good, Hal. How are you?"

"Good. Hey, do you think you might want to learn how to drive a truck someday?"

"You bet. When can I start?"

"I'll talk to my boss and let you know."

"Wow. Thanks. I'll be ready."

Once he was tall enough to see over the steering wheel and to comfortably reach the pedals, the eager-to-learn, teenaged

Teamster was taught how to drive tractors around the yard. Earle was big, burly, loud, and intimidating, but those who knew him considered him a good man. He was the same Rapoza nephew who gave McLean his nickname, and he became Buddy's driving instructor on weekends. He taught Buddy how to drive a rig in the yard at Durago's when business was done for the day. Buddy was a quick study, and, after he had a good feel for moving the eighteen-wheeler forward and around the yard, young McLean learned the skill of backing in and dropping trailers. He became proficient at utilizing his side-view mirrors when backing straight to a dock and in judging the distance between the rear of the trailer and the dock.

"Take it slow," instructed Harold softly to Buddy as he began backing the tractor-trailer toward the loading dock. "Keep it nice and straight, and touch that dock evenly. There you go, that's very good, now pull forward fifty feet and do it again."

Eventually the youngster was backing the trailer between two other trailers spaced one open dock space apart. Harold had Buddy repeat the task many times so that he became confident with the rig. Then Harold had Buddy pull the big truck up parallel to the dock and perpendicular to two trailers one space apart. "Now you're going to turn out like you're on the street, and you're going to back in between these trailers. There's going to be blind spots that you'll have to get used to. But we can stop and get out and take a look the first few times. But soon you'll be able to back in without having to get out and look."

"Okay, Hal. Whatever you say," responded Buddy.

Buddy loved the work. He relished every chance he had to drive trucks in the yard and earn high wages from unloading and loading the trailers. He looked forward to the physical challenge of handling the heavy freight.

When school was dismissed, Buddy would go straight home, place his books on a table in a corner of the dining room, go out to the kitchen, and have an afternoon sandwich at the table as he chatted with Mary Rapoza.

*April 25, 1944*

"How was school today, dear?"

"It was good, Ma."

"Did you learn anything?"

"Nothing important."

"What's important to you?"

"Making lots of money."

"How are you going to do that?"

"Driving a truck."

"Really? Don't you want to aim a little higher?"

"Sure. Maybe someday I'll own my own truck and start a business for myself."

"Now that sounds ambitious. I'd be happy to see you in business."

"Yup. I have to go, Ma. I'll see you later."

After chugging down his glass of milk, Buddy flew out the back door, hopped on his bicycle, and pedaled off to Washington Street in Somerville. Other days, he would bike over to Charlestown, where, despite his age, lack of size, and experience, he outworked men in their twenties. The grueling manual labor strengthened the young lad's body, character, and bank account. He enjoyed his job and the compensation. It set him on a path toward the goal of financial independence. It was Mary Rapoza who instilled a strong work ethic in Buddy. He maintained that frame of mind throughout his life.

# Jean Kelley

*October 17, 1944*

One balmy afternoon, Buddy was talking with his friends John Hurley, Howie Winter, and "Pushka" Murphy outside after school. The four boys abruptly halted their conversation as a shapely girl came walking by.

Buddy smiled at her and said, "Hi there. What's your name?"

"Jean Kelley."

"I'm Buddy McLean. Do you live around here?"

"Right down the street. What's your friends' names?

"Oh, you don't want to know them. They're bad news."

"Maybe I don't want to know you either," said Jean as she began to walk away.

"This is John, Howie, and Marty, and we're all good guys. I was just kidding," Buddy stated anxiously.

"Do you want to walk me home?" Jean asked.

"M-m-m-me? Sh-sh-sure!"

From that moment on, Buddy and Jean began seeing each other. In the beginning, they had many movie dates at the Capitol Theater on Broadway. Although he was athletic, Buddy was not much of a dancer.

After a school dance, Jean told her sisters, "I had to pay some guys to cut in because he was stepping on my toes."

They all laughed, then one sister remarked, "He's so handsome, though."

"Yeah, he is," answered Jean. "And he's a gentleman, but it's too much. He's a pain in the ass."

*November 5, 1944*

Another Somerville girl named Joan Vercellini went on a date with Buddy to the movies.

"He was very nice," recalled Joan to four neighborhood friends a few days after the date. "Just a kiss on the cheek."

"He's seeing Jean Kelley, too," said one of her friends.

"Listen, every girl on Winter Hill has a crush on Buddy McLean. If he asked any of you to the movies, who would say no?"

None of the girls answered.

"He'll end up going steady with Jean. She has that fabulous body."

"That's probably how she'll win Buddy," laughed one of the girls.

They all nodded in agreement.

*August 12, 1945*

"Buddy, are you almost ready?" asked Mrs. Rapoza on a bright Sunday afternoon.

"I'm ready, Ma."

"Set the table, would you, dear?"

"All right, Ma."

"And don't forget to set a place for Father Hogan."

"I know, Ma, I'm the one who invited him over, remember?"

"That's right. Sorry, dear."

"Don't worry about it. Hey, me and the Father can eat on the front steps."

"Heavens, no!"

"And then we can throw the football around in the street."

"You will do no such thing."

"I'm only kidding with you, Ma."

"He'll be here any minute," said Mary as she walked into the dining room to see Buddy setting the table. "You two have been friends for a while now."

"Yeah, ever since I started helping him at Sunday Mass. He's a good guy, Ma."

"What were you two talking about after Mass?"

"We were talking about those bombs that were dropped on Japan last week."

"What did the Father have to say about that?"

"He said it was a tough decision for Truman to make, but that he thinks that the president did the right thing."

"But what about all those innocent people, children, burned. My God, I hate thinking about it."

"Father said, 'Japan is tough. They weren't going to quit.' Then he told me, 'Over five million more Japs would have had to die before they would give up. And it would also mean that a million more Marines would die. And on top of that, Japan tortured and killed a million people when they invaded China.' I have to agree with the Father on that one, Ma."

"You're probably right. He's here," said Mary, looking out the front window. "Let's not talk about the war during dinner, okay, dear?"

"All right, Ma. I'll save it for the front steps."

Through the influence of Mary Rapoza, Buddy became a religious and loyal parishioner at Saint Benedict's Church in East Somerville. He volunteered as an altar boy for a few years and would help take in money collections every Sunday. He looked up to Father Hogan and saw him as a fine advisor and a knowledgeable teacher. The priest later became a great friend and a confidant during Buddy's adulthood.

When Buddy obtained his driver's permit at fifteen, he drove a pickup truck for the electric light company in Somerville. Due to the war, there was a shortage of workers. Because of that, Buddy could drive around town with just a permit. The work was only temporary, but he saved up enough money to buy his first car and a motorcycle.

*February 2, 1946*

On his first long-distance excursion with the new car, he ruined it on a return trip from visiting a friend in Bangor, Maine. According to Buddy, "Some guy driving a logging truck cut me off on the turnpike, and I went off the road and rolled it over."

The car was totaled, but Buddy was not injured.

# Daredevil

On an early Sunday morning, Buddy was sitting on his motorcycle at the side of the street on the Somerville side of the Craigie Bridge. The engine was running. He had a few friends with him.

"What are we doing here?" asked John Hurley.

"Relax, you'll find out."

A boat came down along the Charles River and what little traffic that was around was stopped by the bridge operator. As the bridge began to rise, Buddy told his friends, "This is it; boys," and he began to rev the engine.

"What are you doing?" screamed Hurley.

When the bridge angled up to twenty degrees Buddy took off around the idled traffic and toward the bridge. At almost twenty-five degrees the bike zoomed up the rising bridge.

"There he goes. He's fuckin' nuts."

Flying at seventy miles per hour and traveling airborne for close to one hundred feet, McLean landed safely on the Cambridge side of the bridge as it continued to rise.

He spun the bike around and smiled at his friends, who were shaking their heads in disbelief.

Later that day, Buddy's friends spread the word around Somerville about his leap over the Charles. When Jean found out about Buddy's escapade, she told him, "I'll never get on that damn thing with you, you crazy bastard."

# The Teamsters

*May 11, 1946*

Throughout their mid-teen years, Buddy, John, Howie, and Pushka worked for Fay's Transportation and in the Teamsters Union with Durago Trucking. They loaded and unloaded freight, but they also made local deliveries for Fay's throughout Greater Boston. For the local drop-offs, the Somerville teens drove a midsized box truck. It was a nice opportunity for them to gain experience delivering freight and to show responsibility.

As they glanced at their paychecks one Friday afternoon, the boys noticed that they had received a raise. "You see this; fellas? This means they like us. They want us to stay. Just keep doing what we're doing, and we're gonna have a lot of money."

"You think so; Buddy?" asked John Hurley.

"Yes. These guys will remember us. And someday we might have a business, and they might want to help us out a little."

His pals smiled and nodded in agreement.

It was during the time, while working for Durago's Transportation, that Buddy became an outstanding truck driver. From Local 25 Teamsters Union drivers Pat Culligan, Harold Earle, Arthur O'Rourke, and Billy McCarthy, Buddy received expert training in moving tractor-trailers. He enjoyed listening to the men talk about truck driving. He developed a fascination for trucking and wanted to be taught everything there was to know about it.

## June 19, 1946

Late in the afternoon, a few truckers were gathered on the loading dock at Durago's. They were drinking beers while they talked about their day and their plans for the weekend. Harold noticed Buddy standing nearby and invited him over.

"What are you still doing here?"

"I just finished sweeping the trailers."

"You want a beer?"

"Sure, thanks."

Arthur asked Buddy as he sipped his beer, "How come you're always around when we're here?"

"I like listening to you guys talking about truck driving."

"Is that what you want to do?"

"Yup. As soon as I can, and who better to learn from than you guys?"

The men smiled and nodded as they listened to the young McLean. When Buddy finished his beer, he thanked the men and said, "So long." He jumped off the dock, got on his bicycle, and began pedaling home for dinner.

"There's something about that kid. I never met anyone like him," stated Billy.

"You're right, Bill. He's a one of a kind," said Pat.

"Yeah, he's smart, hardworking, and he's a nice kid," added Arthur.

"Mary did a nice job with him. She raised him from a baby. Now he wants to be one of us. I say we take him in," finished Harold.

The men nodded in agreement.

*January 10, 1947*

After a year and a half of training, all of Buddy's teachers agreed he was ready to go out on the road. Arthur O'Rourke decided to go in and talk to his employer. He knocked at Durago's office door.

"Come in."

"Hi, Boss. You got a minute?"

"Yeah, sure. What's up, Arthur?"

"It's the kid, Buddy McLean. You know we've been training him."

"Yeah, how's it going?"

"He's great. We think he's ready."

"How old is he?"

"Seventeen."

"That's too young. We can't have a young kid like that driving freight over the road. We'll lose business, or even worse, we'll get sued."

"Mr. D, you know you can trust me, and I would never steer you wrong. This kid is the real deal. He's as good as any of us right now, and, pretty soon, he's going to be better than all of us. You don't want to lose him. Someone else will grab him if we don't give him a chance. I'm telling you, he's going to make us look great. Give him one chance, you won't be disappointed."

After a short, silent moment, a deep breath, and a long sigh, "All right, Arthur. I'll send him out to Worcester, but I'm gonna have a supervisor sitting next to him."

"That's great, Boss. You won't regret it."

Buddy made the delivery without a problem. The company sent someone with Buddy two more times. Both times, the assignment was performed flawlessly.

At that point, Buddy was dispatched alone. It was a sight never seen before or, most likely, ever again. People stared in disbelief at the seventeen-year-old boy embarking on long journeys, driving a tractor with a forty-foot trailer in tow. Once the Durago customers observed and evaluated his driving and delivery skills, they began to request him. "Yeah, next time you have a delivery for us, have the kid drive it out here." They found Buddy to be courteous and very reliable for his age.

And whenever Buddy received praise for his truck driving skills, he deflected the accolades to his trainers. "I owe it all to those guys. They took me into their group when I was a young kid and knew nothing. They made me one of them. They're great guys, and I'll never forget that."

And despite all the time he spent training and working with the Teamsters and playing sports with his friends, Buddy was having a nice relationship with Jean. Though he was no longer a student, Buddy took Jean to her prom.

Prom night, 1947

*October 1, 1947*

Arthur O'Rourke was a good friend and advisor to Buddy. During a ride home one evening, he tutored Buddy. "When you are traveling in bad weather, make sure you stay in the lane that most of the traffic is driving in. This will help prevent you from slipping and sliding off the road. And take your time. Don't be in a hurry. The main thing is to get there safely. Before you leave the terminal, make sure you inspect the rig. Check everything. Always double-check the back door to see if it's secure and locked. Check all your lights, your brakes, your hitch, your tires. I routinely check under the hood to see that all the fluids are topped off. There's nothing worse than breaking down in the middle of nowhere."

"All right. Good. I'll make a complete inspection before I take off. What else?"

"Always try to stay on the highway as long as you can. It's quicker and safer. Even if the traffic is slow or backed up, unless they detour you off the highway, try to stay on it."

"What if I know a side road or a shortcut?"

"No, stick with the highway. A lot of times, the side roads are more congested than the highway because everyone is thinking shortcut. Just stay with the direct route, you'll get there eventually."

"Okay, what else?"

"You have to have good maps in the cab with you, especially when you are delivering out of state. If you think you're lost, pull over and look at the map. Make sure your flashlight batteries are working and keep spare batteries in the cab. Put on your gloves before you get out of the cab. You never want grease on your hands. It's not professional. I have a baseball bat under the seat, and a lot of guys carry handguns. Have your license and registration handy in case you get pulled over."

"Okay, I'll remember all that. Is there anything else I should know?"

"Yeah, you have to know the union contract like the back of your hand, so no one pulls the wool over your eyes. And make sure to vote in all Local 25 elections and in national elections. It's important. Don't forget."

"I won't."

"I'll remind you."

"All right. Hey, if you're not doing anything Friday after work, my Ten Hills team is playing against a bunch of guys from Cambridge."

"That sounds good, I'll tell the rest of the guys."

# He Coulda Been Great

*October 3, 1947*

On a late Friday afternoon, two Somerville High School football coaches chatted in their office after the players had gone home from practice.

"Joe, where are you going now?"

"Home, why? What's up?"

"Drive down to Foss Park. There's a big pickup game starting in a few minutes. I want to show you someone."

"Who is it?"

"The kid's name is Buddy McLean."

"I know him—tough kid. He quit school last year."

"I know all that. Have you ever seen him play football?"

"No. Is he good?"

"He's fuckin' fantastic. He breaks people in half, and he's not just playing against kids. He's down there banging the shit out of college players, and other good players from all over Boston."

"Is he a linebacker?"

"Yup, he's the best I've ever seen."

"And he never played organized football. Too bad he didn't stay in school. I'll take a ride down there."

*October 9, 1960*

On a late Sunday morning, a large congregation of men had gathered at the Capitol Bar on Winter Hill. The men were discussing the bets they had made on that afternoon's upcoming football games. One man, a behemoth nicknamed Ox, loudly asked, "How come McLean never bets on these games? His wife won't let him?" He "hee-hee-haw-haw" laughed at his own joke.

John Hurley marched up to Ox and threatened him with, "You shut your fuckin' mouth or I'll shut it for you."

"No, you won't, Hurley, and neither will your tough friends. I'm working for the McLaughlins now."

"Then why the fuck are you in here?"

"It's a free country, I'll go wherever I want."

"You'll leave now on your own or you'll be leaving in an ambulance in about a minute."

Ox looked around the room. He did not see a friendly face. "Fuck all of you assholes. I'll spend my money down in Charlestown."

He slapped a twenty-dollar bill on the bar, stood up, and walked out. After the front door closed, one man asked Hurley, "Why doesn't Buddy ever bet?"

The silent barroom listened intently. Hurley slowly shook his head. "He doesn't bet 'cause he hardly ever wins. Bad luck. That's all it is."

"Is that because he doesn't understand the game?"

"Fuck no. He just knows the odds are against him, and he'd rather do other things with his money. And let me tell you guys something, Buddy was a great football player."

"I don't remember him playing in high school," stated one man.

"That's because he dropped outta high school when he was fifteen, but he played around Somerville, and he was fuckin' great. I mean it."

"You grew up with him, John. What was he like? How good was he?"

"On offense, he was a fast, hard runner, and he could throw the ball sixty yards, perfect spiral. He had good hands, too. On defense, he was even better. He'd fire through the line and blitz that fuckin' quarterback like he wanted to kill him. Scared the shit out of all of them. He loved hammering the quarterback to the body, using only his shoulders. He hardly ever arm tackled anyone. His hits were major fuckin' collisions, and he would have been a tremendous player in high school. But, his goal in life was always about making money, ahead of playing sports and also, eventually ahead of going to school. The Teamsters got him started. That's why he's such good friends with them."

# The Rise of a Street Fighter

*December 6, 1947*

Bill McLean came by Mary Rapoza's house on a Saturday afternoon to speak with his son.

"I can get you some part-time work on the docks if you want it."

"As a scalawag?"

"Yeah, but if you stay with it, eventually you can get in the union. You can make a good living down there, and it's a hard job to get."

"Loading and unloading ships."

"Yeah. It's hard work, but you can handle it. I might be able to get a few of your friends some work, too."

"All right, I'll do it. And I'll see if some of my pals want to work."

Along with the full-time job he already had with the Teamsters, Buddy began working on the precarious, often unruly and violent docks of Charlestown and East Boston. Until this point in his life, Buddy had not been in many hard-core fights. Most of his scuffles were schoolyard scrapes, neighborhood disagreements, or brawls before, during, and after football games. He was known as a strong, tough kid, but the Boston ship docks introduced young McLean to life-threatening abuse.

*December 19, 1947*

A group of beefy, card-carrying ILA (International Longshoremen's Association) thugs enjoyed beating and extorting the scalawags (nonunion workers). When the gang confronted him on payday, Buddy refused to concede.

"I earned my money. I'm not giving you guys a dime."

"Oh; really?" asked the gang leader.

"That's right. Now get out of my way."

The five big men surrounded Buddy. The leader pushed Buddy back into another man's bear hug. The gang rat-packed him, taking turns punching and kicking the teen when they had him down. They took his money and his new jacket and warned young McLean to, "Keep your fuckin' mouth shut and never give us any shit again, or next time it's going to get worse."

As he slowly struggled to his feet, Buddy watched the men walk away, laughing as they piled into a car. With his face badly swollen, bruised, and bloody, he turned and walked away. Tears began to streak down his cheeks. He was disgusted with himself. *How could I let this happen?* His body began to shiver as he walked home in the frigid, cold Boston weather. Passing through Sullivan Square, Charlestown, into Somerville, Buddy anguished over the beating he took. A fury within him began to rise. Bothered to no end, but not sure what to do: *I can't tell anyone. I'm no rat. But I'm not going to take this. I have to get even. I'll get a gun and shoot every last one of those bastards.*

A few days later, Teamster truck driver Billy McCarthy, Buddy's friend from Durago's Trucking and by then a union representative of the Local 25 Teamsters Union, bumped into Buddy coming out of old man Raymond Grande's pizza shop.

"What the hell happened to you?"

Looking down, then away, Buddy replied, "I really don't want to talk about it."

"Well I do. Now go back inside."

They sat at a table and Billy started, "Tell me the whole thing, right now."

When Buddy finished, Billy advised, "Don't shoot the bastards. You'll end up rottin' in jail for the rest of your life."

"What should I do then?" asked Buddy.

"Be smart, be alert, and be aware, at all times. Know where they are. Be ready. You can outrun them if you have to."

"I don't want to run. I want to fight back."

"There's too many of them. Why don't you start working out at the Y then? It'll put some size on you and make you stronger. Then, when those bums try to pull some shit, they'll get more than they bargained for."

"Yeah, I will, but what should I do in the meantime? How do I keep them off me?"

"Hang with your pals and people you trust. Don't get caught alone. Don't carry too much money on you. Have your old man give you the money at home, not on the dock. Be ready to run if you have to. You want me to come down there with a few of my friends?"

"No, I'd rather handle it myself. I don't want someone else fighting my battles for me."

"I like that. It's better that way. You'll get even one day."

Buddy nodded in agreement. He shook hands and hugged his friend. He then looked forward to making himself bigger and stronger.

He did not waste any time. He joined the Y that same day. Buddy took to his workouts with enthusiasm. He spent all his free time lifting weights and punching the heavy and speed bags at the Somerville YMCA.

Somerville YMCA

*January 2, 1948*

A well-known Somerville man named Joe McDonald had just returned home from serving in World War II. McDonald was a decorated Navy veteran, and he also worked out at the Y. He was twelve years older than Buddy and, at that time, "Joe Mac," all five feet, seven inches of him, was considered the toughest man residing in Somerville. The war veteran noticed Buddy torturing himself in the gym every day for a week. One afternoon, McDonald decided to approach the youngster.

"Hey kid, you want to work the bag with me today?"

"Yeah, sure."

"Let's go."

After getting acquainted, Joe Mac gave Buddy some advice, direction, and coaching, which seemed to step up his progress

Joe McDonald

and confidence. Then he showed the eager-to-learn teen the benefits of long-distance running. They began running the track inside the Y.

"You got to have lungs that don't quit. The worst thing that can happen to you in a fight is you get tired."

"Let's go then."

The Somerville YMCA had an elevated, banked wooden track, which ovalled around the basketball court. In each of the four corners were mounted punching bags, two with speed bags, and the other two had hanging heavy bags. There was a good-sized weight room and a long, tiled swimming pool. In the winter of 1948, this building became Buddy McLean's second home.

When he was not working at the Charlestown Docks, Durago's Trucking, or for Fay's Transportation, Buddy was at the Y. The East Somerville teen made a quick upgrading to his physical conditioning, including his strength, speed, endurance, and punching ability. He developed hard calluses on his hands from performing endless pull-ups and on his knuckles from punching the bags bare-handed. He became a master of push-ups. From Joe Mac's tutelage and encouragement, Buddy exhausted himself with military push-ups, one-hand push-ups (switching from one hand to the other), and handstand push-ups (with his feet braced against a wall).

One afternoon, drenched in sweat and gasping for air, young McLean made his way to the bubbler and began gulping the cold water. As he came up for air, the attendant in the gym warned Buddy, "Slow down, kid, you're going to make yourself sick."

"I'm fine."

"Yeah, well if you're gonna throw up, get to the bathroom."

Buddy headed back out to the track. *Keep it going. Don't stop.*

Buddy saw Joe McDonald waiting for him. *This guy is awesome. I'm lucky to know him. He's helped me develop these skills I didn't know I had. Thank you, God, for bringing us together.*

Joe Mac was an excellent boxer. He taught Buddy basic combinations and had him repeat the sequences many times in front of a mirror, on the hand pads, and on the heavy bag.

He instructed Buddy, "Push off your back foot when you're throwing straight punches and pivot on the ball of your front foot when you are transferring your weight from your left foot to the right foot for a left hook. Turn your left hip, let the hip bring the arm around. Make perfect circles when you throw your left hook to the head or to the body."

Then they worked at executing powerful uppercuts. "I want you to work from a slight crouch and drive your legs and body up when you fire uppercuts. Don't let your hands drop; just lower your body a little bit, then shoot upward." These intricate improvements doubled the strength of Buddy's punches.

*Geez, this guy sees everything*, thought young McLean as Joe Mac harped on him. "Keep your feet spaced shoulder-width apart, with your left foot a walking step ahead of the right."

He constantly reminded Buddy to, "Teeter on the balls of your feet, keep your chin down, bite down on your teeth, breathe through your nose. Hands up, chin down! Elbows in, feet close, teeter, relax, relax, breathe, then be quick, be quick! Explode when you see the opening. Don't waste any punches, make them all count. That's it. Keep doing it, just like that. Repetition, over and over again, until it becomes second nature. We're looking for perfection."

*This is great, just do exactly as he says. He knows this stuff inside out.*

The finishing touch was the wisdom Joe imparted after one Saturday morning workout. He put his hands on Buddy's shoulders and squeezed firm. He looked hard into the eyes of his young protégé and told him, "It's going be a big mistake for someone looking to start a fight with you. Just remember this: when it happens, you don't stop punching. No matter what happens, you never stop."

Joe's words were simple and direct. Buddy felt a rush of awareness and confidence that penetrated the core of his soul. The master had instilled a sense of warrior spirit in his young disciple.

From that moment on, Buddy knew, *Joe McDonald is the best friend I'll ever have.*

"Okay, Joe," Buddy responded, "I won't forget. Thanks for helping me." He then grabbed Joe and hugged him. "Thanks again."

Joe told Buddy, "It's better if you take care of those bums yourself. But you let me know what happens. Keep me informed."

"I will."

# Who the Hell is That?

*February 13, 1948*

Buddy had been avoiding the dockyard goons. Now, after six weeks of training with Joe McDonald, he felt ready and was anxious to run into them. It happened outside on the Charlestown docks, during a lunchtime break. Buddy was with a group of friends and coworkers. He was sitting on a four-foot stack of pallets eating a sandwich when he spotted the leader of the gang and his enforcer approaching.

"You see who's coming?" asked a young coworker.

"I see them."

Buddy's heart began to race. His breathing became shallow. He felt the burning sensation of adrenaline on the back of his neck, and his hands began to tremble. He placed his hands on his thighs—the sandwich was still in his right hand. He glared hatred at the two men as they walked toward him, yet he remained motionless. *Don't stop punching, don't stop.*

The leader spoke to Buddy, "Where've you been, kid. We've been looking for you. You owe me some money. Fork it over."

Without uttering a word, Buddy suddenly frisbee-snapped his sandwich into the leader's face and sprung onto the enforcer. Although the enforcer was much larger, Buddy immediately overwhelmed him with a ferocious attack. Wham. Bang. Boom. Left jab, right cross, left hook, all to the head. Bang, bang, bang. Hard, continuous shots to the body.

"Holy shit, look at that," shouted one of the workers.

As the big man backpedaled, McLean unloaded two dozen machine-gun punches to the man's head and body. In seconds, Buddy had the enforcer down and on his back, and he kept firing away.

"What the fuck? He's going to fuckin' kill him," yelled another spectator.

The gang leader was momentarily stunned by Buddy's speed and aggression. As a crowd closed in to watch the assault, the leader gathered himself, pulled out his longshoreman's hook from the ring fastened to his belt, and ran up behind Buddy. The leader reached back with his hook and was about to start his forward-downward swing on Buddy when, from the sideline, Buddy's friend Tommy Ballou rushed in and sank his hook into the leader's right trapezius muscle. The crowd stood frozen. They were shocked at the split-second, vicious violence that was taking place in front of them. As Buddy was pounding away at the dazed and defenseless enforcer, his concentration was interrupted by an ungodly scream. "Shieeee fuuuuckk!"

Tommy Ballou

Reacting to the gang leader's ear-piercing shriek, Buddy turned and went after him. He grabbed the hook with both hands and ripped it from the man's shoulder. While the leader was on his knees emitting deafening screams, Buddy held the hook with his right hand and walloped a left uppercut under the man's chin, dropping him to an unsteady sitting position and ending the whaling. Then he began hammering the leader's head with the curved steel until he was flat on his back and unconscious. The seemingly crazed McLean hovered over his captive, intending to kill him. He gave the bloody, motionless gang leader a few more blows to the head with the hook as Ballou managed to prevent a homicide by pulling Buddy away from his tormentor.

Not certain about what was going to happen next, Buddy pushed away from Tommy to be ready for a possible second wave of hooligans. Breathing heavy and rotating himself within the circle of longshoremen, Buddy scanned the crowd for another attack.

"Come on! Who's next? Right now!"

No one said a word to Buddy or moved toward him. The large circle of men slowly began to disperse. As they did, one said to another, "Unfuckin' believable."

Buddy threw the longshoreman's hook end over end a good distance into the harbor, then he and Tommy quickly and quietly walked away, leaving the two browbeaters crushed and bloody.

As they were walking away, Tommy quietly said to Buddy, "That was fuckin' great."

With his body still shaking, Buddy responded, "Yeah, it felt pretty damn good, too."

In less than one minute of nonstop, near-death violence, Buddy McLean's life changed forever. Word spread fast. Strong, heavy-duty, unbreakable longshoremen looked at the polite, quiet kid with the lightning-fast hands and treated him differently.

Many became courteous and respectful to the young scrapper. He started gaining more friends.

\* \* \*

The next morning, Buddy could not wait to tell Joe McDonald about his conquest at the dock.

"Joe, it was unbelievable, everything that you said was going to happen, happened. Those guys are done."

"Hold on a minute. I'm glad you took care of those bums, but now you have to watch out that they don't try to sneak up on you. Make sure you have plenty of friends with you all the time down there, guys you can trust so your back is always being watched."

"You mean like Tommy Ballou?"

"Yeah, him, and get a few others. Have your own little crew of friends who have balls and are ready to fight. Then you guys always stick together. And another thing . . . there's going to be other guys who won't accept the truth about what happened, and they will challenge you. So be ready—that is also going to happen."

*February 18, 1948*

Sure enough, Joe's prediction came true. Buddy took note of those sizing him up among the older, bigger, nonbelieving longshoremen. There were several who did not consider that the baby-faced newcomer had dismantled the gang. He had continued his intense, time-consuming sessions with Joe Mac at the YMCA, knowing he had to be ready for any retaliation or challenge.

Almost on cue, more than a few barrel-chested, broad-shouldered roughnecks demanded their turn. Buddy obliged every one of them, but made sure he had Tommy Ballou, John

Hurley, and a few other pals watching his back. Ballou would be credited a few years later for coining the well-known description of Buddy McLean: "He looks like a choirboy, but fights like the devil."

Buddy got banged around a bit when trading punches with some of the older hard-hitting longshoremen on the waterfront, but, through his physical conditioning and indomitable spirit, he wore down each opponent. The young scrapper also discovered that he could take another man's best shot and not miss a beat. After a little more than a year, and roughly two dozen matches, it was common knowledge that the toughest of the six hundred men working on the Charlestown docks was Buddy McLean.

He was eighteen.

# An Introduction to Crime

*April 29, 1948*

On an early, warm evening, as he was heading home after work, Buddy passed a group of men loading large boxes into the trunks of their motor vehicles. One of them said to young McLean, "Hey, Buddy, this one's for you," and handed him one of the boxes.

"What is it?"

"Cigars. Cubans. You can get a hundred bucks easy at any smoke shop in Somerville."

Buddy threw the box on the front passenger seat of his car and headed for home. At the first cigar store he came upon on Broadway, Buddy pulled over. He walked into the shop and placed the box on the counter. The owner asked, "What the hell is that?"

"Cubans, fifty boxes in the case."

"Where did you get them?"

"Hot off the docks."

"I'll give you a hundred bucks for it."

"No, two hundred."

"You fuckin' punk, you think you're coming in here and telling me how much I'm going to pay?"

"We both know two hundred is a bargain. If you don't like it, I'll try your competitor up the hill."

"I'll give you one-fifty."

"No deal, I'm out," and Buddy grabbed the box and turned toward the door.

"Hold on, hold on. I'll give you the two hundred," said the shop owner as he pulled a wad of cash from his front pocket.

Buddy stuffed the money in his front pocket and exited the shop. He jumped in his car and drove home. He walked in through the back door to the kitchen, where Mary Rapoza was preparing dinner.

"Hi, Ma, what's for supper?"

"Steak and potatoes, dear, how was your day?"

"Good, I have something for you."

"What is it, hon?"

"This," and he handed her one hundred dollars.

"What is this? Where did you get this money?"

"Down at the dock. It's bonus money, Ma. They gave me two hundred dollars. I'm giving you half of it, and I want you to go out and buy something nice for yourself."

"Oh my. I can't. You shouldn't, please, Buddy."

"Ma, you've always taken care of me. It's time I started doing things for you. Let me give you this money—it will make me happy."

"All right, dear, thank you," and she began to cry.

Buddy smiled and walked into the living room. He picked up the phone and dialed his father. After Buddy explained what happened, Bill McLean told his son, "Yeah, it happens all the time. We can't control it. Just be careful you don't get caught. You would lose your job. It's very hard to top a job on the docks."

"Okay, I'll be careful. See you tomorrow."

Though he appreciated the extra cash, Buddy did not have much faith in the aptitude of some of his cohorts. Nor did he trust them. He decided to go in a different direction.

*June 22, 1948*

On a bright, eighty-degree afternoon during a lunch break, Buddy ran some thoughts by his friends John Hurley and Tommy Ballou. They were sitting on a bench looking out at the massive, green-steel Tobin Bridge, spanning across the calm flowing Mystic River, the bustling Boston Harbor beyond it. A slight breeze came off the water, cooling the young men. As Buddy finished his sandwich and drink, he turned to his pals and suggested, "Why don't we start doing our own planning."

"Planning for what?" asked John.

"For grabbing stuff off the docks."

"What's wrong with the way it's going right now?" asked Tommy.

"Think about it. We're taking orders from guys who aren't that bright, not very careful, and I don't really trust them. Plus, we're the ones taking all the chances and doing all the work. They just drive off and sell it. I seriously doubt that we're getting an equal share of the profits."

"What do you want to do then?" asked Hurley.

"I know a guy over in Cambridge who has a warehouse and some trucks. He'll let us use the place and a couple trucks anytime we want. He'll even have his guys drive for us if we want. We'll have to give them a cut, but we can work out of their warehouse and sell our stuff in Somerville. How's that sound?"

Tommy and John looked at each other, raised their eyebrows, smiled, and nodded in agreement.

"When do we start?" asked Hurley.

"The next time there's something good coming in."

"Yahahh!" boomed Tommy.

*June 26, 1948*

On a Saturday afternoon inside Raymond Grande's pizza shop, Buddy asked a few trustworthy pals, "How would you guys like to make a little extra money?"

"Sure, Buddy," exclaimed Russ Nicholson, "what do you got?"

"Different things down on the dock. It could be anything and everything. We just grab it and sell it, fast. Do you guys want to get in on this?"

Russ, Howie Winter, and a few other young men looked at each other and nodded. "When do we start?" asked Russ.

"I'll let you fellas know. Just be ready to go."

Buddy's handpicked circle of friends were smart, smooth, quiet, and fast. The stolen freight was usually moved to a warehouse on Warren Street in East Cambridge. From there, the merchandise, whatever it might be—shoes, sneakers, coats, tires, cases of tuna, anything they could move quickly—was sold at a discount rate. It was a simple method that was lucrative, and the chances of getting caught were slim.

Buddy was the mastermind. He would plan and organize the group. Then they would grab the merchandise and make a clean getaway. They became very effective at pilfering merchandise from Boston docks.

*August 7, 1948*

After a morning workout with Joe McDonald, Buddy updated his advisor on the progress of his shipyard larceny business. "Yeah, Joe. It's going pretty good so far."

"How's it working out with the guys in Cambridge?"

"It's been perfect. Thanks for introducing me to them. We use their warehouse, their trucks, some of their men. It's worked out good."

"All right, let me know if you need anything."

"I will, thanks. You don't want to get in on this?"

"No, that's your business. I have my own affairs to attend to."

"Okay, Joe, I'll have to find someone else to help me move all those diamonds I grabbed the other day."

"Don't be a wiseass."

Right from the start, Buddy's business was off and running. His days became extremely busy. He possessed both Longshoreman and Teamster membership cards. Plus, his group was putting together a nice string of successful pilfering. The cash flow seemed endless. Although he did not care for it, Buddy was becoming well known. People respected his intelligence and the boldness he displayed in planning and executing each heist.

That was the beginning of the Winter Hill Gang.

# Businessman

*August 9, 1948*

Early Monday morning, at a local diner, a Somerville trucker named John Canty approached Buddy. Canty was a Teamster working for J.J. Minnihan in Charlestown. He was also on a waiting list to become a Somerville cop.

John Canty

"Hey, Buddy. How are you?"

"Good, John. How are you?"

"I'm all right. Hey, listen, I want to give you a heads-up. The cops are going to start looking into the heists down at the docks."

"Oh, yeah?"

"Yeah. There's a lot of pressure coming down from the statehouse because of all the customer complaints."

"So, we'll start seeing other uniforms on the docks, and not just the security guards?"

"Not only uniforms."

"Detectives?"

"Yup, undercover, meaning they will be disguised as longshoremen. Any new face down there could be a cop."

"All right, John. Thanks."

Just as Canty had warned, the police started an investigation. Although the inquiry came to a dead end, Buddy resolved to try something else.

### August 13, 1948

Buddy decided to become a legitimate businessman. After a Local 25 union meeting had wrapped up, Buddy gathered a few Teamsters together.

"I want to buy a truck and start making deliveries."

"You want to start up a company?" asked a Somerville Teamster named Bobby Mahoney.

"Yeah, what do you think?"

"I'll do it with you, Buddy."

The two young Somerville men started Traveler's Transportation, a trucking company that later became known as Columbia Transportation. Howie Winter also became a partner. Beginning with one rig and operating out of South Boston, the three partners took turns making deliveries up and down the East Coast and all the way out to the West Coast. Buddy was somehow able to hold down his two other jobs, working on the docks, and driving a truck for the Teamsters, without disrupting his side business. He was always on the go and did not get much sleep. Mary Rapoza warned him, "If you keep that up, you're going to work yourself into an early grave."

"I'm making good money here, Ma. You should be happy about that."

"I know you're doing very well for yourself, and I appreciate the money you contribute to the house every week. I just don't want to see you get run-down, that's all."

"It'll be fine, Ma. I'm the last guy you have to worry about."

"I'm very proud of the hardworking man you've become."

"Thanks, Ma."

*Hopefully, she never finds out about the other stuff.*

# Reckless

*September 16, 1948*

More stuff came along. On a cloudy, cool weekday afternoon, Buddy and Tommy Ballou were about to make their way home from South Boston. They had just finished their work assignment for that day, which was loading lobsters and ice on a truck destined for New York. They happened to be walking past a large box truck packed with cases of liquor. The truck was parked near the exit of the Southie trucking combine. The driver had left the door of the vehicle open and the engine running while he went into the dispatch office to pick up some paperwork.

Inaudibly but excitedly, Tommy urged Buddy, "Let's take it."

With a stern look, Buddy asked him, "Are you crazy? The driver is right there," pointing to the man in the window with his back turned.

"Maybe I am, but we can't pass up an opportunity like this. C'mon, let's grab it."

"We're probably not going to get very far."

"Are you fuckin' kidding me? The way you drive? They won't catch us. We can sell this to every bar in Charlestown and Somerville. Come on, this is a major score. Let's do it. You drive."

With reckless abandon, the pair scrambled into the truck. Buddy shifted it into gear and hit the pedal as the driver was walking out of the dispatch office. He screamed at the teens, "What the fuck you kids think you're doing? Stop that fuckin' truck right now."

Buddy gunned it out of the combine. He waved to the enraged driver as they left the yard.

Not more than two blocks down the street, they encountered their first Boston Police squad car on Summer Street. The squad car, coming at them in the opposite direction, swerved in front of the box truck. Buddy, in turn, swerved around the squad car and proceeded to zoom down Summer Street as the speedometer nudged past sixty.

"Wow, nice move. I'm glad you're driving."

"Yeah, me too. Now hold on tight."

Roaring past South Station, Buddy pulled a hard right turn onto Atlantic Avenue and accelerated along the Boston waterfront toward the North End. Passing cars, he weaved in and out of traffic. The police pursuit continued north on Atlantic. At the intersection of Atlantic and Northern Avenue, a second squad car joined in the pursuit.

"We've got more company," exclaimed Tommy.

"I know; I saw him. We're not going to be able to outrun them. I'll try and shake them in the North End."

"Those streets are narrow. And crowded. We might have to abandon ship."

"Not just yet. Let's see what happens."

"Holy fuckin' shit. Did I ever tell you, you have big brass balls?"

"No, you never mentioned it."

"Well, I'm telling you right now. You got big ones. You're one of a kind all right."

"Yeah, let's talk about that later. This is going to get real tight now. Hold on."

With the Boston Police hot in pursuit, Buddy thundered the big box truck into the North End. Tommy had his nose out the open window. "Hmm. Smell them sausages," he exclaimed.

"You want to stop and get one?" asked Buddy.

"Can we?"

"The cops will probably insist on joining us," replied Buddy.

"I guess I can wait," chuckled Tommy.

The squad cars pursued the liquor truck into Boston's North End. After cornering an inflexible right bend on Atlantic, Buddy cut a sharp left turn onto Richmond Street and floored the pedal. A quick left-right put him on Parmenter Street. At the intersection of Parmenter and Hanover, Buddy cut it hard to the right, catching the right sidewalk on the turn, which lifted the truck onto the two left wheels. The friends leaned all their weight to the right to regain control and see around the corner. At the same intersection, the lead squad car slammed into an automobile driving down Hanover Street that Buddy had barely missed.

Tommy leaned out his window and looked behind. "That's one down," he yelled.

"There might be more coming, and stay inside. You don't want anybody to get a good look at you. I hope nobody recognizes us."

With one cruiser still after them, Buddy floored it up Hanover Street as horrified North End residents gawked from both sides of the busy street. After powering the truck seventy-five yards up Hanover Street, Buddy maneuvered a hard left turn onto Prince Street. As he floored the pedal, Buddy blared on the horn all the way down the hill to warn drivers and pedestrians. He rumbled the big truck the wrong way on a one-way street. At the end of Prince Street, he veered close to the left sidewalk for a suicide left turn onto Commercial Street.

"Oh shit-shit-shhiiit!" bellowed Tommy as Buddy grabbed him and leaned all their weight to the left as the truck banked the corner, barely missing the brick building and the light pole on the sidewalk. The vehicle veered across Commercial Street onto the right sidewalk, slightly scraping a brick wall before returning to the street.

The second squad car was not as lucky. The cop lost control of the vehicle and rammed into another automobile that was driving northeast on Commercial Street.

"The second one's gone, too," reported Tommy.

"Keep looking for more," answered Buddy.

Buddy sped the truck onto Commercial Street for a quick, wide right turn onto and across the Charlestown Bridge. He zipped through City Square in Charlestown, where he saw a patrolman on foot who seemed oblivious.

"Eyes straight ahead, Tommy."

"Yup."

Continuing through Charlestown on Rutherford Avenue at a reduced speed, Buddy and Tommy kept looking around for more police cruisers. There were none. They made it through Sullivan Square and into Somerville, where they pulled in and backed up to a loading dock behind the gigantic First National Supermarket Distribution Center next to the Mystic River.

"I know some guys here who'll help us out."

Buddy quickly organized a few friends at the center to help them unload the truck and reload the cases of liquor onto two smaller box trucks that belonged to First National. After emptying the large box truck, Buddy moved it to the far side of the lot, where he quickly wiped it down for fingerprints. The truck would be recovered later by the Somerville Police.

"Okay, Tom. You and I are going to get the hell out of here."

"All right, pal, let's go."

Then, Buddy and Tommy drove the small box trucks to the warehouse on Warren Street in Cambridge, near the Somerville line. They unloaded the cases of liquor at the warehouse and returned the box trucks to the First National Distribution Center.

As the pair walked away from the empty trucks, Tommy remarked, "Wow, that was unfuckin' believable."

"Yeah, we got lucky. I'd rather not talk about it until we get rid of all that booze."

"All right, pal."

"Let's just hope that nobody recognized us."

"Right."

"And I think we should stay out of Southie for a while."

"Good idea."

Buddy and Tommy began soliciting bar and liquor-store owners in Somerville and Charlestown, offering large discounts on the stolen alcohol. Using their cars to deliver the cases of liquor, every bottle was sold in less than a week. After paying the men who helped them, Buddy and Tommy netted themselves a couple thousand dollars each. The partners were questioned, along with many others, but the crime was never solved.

*September 25, 1948*

Standing outside the Sweet Shop at the corner of Broadway and Temple Street on Winter Hill, Buddy reflected on the getaway through the streets of Boston. He announced to Tommy and a few friends, "We're never going to do that again."

Tommy responded, "Come on, pal, that was one hell of a ride. Nobody else would have the balls to do what we did."

"Yeah, but we could've killed someone."

"Yeah, but we didn't. And besides that, now we'll be famous."

"That's just what we don't want. We'll end up in jail. From now on, we plan ahead."

"All right, Buddy, whatever you say. I'm with you."

And so were the rest of the group. And the thefts kept coming.

# Gaining Notoriety

The eighteen-year-old McLean and his friends began frequenting the Alibi Club on Main Street near City Square, Charlestown. Buddy began to make a lot of friends who lived in Charlestown, and the Alibi was *the* hotspot for meeting girls and for fighting sailors. He was going steady with Jean, and Saturday night was date night for the couple, but Friday night became fight night for Buddy McLean.

With the extraordinary number of sailors patronizing the Alibi, plus the tough Irish Townie regulars drinking alcohol and pursuing women, it was natural there would be many confrontations.

*October 1, 1948*

The legend of Buddy McLean's hand-to-hand combat skills began on a Friday evening around eight o'clock. He was sitting at a table having drinks with John Hurley and Tommy Ballou. A group of four Charlestown girls walked over to the table and greeted John and Tommy. The girls were anxious to meet the handsome McLean, who did not look like he should be associating with tough-looking Townie boys. Tommy introduced Buddy to the girls.

"Hi, girls. Nice to meet you. Why don't you sit with us and let me buy you pretty ladies some drinks?"

The girls all smiled and giggled as one of them responded, "Okay."

During a little small talk between both parties, a dozen sailors sauntered into the club from the Navy Yard down the street. One of the larger sailors looked over at Buddy's table and bellowed, "Look at the tits on that blonde."

Buddy immediately excused himself from the table and walked over to the group occupying the bar. John and Tommy squared their chairs to face Buddy, preparing to rush in and assist. Buddy told the sailor, who had four inches and fifty pounds on him, "Don't be ignorant like that. If you don't have anything good to say, then keep your mouth shut."

"You want to be a fuckin' hero, kid?" asked the sailor.

"No. I want you to apologize to that girl."

"I'll give you one fuckin' chance to tuck your fuckin' tail and run back to your slime-bucket friends over there and them little whores."

"You're not going to get away with that."

Gesturing toward the other sailors, the big man responded, "You guys believe this little fuck? I take shits bigger than him. He thinks he's going to teach me a lesson. Ain't that right, little man?"

"Yeah, I am."

"Ha! All right, tough guy, let's see what you got."

Buddy was standing three feet from the big sailor. He pushed off his right foot and blasted a straight right fist into the sailor's stomach, knocking the wind out of him. Buddy pivoted on the ball of his left foot and circled a flawless left hook to the big man's rib cage. As the man's hands dropped and his chin came forward, Buddy nailed him with a perfectly executed straight right ring-finger knuckle just below his lower lip and finished with a wide circular Sugar Ray Robinson left hook, this time along the man's right jawline.

The sailor crashed back to the bar and dropped to one knee as he grabbed for the bar rail. The sailor was lifted by his friends and helped to a chair.

"Anyone else?" asked Buddy.

"What the fuck's going on here?" demanded another good-sized sailor who apparently missed the action while he was in the men's room.

"This kid just pounded Danny. Now he wants to fight someone else," spoke up a nonchallenger as he pointed his thumb at Buddy.

"All right, kid. You've got another one. Let's go."

"Do you have a problem with me and my friends having drinks with the ladies over there?" asked Buddy.

"Your fuckin' lady friends are whores, and you and your pals are fuckin' queers. What do you think about that?"

"Now we've got a problem," responded Buddy.

The two circled each other as the onlookers backed up to give them room. The sailor took a wild roundhouse swing at Buddy that missed by a foot.

Buddy smiled at him and asked, "Were you trying to hit me?"

"You fuckin' little shit," boomed the big sailor.

The enraged seaman blitzed young McLean and attempted a high body tackle. Buddy sidestepped to his right and ducked under the man's meaty arms. The sailor turned back to his left and was met with a Buddy McLean right cannonball to his left eye. The big guy was dazed. Buddy closed in on him. Wham. Bang. Boom! A straight right to the chin, left hook to the jaw, and a second right bomb to the sailor's left eye ended it.

The big man waved his hand and said, "No more."

"Jesus, that fuckin' kid can hit," stammered one of the onlooking sailors.

"Oh . . . my . . . God! Did you see that?" asked one of the girls to the others.

"Ho . . . ly . . . shit," was the only sound the bartender made.

Tommy and John walked over and stood close to Buddy. Tommy announced, "Now it's our turn, sea dicks. Fight us now or get the fuck out."

The sailors huddled together, unable or unwilling to make a move.

Buddy quietly asked Tommy, "Sea dicks?"

"Yeah, good one, huh?"

Buddy advised the sailors, "Fellas, you should probably take off. You don't need this. You guys should go to another bar."

After giving Buddy and his friends a good long look, one of the sailors spoke up, "Let's go, fellas. Everybody out. Let's go. And you, there's gonna be other guys from the Yard who are gonna come looking for you."

"You know where to find me," answered Buddy.

And they came. There were several thousand sailors stationed and bunking at the Charlestown Navy Yard. The news about this tough young fighter spread like wildfire throughout the base.

## October 27, 1948

The barracks were packed on a Wednesday evening. One seaman raved, "You have to see this kid from Somerville. No one can take him. He's down at the Alibi every Friday night. He stands at the front door waiting for anyone who wants to fight him. There're tough guys coming from all over Boston to try him. He'll duke it out with anyone, even guys who outweigh him by a hundred pounds. Some nights, he'll have five or six fights. Most of them are finished in under a minute."

"Is he a professional boxer?"

"I don't know, but he should be. But it's not just that, it's the way he comes at you—he moves in so fast. Bam! He's on you.

71

Then it's nonstop, incredible punches, one right after another until you're down."

"Doesn't he get hit?"

"Yes, he does. But it's like he doesn't feel it. He punches right through it. He never backs up. And it doesn't matter how big, how fast, how tough, or how talented the other guy is. You have to see him to believe it."

"What's he, fuckin' Superman? What makes him so good?"

"I heard he trains all the time. He's always ready."

"He trains for bar fights?"

All the men laughed.

"Yeah, he does. He doesn't want to lose. Plus, his friends bet on him, and he doesn't want them to lose either."

"What else about him?"

"Well, like I said, he's young and not that big, kinda lean. He's got a baby face and he's real quiet, not cocky at all."

"He lets his fists do the talking?"

"Yeah, that's it. And he'll fight at the drop of a hat."

"Well, who wants to fight him? Anyone?"

No response.

"Good, I'm glad you guys are smart enough to know better. Just go down there on Friday night and see for yourselves."

# Starting a Family, and the Reputation Grows

*Saturday, May 7, 1949*

Buddy and Jean decided to get married. They did not have a typical Irish Catholic wedding. Jean was pregnant, so they walked over to see Father Conners at Saint Ann's Church in Somerville. He performed the ceremony, and the newlyweds moved into a three-room apartment on the third floor of Mary Rapoza's house, the home Buddy grew up in.

It was shortly after Buddy got hitched that his father, Bill McLean, asked his son for some assistance with a problem down at the docks.

"What's up, Dad?"

"Some punks from East Boston stole a shipment of winter coats from my area today."

"Are you sure they were from Eastie?"

"Yeah, Billy Dunn saw them driving away, and he recognized one of them."

"From East Boston?"

"Yes."

"Does he know the kid's name?"

"No, but I guess they hang out at a club over there."

"What'd your boss say?"

"He said if I don't get it back, I'll have to pay for it myself."

"I think I can find out about these guys, then I'll take a ride over there and get it back."

"All right, thanks. Just be careful. Maybe you should bring a few of your pals with you."

"I can handle it."

Buddy did a quick investigation with his coworkers, then drove by himself to the thieves' hangout, a social club in East Boston.

Buddy walked into the smoke-filled club, where six men were playing cards at a round table. He spoke directly to one man, whom he recognized as a longshoreman.

"Those coats you took in Charlestown this morning are the responsibility of my father. I want every one of them returned today, or I'm coming back here tomorrow."

He did not wait for a response. He turned and walked out of the club.

"Who the fuck was that?" asked the group's senior, a local mob boss.

"That's Buddy McLean," responded the longshoreman who Billy Dunn had spotted making the getaway.

"Oh," said the boss. "From what I hear, he's the last guy you want to fuck with."

"That's right, he is. We definitely don't want him as an enemy."

"All right, then. You guys bring the shipment back right now, to wherever he wants it to go. Give him a hundred bucks for the inconvenience. And next time, make sure you know who you're stealing from."

*March 31, 1950*

On a Saturday afternoon, Jean gave birth to the couple's first child, a son, James Dennis. The family needed more space, so

Buddy with baby Jimmy

they relocated to a good-sized apartment on Otis Street in East Somerville. Buddy absolutely loved being a father and always enjoyed being with his family. The McLeans would remain at this dwelling for the next ten years. The new address for the family was directly across the street from the Somerville Vocational School. The school's parking lot served as a great play area for the McLean children through the 1950s.

6 Otis Street

*May 2, 1950*

"There he goes again," stated Otis Street neighbor Tom O'Brien.

"Where's he going?" asked Jimmy Sullivan as they watched Buddy McLean jog down the street.

"Down to Foss Park for his evening workout."

"Getting ready for another night of brawling?"

"Yep, that's what he does."

Slowly shaking his head, Sullivan wondered, "That's crazy, all that fighting. Why doesn't he just stay home with his family?"

"Listen, he's got tough guys from all over Boston looking to fight him. He's not going to back down . . . ever."

"Well, he's getting quite a reputation as a skull basher, that's for sure."

"Yeah, he certainly is. But you know what? You'll never meet a nicer guy, a harder worker, or a better neighbor."

"Yeah, I guess you're right."

# Irish Thunder

*May 7, 1950*

On a beautiful Sunday morning, a dozen Somerville firefighters were gathered in front of the department's headquarters at the intersection of Highland Avenue, Medford Street, and the McGrath-O'Brien Highway. In following their regular routine, the firemen discussed the previous night's activities over coffee and donuts. Their Saturday evenings were mainly uneventful, except for the two who were driving down Broadway around six o'clock.

Foss Park

As they were passing Foss Park, the two young firefighters saw a large group of people watching a fight. The driver pulled over so the pair could have a look. They walked up to see Buddy McLean pounding on an Everett High School alumnus, who happened to have been the star linebacker on the Crimson Tide football team a few years earlier. The linebacker's face was a bloody mess from the relentless assault he was receiving from his far superior adversary. The leatherhead attempted to tackle McLean at his thighs. Buddy sprawled across the linebacker's wide back and circled to the left in a quick slide step, then wrapped his left arm around the football player's neck and squeezed. McLean stepped in front of the star and tossed him over his left hip. The young man landed hard on his back. The fall knocked the wind out of him, and he was dazed from banging his head. Buddy was instantly sitting on the linebacker's chest with his knees pinning the Everett lad's arms. Buddy clamped onto the player's throat with his left hand and readied his right fist. The linebacker winced and turned his head.

Buddy asked him, "Had enough?"

The football player replied, "I'm done."

Buddy stood up and asked the crowd, "Are there any more tough guys here?"

Nobody, including the eight Everett chaps wearing Crimson Tide football jackets, responded. McLean walked away with a few friends.

The firefighters were told by another spectator, "That was McLean's third fight of the hour."

"Holy shit, no kidding? How'd the other two fights go?"

"The other two were as lopsided as the one you just saw."

One of the firefighters wondered, "Where's he going now?"

Another spectator predicted, "He'll go home, take a shower, change his clothes, then he'll take his wife out for dinner and some drinking and dancing. And there's always a good chance of a couple more fights."

"Incredible."

After a few seconds of silence, one firefighter spoke up and backed his claim by stating, "I have never seen a man fight with such ferocity, yet tough guys want to try him all the time."

"It has to be that baby face of his, plus, he's not that big," responded the storyteller. "Plus, they haven't seen him go. But boy oh boy, can he ever go."

The captain agreed. "Buddy McLean is extraordinary, and he can absolutely pulverize the best fighters the region has to offer."

But he also added, "You all really need to understand this—if McLean likes you, he's the best friend you'll ever have. Indestructible loyalty and generous to a fault. Treat him with respect, never lie to him, and you're all set."

All the firefighters were Somerville residents. All of them were physically capable, hardy men who would not hesitate to run into a burning building to save a life. None of them questioned the assertions, nor did they express or show any interest in challenging McLean. After a silent moment, the firefighters went about their business. But it would be far from the last time they would share a story of Buddy McLean.

# Mentoring Buddy

## April 9, 1951

Mary Rapoza passed away. Buddy took it very hard. *She was everything to me. I never got to pay her back for all she did. What am I going to do? Oh God, what do I do?*

He became a bit distant from people for a while. He immersed himself in agonizing workouts. He became a fitness specimen, far beyond any professional boxer or other professional athlete. When he was around family and friends, he was quiet. On the streets of Somerville and Boston, however, anger issues arose.

## April 13, 1951

For the next three days, Buddy walked from one barroom to the next, entering almost every bar in Somerville. On each visit, he ordered a shot of whiskey. After downing his shot, he announced to the patrons, "If any of you want to fight me, let's get it over with right now."

In most of the bars, there were no takers. But he fought almost a dozen men in the three days. Each one was finished in under a minute. The next weekend, he did it again, this time in Charlestown. The results were the same, except that there were fewer challengers.

## May 2, 1951

Joe McDonald found out what Buddy had done. He phoned his friend and said, "Come by the house."

Fifteen minutes later, Buddy was ringing his doorbell. He asked his friend, "What's up, Joe?"

As they walked into the front parlor, Joe told Buddy, "You have to slow down there, champ. If you fight too much, someone's going to get a lucky shot in on you because you're not at your best. You don't have to go looking for them. If somebody wants to fight you, let them come looking for you."

"I just keep hearing about all these guys who say they can beat me, and I got fed up with it. So, I figured I'd get them all and be done with it."

"I know. There's a lot of wise fucks out there who talk tough, but most of them can't back it up. They're a waste of your time. Everyone knows you're the best around. Trust me. Don't go looking to prove anything. Just be the nice kid I know who doesn't take shit from anyone."

"You're right, Joe. From now on . . ." and he began to cry.

"What is it, kid? What's bothering you?"

"It's my ma. I miss her, and I feel like I never really paid her back for everything she did for me. That woman was a saint."

Joe hugged Buddy and told him, "She was a fine ole gal, all right. But let me tell you something. I miss mine, too. And she's been gone for a while now. It takes time, but you'll get past it. You have to. You've got your own family now."

"I know. You're right."

"Why don't you go talk to Father Hogan? He's a good guy, and you two have been pals for a long time. Might do ya some good."

"That's a good idea, Joe. I'll do that."

"Then come by and see me next week. I might have something for you."

"All right."

When he left Joe McDonald's house, Buddy walked down Broadway to Saint Benedict's for a visit with Father Hogan. The two had a long chat, after which Buddy felt a little better. *Father was right. Ma would want me to carry on and take care of my family. No more looking for fights. But I'm never walking away from them either. Forgive me, God, Ma, and Father Hogan, but I'll never back down from a fight or take shit from anyone.*

*May 10, 1951*

The following week, Buddy stopped by Joe's house after lifting weights at the Somerville Y.

"Come on in," invited Joe as he walked toward the kitchen.

Buddy followed his friend, sat down at the table, and they clinked ice-cold beer bottles.

They each took a long swig, then Buddy started, "You think you might have something for me?"

"Yup, lobsters, up in Portland. What do you think?"

"Give me some details."

"They're supposed to be going to New York. But you're going to bring them into Boston."

"How am I going to do that?"

"I have an old Navy pal who works down on the docks in New York. He'll send me all the necessary paperwork from the company that's ordering the lobsters. And if the people up in Portland ask for it, you and whoever is with you will have all the right credentials. Oh, you'll also have New York license plates, and a New York registration."

"Wow, it sounds easy."

"It should be, for you."

"Where am I dropping off?"

"South Boston, I'll be meeting you there. They're going to pay us eight thousand dollars. The split will go one thousand each for my friend in New York and for your helper. Then, three grand to you and three grand to me. The entire job should take less than ten hours. What do you say?"

"I say yes, let's do it."

"One more thing, does anyone up there know you?"

"I've never been to the Portland docks."

"Well, I have. That's why I'm not going. And just to be safe, you should probably disguise your face, in case you have to go back up there another time."

"I'll get a crew cut and wear fake eyeglasses."

"That should work."

And it did. Security personnel let Buddy drive in and out with no delay. Buddy was packed and gone two hours before the real truck from New York arrived. On the ride back, Buddy smiled, *Good ole Joe. He was right. That was easy.* He beamed the whole way home.

# That's Buddy's Seat

*March 20, 1952*

Though he promised Father Hogan and Joe McDonald that he would try to curb his fighting, Buddy still had some issues with his temper.

A group of young men were drinking in Mike Khoury's State Spa. The conversation eventually turned to Buddy McLean.

"That's his barstool right over there, the last one down. Nobody sits there, even if he's not here," said one of the men, pointing toward the end of the bar.

"Oh really? What happens if I sit there?"

"You're taking the chance of getting the shit beat out of you if he walks in."

"Why, what's the big deal? It's just a fuckin' barstool."

"It's all a matter of respect with him. If he's in here drinking and you give him a long look, or sit on his barstool, or stand in his way, or say something he doesn't like, you are putting yourself at risk. If that ever happens, you better apologize, and then get the hell out of here."

"You're shitting me."

"No, I'm not. And don't let that fuckin' college-boy face fool you. If he's drinking, he's not to be fucked with. Ask anyone who knows him."

"What? An Irish temper?"

"Yup, razor sharp. Last week, he was in here. He got mad at some guy showing off his pretty girlfriend, at a table over there. Buddy made the guy sit under the table while he bought the girl a drink."

"The guy sat under the table?"

"Yup, it was that or take a fuckin' beating. The guy knew who McLean was."

"I guess they won't be coming back in here."

"Probably not, and you'd be smart to not bother him when he's in here."

# John Canty

John Canty (wearing leather jacket)

## *March 12, 1954*

John Canty had been friendly with Buddy McLean from when they both drove trucks for the Local 25 Teamsters Union, before Canty joined the Somerville Police Department. Canty was a big, strong, tough Irishman, a man not to be made angry. As tough as he was, Buddy McLean was a bit leery of only two men: John Canty, and the super-strong longshoreman, Richie Fiore.

In the Capitol Bar, Buddy explained his reasoning to a few friends. "Those two guys are unstoppable. They're the nicest guys you'd ever meet, but don't piss off either one of them. They're too damn strong. You'd need a cannon to knock them down, and you better not miss. I saw a thousand pounds of canned vegetables fall on top of Fiore down at the docks. Everybody thought he was dead. We all came running to help him, but Canty got there first. He grabbed the pallet and lifted it, by himself. Richie got up on his own, shook his head, brushed himself off, and went back to work. Canty stayed with Fiore for a minute, then he went over and climbed into his rig and drove off. They both acted like nothing had happened. I would never want to fight either one of them."

## June 28, 1954

It was a warm summer evening, around eight o' clock. Canty, working the four-to-midnight shift, received a call from dispatch about an elderly woman who had been beaten and robbed as she was walking along the sidewalk after leaving St. Ann's Church. Canty pulled up to the scene of the incident and radioed in for an ambulance. He jumped out of his cruiser and rushed to the injured lady, who was surrounded by concerned neighbors. Although her face was bloody and swollen, the woman was coherent enough to provide Canty with a description of the three teens and the one who had beaten her and taken her red pocketbook.

After making sure the woman was safely loaded into the ambulance, Canty got back on his radio and notified every on-duty Somerville cop of the incident and gave them a description of the perpetrators. Upon completion of the transmission, he hung up the two-way and slammed his hands on the steering wheel. Canty was furious that someone would commit such a brutal and cowardly crime to a harmless woman in his hometown, and worse: *Right in my area, those fuckin' punks.*

Steaming mad, he drove up toward Broadway. After turning right on Broadway and left onto Temple Street, he saw Buddy McLean driving toward him. He flashed his lights at McLean, and Buddy stopped in the middle of the street.

"What's up?" asked Buddy.

"We just had a bad mugging of a woman outside St. Ann's."

"Is she going to be all right?"

"Yeah, but her face is a mess."

"Damn. Any idea who did it?"

"Three punks. They ran away with her bag, toward Broadway. Probably local kids."

"Probably from the projects."

"Good point. I'll take a ride down there," stated Canty.

"Let me do it. I know a lot of kids down there."

"All right. It's a red pocketbook. Let me know what you find out."

"I will," replied Buddy.

Buddy pulled into the projects, where he found a small group of tough-looking teens boxing near the playground. *These guys will be perfect for what needs to get done.*

"Hey, fellas, I'd like you guys to do me a favor."

"Sure, Buddy. What do you need?"

"Three kids your age just beat and robbed a woman coming out of St. Ann's Church. I think they live down here. They took her red handbag and ran off. The lady is in the hospital. I want you guys to find them and get me that red bag, and I want all her money in it. And I want you guys to give those punks a good pounding so they'll think twice before they try anything like that again."

The boys looked at each other and nodded.

"No problem, Buddy. We have a good idea who it is, probably the O'Brien brothers. They do a lot of quick grab-and-run shit like that. They have a few other kids with them, but we'll get all of them. And we'll be glad to pound the piss out of them."

"All right. Good. When you get that lady's bag, bring it to me up at the Capitol Bar."

"We'll get it done."

Buddy waved to the kids and drove off.

Within one hour, the Somerville Police received an anonymous phone call informing them that the beaten woman's red handbag could be picked up at the front doorway of Marshall Hall. John Canty drove to the hall, which was across the street from the Capitol Bar on Winter Hill. He stepped out of his cruiser, walked up to the building, and grabbed the bag outside the front door. As he walked back to his vehicle, Canty wondered, *No one snatched the bag while it was sitting in plain sight.* He surmised the bag was being watched, or the neighborhood knew who placed it there and to stay away from it. Once inside the cruiser, John inspected the contents. Everything seemed to be in order, including the woman's cash. A second later, he noticed a roll of cash with an elastic around it at the bottom of the bag. He slowly shook his head as the smile came across his face. "Buddy," Canty muttered. "I love that kid. And he's the one guy who could get this done, and so fast."

John Canty was known throughout Somerville for his nickname, "Matt Dillon," after the character played by James Arness on the television show *Gunsmoke*. Canty was tall and broad like Arness, but he also had very high morals, similar to Matt Dillon. He later taught those moral values to his sons, who also wanted to become cops:

"Booze, broads, and bribery will kill you."

"Be nice to the little everyday people."

"Don't ever let the badge become bigger than the man wearing it."

"There are good guys, there are bad guys. And there are bad guys who are good guys. You have to know the difference."

"The job comes with power. Use it to do good things."

Canty always felt that he was put on earth to help people in need. He did not understand why many others did not think the same way. There was one man in Canty's mind who was the exception. And he held a high regard for him.

*August 6, 1954*

One late afternoon on a warm Friday, John Canty was assigned to oversee the eviction of an Italian family from an apartment on Short Pearl Street. He drove down there and saw the family sitting on the front stairs. The wife and four kids were crying. The husband was standing on the sidewalk trying to reason in broken English with his landlord. The landlord kept shaking his head no to everything the man pleaded for. The movers were getting ready to remove the family's possessions to the sidewalk. From the corner of his eye, John saw Buddy McLean crossing the street toward him. He was having a beer at a friend's house out on the front porch, and he overheard some of the commotion. Buddy walked up to Canty and asked, "What's going on, John?"

John explained to Buddy, "These folks are being evicted for not paying their rent."

Buddy looked at the evictee and his family for a moment, and then at the landlord. He asked the landlord, "How much does he owe you?"

The landlord told Buddy, "He's behind four months on his rent, and he owes me four hundred dollars."

Buddy looked at the Italian, who was a total stranger, and he asked him, "Why aren't you paying your rent?"

The man answered, "The people I work for, they cut back, and now I have trouble finding a job."

Buddy looked to the landlord, then asked a few questions about the Italian man. "Is he a good tenant, a hardworking man, a good family man? Does he usually pay his rent on time?"

"This is a wonderful family, and he is a good, hardworking man. He's always paid the rent on time, for close to ten years now. I feel lousy about doing this. I don't want to throw them out, but I have a mortgage to pay."

Buddy nodded at the landlord and looked over at the Italian man and his family for a long moment. Then Buddy turned back to the landlord while reaching into his pocket, and he pulled out a large roll of cash. He began peeling off twenty-dollar bills. Buddy handed the landlord four hundred dollars and said, "Now he's caught up." Then Buddy counted out another six hundred dollars, handed it to the landlord and said, "Now he's ahead six months."

The shocked landlord thanked Buddy and walked over to the movers to tell them their services were not going to be needed. Buddy turned to the confused Italian man, put his hand on the man's shoulder, and told him, "You come see me at the Charlestown docks on Monday morning and I'll find you some work. You can pay me back over time."

The man was so happy, there were tears in his eyes as he shook Buddy's hand, then hugged him. The family rushed over to Buddy to hug and thank him. As the kids and the mother were squeezing and thanking Buddy, he looked over at John Canty and slowly shook his head with a big smile on his young face.

Canty later admitted to his wife, "I felt like giving him a hug, too. Instead, I smiled back, gave him a wave, and walked back to my cruiser. As I was driving off, I thought to myself, there's no one else like Buddy McLean. He truly has a heart of gold."

# Somerville's Golden Boy

At just twenty-four years old, Buddy McLean was becoming a Greater Boston celebrity. He was a tough-as-nails, hard-working Irish-American lad who also enjoyed hijacking trucks. This seemed to generate a large fan base among the unbreakable union men of Teamsters Local 25 and the calloused longshoremen working the docks of Boston. To go along with extreme community generosity, Buddy's handsome face and quiet-but-friendly demeanor confused people because of his fighting and law-breaking reputations. He was liked and admired by many people.

*August 28, 1954*

Fourteen-year-old Al Boudreau of Somerville and his friend Johnny Racioppi, from the Mystic Avenue Projects, were having a bite to eat at the Mystic Diner down the street from the projects, close to the Charlestown line and Sullivan Square. Suddenly, Buddy McLean, driving a black Ford, pulled over directly in front of the diner. A Somerville police cruiser, blue lights on, pulled in behind McLean.

"Johnny, look. It's Buddy McLean. Let's see what's going on."

The boys hurried out the front door to the sidewalk. The cop and Buddy both got out of their cars and quickly walked toward each other.

"License and registration, McLean."

"Here it is," and he fired a straight right punch into the cop's gut.

The cop went down like he was shot. Buddy looked over at the boys and winked. Then he walked back to his car and took off. The boys looked at each other in disbelief and slowly shook their heads. After a while, the cop pulled himself up and walked, bent over, back to his cruiser. He had no desire to chase Buddy. He made a turn and headed down toward Foss Park.

As the word spread throughout the city, most people assumed it was one of the Bavin brothers. They were not well liked in the community . . . or by Buddy.

McLean was friendly and respectful to most of Somerville's finest. And they pretty much felt the same way about him. They tended to ignore his illegal activities.

## August 31, 1954

On a weekday evening, a Somerville patrolman stopped at a Winter Hill liquor store to pick up some beer. The officer was still in uniform, having just finished his shift. He parked his car and walked into the store.

"Freeze, you son of a bitch."

From behind him, a masked man pushed the barrel of a handgun against the back of the patrolman's head. In front of the cop, another masked bandit was robbing the store's owner at gunpoint.

"Get down on your belly and keep your fuckin' mouth shut."

The patrolman complied, and the man from behind disarmed him.

"Now what are we going to do?" asked the bandit who disarmed the cop.

"See if there's any more cops outside, 'cause I got no problem killing these two motherfuckers. Go look out the window."

The second robber walked toward the door to have a look outside. He saw nobody.

"It's all clear. Let's get the fuck out of here."

He turned around and walked back toward the prone patrolman while the other was finishing the robbery.

"I think we should kill these guys in case they know us," said the backup bandit.

"All right, go ahead. You shoot them," replied the robber holding the money in a brown paper bag.

The store owner began to pray. The cop began an attempt at reasoning with the robbers.

"You guys don't have to kill us. We have no idea who you are. You can make a clean getaway. Just walk out the door."

"You know what? I fuckin' hate cops. But there's nothing worse than a fuckin' liar who's wearing a badge."

Suddenly, the front door opened and in walked Buddy McLean. "Oh shit," blurted one gunman. They were stunned and began to quiver.

Instantly assessing the situation and without hesitation, Buddy spoke to the bandits in a calm, firm voice. "These guys are friends of mine, and I know who you guys are. Give the money back, walk out the door, and I'll forget the whole thing."

The robbers decided to scrap the holdup. "We didn't know they were friends of yours, Buddy. We're sorry about this. Here's the money, and we'll get out of here. Sorry about this, Buddy. And it won't happen again."

As the two headed for the door, Buddy nodded, then advised them, "No more stickups in Somerville. Go down to Charlestown for that." With that, the other men in the store, including the robbers, had a nervous snicker.

*September 19, 1954*

The two would-be liquor store robbers, Sleepy Finnick and Arthur Granderson, approached Buddy on a Sunday afternoon at the Capitol Bar.

"We're sorry about the liquor store, Buddy," said Granderson.

"Yeah, just don't do any of that around here," replied McLean.

"No problem. Hey, I was wondering, could you help me and Sleepy get a truck? We have to move some furniture. We'll pay you a hundred bucks for helping us. What do you think?" asked Granderson.

"Sure, I'll get my truck. When do you want to do this?" asked Buddy.

"How about right now?"

"Give me an hour, and I'll meet you guys right here."

Buddy returned with a large box truck, and Finnick and Granderson piled in. Buddy drove for about a mile, making a few turns along the way, until Finnick told him to pull over in front of a house on Cherry Street. The three men climbed out of the truck.

"This is it?" asked Buddy, seemingly confused.

"Yeah, we're here," cackled Granderson.

"Which house is it?" demanded an anger-growing McLean.

"That one," responded Granderson, pointing to the house.

"You guys are moving furniture out of that house?"

"Yup, that's the one."

Buddy pushed Granderson over a three-foot chain-link fence and into some hedges.

"What the . . ." started Finnick, but was interrupted by a hard slap to the side of his head.

Buddy grabbed the two by the front of their shirts and pulled them in close. "You two idiots. This is my father's house. Don't ever ask me for any more favors. I told you guys to go outside of Somerville for your robberies. If I hear about any house-breaks in Somerville, I'll be looking for you two. And for wasting my time, you owe me a hundred each. I better get paid right now. Hand over your wallets."

He emptied each wallet and dropped them on the sidewalk. Neither man said a word.

As Buddy headed back to his truck, knowing his father was at work and the house was secure, Granderson stated, "Buddy, there's a lot of house-breaks around here. We could be totally innocent."

"Then you two should move out of Somerville," hollered McLean as he drove off.

# As the Family Grows, So Does the Reputation

*June 30, 1955*

On March 24, 1954, Buddy and Jean welcomed a second son, Michael. The boys loved playing with their dad when he came home from work.

"I'll be back in a little while, fellas. When I come home, I'm going to give you boys some horsey rides."

"Okay, Dad," replied Jimmy.

*All right. Let's get this done, then home to the boys.* Buddy forced himself out the door to go off and do his evening workout. On his jog down to the park he thought: *No bars tonight, I'm taking the boys down to Revere Beach. Let Jeannie have a night out with her friends. We'll go down the beach and have some fun. Tomorrow night, take her out to eat. Can't forget, after work, meet with the boys about that trailer coming up from New York—could be a big score. Hot as hell tonight, skip the run, workout by the pool, swim fifty laps. Finish with push-ups, sit-ups and pull-ups. Get back home.*

*July 10, 1955*

In the 1950s, Rocky Marciano dominated the professional boxing heavyweight division. During those same years, Buddy McLean ruled the streets of Boston.

John Hurley was in a Charlestown saloon when he overheard a bunch of men arguing back and forth.

"You don't know what the fuck you're talking about. Marciano would knock McLean into next week."

"Fuck you! McLean can't be stopped. He's the one guy who can outlast the Rock."

"You're crazy. Ask Hurley. He's friends with McLean. He'll even tell you. He can't beat Marciano."

"What do you think, John?"

Hurley thought for a moment, then answered, "If the two of them were standing side by side hitting heavy bags, it would be hard to tell which one is the champ. Both men have great physiques. They're about the same height. Marciano is maybe eight to ten pounds heavier and has thicker legs. Buddy is broader in the chest and shoulders and back. They both have great arms. Buddy's are longer. Marciano definitely has the more powerful punch. He fights out of that low crouch. Buddy is more of a straight-up fighter. He punches more continuous, and he's faster and more accurate than the champ. Buddy also has better balance and more coordination than Rocky. I watch Buddy hit the heavy bag. He's smooth as silk, like he's not really trying hard. But it sounds like thunder, and he'll work on one combination a hundred times before he goes to another.

"They both can go all day and take any man's punch. I would say Buddy is the stronger of the two. He lifts weights, Rocky doesn't. I saw Buddy lift up a man who outweighed him by a hundred pounds and slam him back down. The fight was over right then and there. Buddy works up to sixteen hours a day loading and unloading freight, then he runs ten miles. Marciano likes to run wind sprints down there in New York City, at Central Park. His trainer throws him passes with the football for a couple hours a day. When he's training for a fight, Rocky does a shitload of sparring. Buddy stays sharp with all his bar and street fights. They're both in phenomenal shape, and they're both great athletes."

"All right, so who wins the fight, John?" asked one of the men listening to Hurley.

"In a boxing match, you have to say Marciano wins because of ring experience. Plus, he's the champ, but he won't knock Buddy out. Marciano is hard to catch, fighting out of that crouch. I think Buddy would have trouble landing hard shots on the Rock, unless they went toe to toe. Then it would turn into a bloodbath. Marciano likes to go body, body, body, then BAM, to the head. He might knock Buddy down, but he won't fuckin' stop him. Buddy will definitely get his share of punches in, but you know Marciano has a steel jaw. And you can hit Buddy with a fuckin' baseball bat, but he's still coming after you. Now, in a bar fight, that's a different story, Buddy will get to him, and I'll tell you why."

Every man in the room leaned forward to hear every word. "No gloves, that's a big advantage to Buddy. He has hands like fuckin' boulders. Marciano doesn't have that. Buddy's strong, too. He's like wrestling a fuckin' gorilla. When he gets a hold of Marciano, and he eventually would, that's when it's over. When Buddy gets his hands on you, you're not going to get away. He'd ram Marciano into a wall or pick him up and slam him headfirst into the floor. In a bar fight, my money is on McLean."

When Hurley finished his explanation, the men were silent and a few nodded to each other. Turning away from the group, John heard one man say, "You'd have to be a fuckin' moron to wanna tangle with McLean." Hurley smiled as he walked toward the door.

*July 17, 1955*

After one of their early Sunday morning workouts, Buddy asked Joe McDonald, "Hey, Joe, you know those boxing tournaments they have at Dilboy every year?"

"Yup."

"Well, it's next week. I was thinking about entering."

"Yeah? I think you'd do pretty good. You're in better shape than anyone I've ever seen. Go ahead."

"Will you work my corner?"

"Absolutely."

"Do you want anyone else with us?" asked Buddy.

"Yeah. Get Bill Cunningham. He's a good man."

The amateur boxing tournament was held at Dilboy Field, Somerville's football stadium. Buddy was slotted in the light heavyweight division, where he weighed in at one hundred seventy-four pounds. The format called for single elimination, and the goal was to finish the festivities in one day. Not many people knew the popular McLean had entered the tournament, based on the number of people watching. More than 300 onlookers were treated to a firsthand, close view of the well-known local boy in action.

Buddy stormed out to the middle of the ring and unleashed wicked body shots to his first opponent. The other man tried to slip away, but Buddy kept charging forward, disregarding the counterpunches to his head and face. Within seconds, Buddy had his foe backed to the ropes. From there, he shifted into overdrive. Exerting explosive speed and power, Buddy let loose an ungodly barrage of crashing blows to the head and body.

The second match was a virtual carbon copy of the first. Each fight lasted no more than sixty seconds, and it was estimated that McLean landed one hundred punches in each fight.

After his first two bouts, Buddy had a two-hour break before his next match, which was for the trophy. Word spread like wildfire throughout Somerville that, "Buddy McLean is boxing down at Dilboy Field. He won his first two fights already, both were first-round knockouts. He still has one more fight to go. Get the hell down there!"

More than a thousand Highlanders, mostly from Winter Hill, hurried down to the sports ground. They swarmed around the boxing ring. There was a lot of pushing and jostling for preferred seating. The McLean crowd was loud and rowdy. The people who had been there for most of the day were overwhelmed by Buddy's fans. The roar from the crowd when Buddy stepped into the ring was as if a tornado had dropped on Dilboy Field.

In the championship bout, Buddy's opponent was a slick, experienced African American fighter from Roxbury, the southwest section of Boston. The instant the timekeeper rang the opening bell, the pumped-up McLean attacked the man as if he was fighting his worst enemy. He fired one missile after another as his rival backpedaled, shuffled, and covered when he was trapped in the corner or against the ropes. The Roxbury lad was able to spin off the ropes and land some combinations to Buddy's head and face. Unfazed, Buddy continued forward, following Joe McDonald's advice: "Hard to the body!"

Buddy lost the first round but won the second with his punishing arm-and-body shots. In the third and final round, the two squared off in the middle of the ring. His fans were screaming for a knockout. "Kill him, Buddy. Knock him the fuck out."

Buddy attempted to land a straight right blast to his foe's head. The projectile grazed the young man's temple as he slipped outside Buddy's right fist and smashed a left hook into the Buddy's right kidney. It was a punch McLean would never forget and one he would use in future fights outside the ring. The kidney blow buckled Buddy's right knee. McLean turned to face his competitor and was met with a bullet right hand on his chin. Buddy's head snapped back, and the Roxbury fellow moved in for the kill. He whipped a left hook at Buddy's jaw, but McLean tucked his chin at the last second and took the punch on his cheek. Buddy instantaneously detonated a short-left uppercut to his opponent's chin, and then a straight right hand to the same spot. The combination staggered the Roxbury fighter back into McLean's corner. The time clock was winding down. Buddy rushed forward, frantic to knock the man out and not leave the outcome of the fight in the hands of the judges. McDonald was shouting, "Finish him."

The last twenty seconds of the battle were total mayhem. As the crowd was roaring, Buddy thundered a dozen one-twos to the head and body. As his opponent tried to escape the onslaught, McLean pulled him back to the corner. The boxer threw a desperate uppercut into Buddy's groin. Ignoring the pain, the infuriated McLean rammed his left forearm into the Roxy's throat, forcing his back to arch over the top rope. The referee tried to drag Buddy away. McLean shoved the referee back and down onto his backside with a hard push from his right forearm while maintaining the pin he had on the Roxy with his left arm. Then, Buddy drove a perfectly straight right hand that connected flush with the boxer's face as the bell rang. The punch turned off the lights in the skull of the Roxbury fellow. He melted to the canvas.

At that point, the officials were not sure how to proceed. "There's a thousand rowdies from Somerville and only a hundred from Roxbury," said one of the judges. "Give the trophy to the Somerville kid and let's get the hell outta here."

The referee disagreed. "Fuck, no. I want him disqualified. He turned that match into a fuckin' hockey fight."

The judges looked at each other, not knowing what to do.

The Somerville fans were chanting, "Buddy! Buddy!"

The organizer of the tournament called over the two Somerville police officers on duty at the field and told them, "We're going to need extra cops down here. It's going to get out of control. You better get all the help you can."

The call went out immediately, and within a few minutes every on-duty cop in Somerville and fifteen more from nearby

Arlington, Medford, and Cambridge converged on Dilboy Field. With thirty of Greater Boston's finest standing at the ready, nightsticks in hand, the ring announcer quickly declared the bout a draw, no winner.

As loud boos and harsh language rained down on the field, Buddy, Joe, and Bill walked from the ring toward the nearest exit. Several hundred fiercely proud Highlanders swarmed the trio. The Roxbury fighter and his handlers left the stadium in an ambulance with a police escort. Their supporters and the tournament officials were detained until the scene was under control. Then they were led to their cars.

On the drive home, Buddy decided, "I don't think boxing is for me, fellas."

"Why not?" asked Bill Cunningham. "You fought great, three knockouts in one day."

"Yeah, but with all the rules and the politics involved in it, plus, it's a huge commitment. I'd have to give up a lot of other things that I don't want to give up."

"Like what, bar fighting?"

"Hey, I don't start that."

Joe Mac chimed in, "Yeah, you don't avoid it either."

Joe and Bill had a good chuckle. Buddy smiled as he slowly shook his head.

"Well, I wouldn't want to let you boys down, so the bar and street fights are still on. Does that make you happy?"

Bill replied, "Yeah, it does, Buddy. We still get to say the toughest guy in Boston is our good friend."

*July 30, 1955*

On a Saturday afternoon, Jean was having tea at her mother's apartment in the Mystic Avenue Projects. Her mother asked, "How did Buddy do at the boxing tournament?"

103

"Oh please, he almost started a riot down there. I don't know what the hell happened, but it took fifty cops to calm everyone down"

"Oh my, I hope he's not going to do that again."

"I know. It's a pain in the ass, all his fighting."

"What do you mean, dear?"

"It seems like every time we go out somewhere, a guy is going to walk up and challenge Buddy to a fight. We might be at a restaurant, a bar, or a club, sitting at a table minding our own business. Sure enough, somebody will walk up to him and say, 'Are you Buddy McLean?' Then the guy might say something stupid like, 'You don't look so tough.'"

Her mother asked, "Then what happens?"

"He doesn't want to make a big scene or mess up someone's place, so he always takes the fight outside. I sit at the table and wait for him to come back. He's never gone more than a few minutes."

"Does he ever lose?"

"Never."

"And this happens wherever you go?"

"Pretty much."

"I've seen him walk in the house with bruises on his face and blood on his hands in the middle of the day!" exclaimed Jean's youngest sister, Mary.

"Yeah, it can happen anytime, that's for sure."

"It sounds like he really enjoys all the fighting," added Jean's mom.

"It's not that he wants to fight all the time. He just never backs down," finished Jean.

Buddy McLean was never one to underestimate an opponent. He did not brag about his accomplishments or act cocky. He was, however, brazen and utterly fearless of anyone or any situation. It was this personality trait that built the foundation of the Winter Hill Gang during the 1950s. It also sent a message to the older Boston gangs: "Make room for the new guys."

# He's Not So Tough

Although he was a super-strong fighter and unafraid of any man or confrontation, Buddy did have a few phobias.

*October 2, 1955*

On a Sunday afternoon, Jean's sister, Joan, was visiting the McLean residence on Otis Street. Sitting in the kitchen, having a cup of tea while chatting away, Jean looked out the window and noticed, "Look, there's a rat climbing up the side of that drain pipe on the house next door."

"Oh my, I'm afraid of those things. I hope you don't have any."

With that, Jean got up and pulled a broom from the kitchen closet. She called out, "Buddy, come out here, and you better come fast."

Buddy was watching football on the TV in the other room. He walked into the kitchen and asked, "What's up?"

Jean handed him the broom and pointed to the rat next door.

"What the hell do you want me to do?"

"Go out there and kill it."

"I'm not going to do that," he said as he started pacing back and forth on the kitchen floor.

"What? Are you of afraid of that little rat?"

"It's not little, and you know I hate those things. I'm locking all the windows. I want you to get an exterminator in here and make sure we don't have any rats or mice."

"That one lives next door. You'd have to exterminate the whole neighborhood if you really want to get rid of them."

"Then do it. Tell all the neighbors. Have the exterminator give everyone a group rate."

"Buddy, just get a cat," suggested Joan. "That will solve your problem."

"I don't like cats either," replied Buddy.

Jean smiled. "How about a dog then? That'll scare off rats, mice, and cats."

"Good idea. We'll get a dog, but I also want an exterminator in here. Fast!"

"Look at the big tough guy," said Jean as Buddy went on to close and lock every window in the house. The sisters sat in the kitchen sipping from their cups and laughing.

Joan had an idea. "Jeannie, I could bring my hamster over here and we can slip it under the covers in your bed."

Jean laughed, "Yeah, then when Buddy pulls down the covers, the hamster would be there and scare the living daylights out of him."

The sisters enjoyed a good long laugh.

"Do you want me to go get the hamster?"

"No, he might kill the hamster, or he might have a heart attack and drop dead right there. I don't want to kill the bastard."

*April 8, 1956*

Another phobia Buddy had was the sight of blood from a person he did not make bleed. He was not bothered by the sight of his own blood or when he made someone else bleed. However, one time, his son Jimmy ripped open his arm trying to climb over a barbed wire fence. Buddy was watching the kids while Jean was at her mother's house. When Jimmy came running into the house, Buddy took one look at his son's blood-soaked shirt and blurted,

"Oh no." He almost fainted. He became light-headed, dizzy, and nauseous, and he went down on one knee. He managed to stay conscious and compose himself enough to wrap a bath towel around Jimmy's arm, then carry Jimmy over to a neighbor for a ride to the hospital. They cleaned Jimmy's arm and stitched him up. He was fine. But Buddy was a different story. Once he got Jimmy into the emergency room, Buddy went off to the men's room to throw up.

He later admitted to Jean, "I don't get it. The sight of all that blood really shook me up."

She told him, "I hope I'm never bleeding and need you to save me."

Buddy replied, "Yeah, I know, but I'll run and get you some help."

They both had a good laugh, then Jean added, "Don't tell anyone else you can't stand the sight of blood, or they'll all think, 'He's not so tough.'"

# Somerville Men

On the lively streets of Somerville, opportunities for making a lot of money through various criminal activities had become a more common occurrence. A few of the bar owners and other men were into the bookmaking and loan-sharking business. They had a monetary agreement with the Mafia to let them do this. Joe McDonald and Sal Sperlinga, another friend of Buddy's, operated independently.

McLean, on the other hand, had his own method for making large sums of money, fast and illegal.

*May 2, 1956*

A group of Teamsters truck drivers from Local 25 were talking about Buddy's other profession one afternoon over a few beers at Driscoll's in Charlestown. Carmine Cafaso, a member in the union, explained to the others how these side jobs were pulled off.

"He sits in the back of that union hall during meetings. He listens to the brass and the other members talking about all the major shipments moving in and out of Boston. He jots down that info in a little notebook. Then he gets his crew ready, and they go to work."

A young Teamster asked, "Simple as that?"

"Yup."

"There's no fuckin' way a hijack goes that easy."

After a long look, Carmine replied, "Well, they used to hijack the freight."

"Not anymore? What's he do now?"

"Now he pays the driver. He makes it look like a hijacking, but the driver is in on it."

"Wow, that's smart, and it does sound easy."

"Yeah, he makes it look easy, but in truth, there is a lot that goes into it."

"What do you mean?"

"You better not go blabbing this around. Your father knew Buddy. He never told you about him?"

"My dad died when I was fifteen."

Carmine nodded and continued, "Well, after he leaves the union hall, he calls his buyers to let them know what is available. If nobody is interested, he'll meet with his guys and they figure out if they want to grab something. Then, he has to find out who the driver is and see if he'll go along with it. And, I might add, he pays that driver very well."

"Is that it?"

Jimmy Sims

"No, he has a guy named Jimmy Sims, who steals a car from Logan, then has him put it back when the job's over. Then, McLean has to set up a site where the hijacking will take place and make arrangements to deliver the freight. There's quite a few people involved in this, but it goes like clockwork. Everyone knows their job, and they all make decent money doing it."

"Wow, I'd like to get in on that."

"Well, he doesn't let just anyone in on this. You have to get to know him first. Then, if he likes you and he trusts you, he might give you a chance. But I should warn you, don't get pushy with him, and make sure to wait for him to ask you. You can let him know you're interested, but that's it, don't push him. And never, ever screw him over."

"Wow, he's something, all right. Who are the buyers?"

"Anyone and everyone, but, sometimes, it's the man down in Providence."

"Patriarca?"

"Yup. Another guy you don't screw with. McLean drops the freight off to him, and from there it goes to parts unknown."

The men all laughed.

"Wow, he's one of a kind," said the young Teamster. "It's a lot more complicated than I thought."

"Yup, but it works. And Buddy and his friends make a good amount of money. And, at the same time, they maintain a low profile."

"You ever work for him, Carmine?"

"Let's just say he's a friend. He's done favors for me, and I for him. And Buddy will sometimes say, 'I like to ride in the back of the bus,' meaning he does not want to draw attention to himself. So, don't bother him, you understand?"

"I understand, Carmine. I won't bother him."

*June 10, 1956*

Over an early morning breakfast, Joe McDonald advised Buddy, "Never put a spotlight on yourself. Hang with your friends, especially the ones you trust. Never draw attention to yourself. Make sure your friends do the same thing."

"Okay, Joe, but I'm doing that already. What's up?"

"I see your partners driving new cars and wearing nice clothes, that's what's up."

"They have legitimate jobs, Joe. They make decent money, too."

"The cops and the FBI aren't stupid. I'm sure they're investigating the hijackings, and they have to think it's a Boston crew."

"I'll meet with the guys and tell them what you said. They all respect you, and they'll follow your advice."

Joe nodded.

Buddy followed up with, "Why don't you come in with us? We'd have a great crew with you running it."

"You're doing fine without me."

"Yeah, but with you running things, we'd be even better."

"I like my situation the way it is right now. There aren't too many people that I trust. You are one of the few. You have a nice little circle of friends there: Howie, Hurley, Big Nic, Tommy, Winn, and Simms. They're loyal to you, because you're good to them. They work well together, everything runs smooth. You don't need another chief. I'll work with just you, and you can organize your crew to complete the job."

"Do you have something for me, Joe?"

"Yes, I have a job that you might be interested in."

"What is it?"

"It's a freight train, six days away from Boston. It's coming to the Allston railyard."

"What's on it?"

"One car, loaded with Columbian coffee beans, the best in the world. You're going to need a trailer."

"Do you have a buyer?"

"Yup, a coffee company down in New Jersey."

"How much does it pay?"

"Fifty thousand."

"That's a lot of coffee."

Joe smiled and nodded. "It certainly is. Now, I know the two security guards who will let you in. They'll lead you right to the car. You back in your rig and load it up. Drive it down to Jersey. I'll go with you, and they'll pay us cash."

"How much for the security guards?"

"A thousand apiece."

"Forty-eight for us."

"Yup, that's six grand each, if we split it eight ways."

"All right, I'll have Jimmy on lookout. Me, Howie, Tommy, John, Billy, and Russ. We'll grab the beans. Where are you going to be?"

"Home, in bed."

Buddy frowned. Joe smiled and said, "I'm going to be a security guard, just in case you need backup."

Buddy smiled, nodded, and said, "Sounds like a good plan. It should go off without a hitch."

And it did.

# A New Friend and Training Partner

*June 30, 1956*

On weekend afternoons, Buddy and his friends liked to congregate outside the Capitol Bar and watch the cars driving up and down Broadway. Buddy began noticing a teenage boy hanging across the street in front of Dawn's Donuts. He was small and wiry. No one ever spoke to him. He just stood on the sidewalk occasionally smoking a cigarette. After watching him standing in the same spot for about a week, Buddy decided to talk to the youth. McLean crossed Broadway and approached the young lad.

"Hey, how ya doin'?"

"Hello," said the teen in a strong Italian accent.

"My name is Buddy McLean. What's yours?"

"Aniello Squillante."

"Nice to meet you." They shook hands. "Do you mind if I call you Nicky?"

"No."

"Do you live around here?"

"Yes, Sargent Avenue."

"Okay, Nicky, I'll see you around," and they shook hands again.

The next morning, Buddy was driving down Broadway when he spotted Nicky standing in front of Dawn's Donuts. Buddy pulled over and got out of his car. He walked up to the teen and asked, "Hey, Nicky. How are ya?"

"Good, Buddy. How are you?"

"I'm good, too. Hey, do you like to run?"

"Run?"

"Yeah, run, workout, you know what I mean?"

"Uh, yes."

"Good, you want to run with me today?"

"Okay."

"All right, go home, put on a pair of shorts and sneakers, and meet me back here in twenty minutes."

"Okay."

When Buddy came back, Nicky was standing there waiting for him. It was the beginning of a long friendship. They started running each day down to the track at Tufts University, and then many laps around it. In typical McLean workouts, push-ups and sit-ups were included.

At the beginning, Nicky had trouble keeping up with Buddy. But McLean kept encouraging the lad, "Hang in there. You're doing good. Don't quit."

*July 10, 1956*

After one of their workouts, Buddy told Nicky, "You're getting better every day, but you know what? You'd improve a lot faster if you stopped smoking cigarettes."

"Okay, I will," replied Nicky.

To make it more fun and challenging, Buddy told Nicky one day, "I'm going to give you a head start today. If I catch you before we get to the track, then you have to wash my car. If I don't catch you, then lunch is on me."

"How big is my lead?"

"One minute, now go!"

Nicky took off sprinting over Winter Hill and down the slope toward Magoun Square. When he got to the square, Nicky looked back over his shoulder to see Buddy flying down the hill. Nicky burst into an all-out sprint, zipping past Trum Field and through Ball Square. As he headed full steam toward Powder House Square, Nicky could hear Buddy yelling, "I'm going to get you, Nicky. Here I come." The footsteps were getting closer. Nicky made it through Powder House and turned right onto College Avenue. He could see the track, less than two hundred yards away. Nicky gave it his last bit of effort racing toward the track. With fifty yards to go, Nicky felt a tap on his shoulder as Buddy sprinted by him.

When he staggered up close to the track, the gasping-for-air Nicky collapsed on the grass. Buddy came over and pulled him up. "Walk with me. Let the air get back in your lungs. Breathe. Slow."

Buddy walked Nicky across the street to one of the houses on College Avenue. He grabbed a garden hose and lightly sprayed Nicky all over. Then Buddy had Nicky sip gently from the hose. Nicky was not feeling well, so Buddy let him rest in the shade as he finished the workout.

When he was done, Buddy walked up to the dejected Nicky and said, "Don't worry about it. You'll get used to this. You were flying down Broadway."

"Not as good as you."

"I've been doing this for a long time, and I had to try my very hardest to catch you."

Nicky looked at his friend, nodded and smiled as he said, "I'm not going to quit."

"That's what I like to hear. Let's go get lunch."

And the two pals started walking back toward Winter Hill.

Buddy and Nicky kept the workouts going for years. As time went by, Buddy introduced Nicky to all his friends. The young

Italian was welcomed into Buddy's inner circle, though he was never part of any illegal activities. However, Buddy did see to it that Nicky was given plenty of work on Winter Hill. When Nicky started bartending at the Capitol Bar, Buddy would come in every so often and say to Nicky, "You ready?"

Nicky would nod to his friend and walk around the bar to where Buddy was standing. Then the two would get down on the floor and pump out fifty push-ups.

## August 18, 1956

On a sunny Saturday afternoon, Buddy and Nicky were standing on the sidewalk outside the Capitol Bar. As usual, many of the folks who drove by honked their horns and waved. Buddy was waving back, and, at one point, he asked Nicky, "How come you never wave back?"

"I don't know any of them."

"I don't know most of them either."

They both laughed, then Buddy said, "Come on, give it a try. It's the right thing to do. Plus, then people will know you and me are friends."

"All right," and Nicky joined his pal in waving to the traffic.

A few minutes later, Buddy mentioned, "I'm getting kind of hungry. What do you say we go down to the Mountie (Mount Vernon) for a couple steaks?"

"All right, that sounds good to me."

"Let's walk down. And I want you to be nice to everyone we see; at least smile at them."

"I'll try."

As they walked along, Nicky thought to himself, *I'm so lucky to have him for a friend. He helps me stay fit, he takes me out to eat, and he gets me work. He's made me part of his group and his family. He's a great guy.*

Buddy and Nicky walked into the Mount Vernon Restaurant on the pub side. The big room and the U-shaped bar were crowded with men having their afternoon meal as well as many who were there just to quench their thirst. One man shouted out, "Hey, Buddy's here!" and everyone turned toward the door. Many long, happy greetings followed as Buddy and Nicky made their way down the bar.

Mount Vernon Restaurant

One of the bartenders hustled over to Buddy's favorite seat and grabbed two men's plates and drinks. "What the fuck are you doing?" was the response.

"Get up, right now, and you, too," the bartender said, cocking his head at the man drinking next to him.

"What are you doing? We're not fuckin' done here," was the response from the second man.

"I'm moving you guys to that table over there. Don't say anything. Just get up, right now."

The men slowly rose out of their seats and walked to the table behind them. The bartender was already there placing their drinks and the plates of food on the table.

"I want to thank you boys for moving so fast. You saved all of us from a sticky situation. Your next round is on me."

As the men got comfortable in their new seats, they noticed Buddy and Nicky getting ready to sit in their original seats.

"Oh, that's what it is," said one of the men.

"What?"

"We were sitting in Buddy's seats. You don't do that around here. That bartender just saved us from having words with the toughest guy in Boston."

"Yeah, I've heard all that shit about him. But look at him, he doesn't look that tough. He's kinda skinny."

"Don't you say a fuckin' word. You'll get us both killed. You fuck with him, and everyone in this bar will be against us. You understand?"

"Yeah, I get it. But just look at him. I mean, he's dressed neat and all that, but nothin' fancy."

"Yeah, so?"

"And I know he drives nice cars, but, other than that, he doesn't come across like he's big-time, making lots of money with his little gang there."

"What the fuck's wrong with you? You want to get the shit punched out of us? Keep your voice down."

"Relax, they can't hear us. But look at him, just a regular guy, like anyone else in here."

"That's 'cause he's smart. He knows not to show off. He's just a regular guy who wants to hang out with his friends. What the fuck's wrong with that?"

"Well, nothin', I guess, but he must be doing something with all that cash, if he's doing as good as everyone says he is."

"Yeah, well, it's a good idea if you just mind your own business and don't bother him. And just remember to thank him before we leave."

"What for?"

"Your next drink, I just heard him tell the bartender to 'Set up the house'."

"No shit? That's gonna cost him a pretty penny."

"And he does it all the time. And if ever you can, you should buy him a drink sometime. He'll remember it, and he's a good guy to have on your side."

"All right, I will. You know, I was in Khoury's the other day, and his friend Howie set up the house, too."

"They're all good guys, but they're kinda quiet. They pretty much keep a low profile, but they're all tough bastards, and they can get fuckin' violent in the blink of an eye, especially him," said the man, motioning his steak knife toward McLean.

"That's why we had to move our seat?"

"That's right, genius."

# Riling Up the Wrong Person

*August 24, 1956*

On a Friday night at Sammy's Patio, a nightclub on Revere Beach, world-class middleweight boxer Paul Pender and three of his friends arrived looking for trouble. At the time, Pender liked to drink, womanize, and fight in local bars.

Paul Pender

On that night, Pender was looking to knock out the bar's reigning tough guy, Joe Barboza, a Boston thug and hitman who later became a friend of Buddy's. Barboza had been a boxer and had made a few negative comments about Pender that got back

121

to him. Pender's ego would not allow that type of criticism from a brawler he was sure he could handle.

Joe Barboza

Barboza was not at Sammy's when Pender and his friends walked in. The bullies decided to stay and harass the customers. The prizefighter walked up to a beautiful, shapely woman who was sitting at a table with her husband and another couple.

"Hiya, gorgeous. Wanna take a spin across the floor with the next champ?"

"I'm married."

"To that bum?" Pender said, pointing toward her husband.

"We don't want any trouble here, Mr. Pender," responded the husband.

"Then you'll shut the fuck up, and I'll have my turn on the floor."

Pender's friends began laughing at the fear and intimidation he was causing. Then the front door opened and in walked Buddy McLean with two of his friends. The bartender smiled and waved to Buddy and taunted the boxer with, "Hey, Pender, this is Buddy McLean. Why don't you pull some of that shit with him?"

Pender looked up to see the legendary street fighter standing in front of him with a physique that was far more developed than his. Pender gulped and replied, "I don't have a problem with you, McLean."

"But you have a problem with these nice folks who are in here having a good time and minding their own business?"

"I thought they were protecting Barboza. He's the one I have a problem with."

"You would be wise to leave now and forget about starting anything with Joe Barboza. He'll end your boxing career. And trust me, your life will be ruined, too."

A large man with Pender spoke up, "Barboza won't fuckin' touch Paul. And we aren't letting anyone jump in, if you catch my drift."

Buddy replied to Pender's friend, "Why don't we settle this outside, and you and I can go first."

Aware of McLean's reputation, Pender spoke up, "No, we're leaving. Let's go, fellas."

"Hey Pender, that's the only intelligent statement you've made since you walked in," chimed the bartender.

"You shut up, or I'll come back another night."

"No, you won't," Buddy interjected. "This man is a friend of mine. You boys have to leave, right now."

Pender's crew looked at each other for a moment, then walked toward the exit. Buddy stood by the front door as they went outside. The Somerville men and several patrons followed the Pender group. A few words passed between Buddy's friends and Pender's.

Buddy said, "Let 'em go. It's past their bedtime."

The Somerville lads and bar patrons had a good, long laugh as the harassers piled into their car. When they passed by the bar, the driver, who happened to be the same big man Buddy had just invited to settle with, rolled down his window, stuck out his middle finger, and shouted to Buddy, "Fuck you, McLean." Then the driver stomped on the gas pedal and tore off down the boulevard.

Buddy went after the car like he was shot from a cannon. With the stop-and-go traffic on the parkway, Buddy caught up to them in seconds. He blasted a huge right hand through the open window and into the driver's temple. Pender's automobile banged into the one in front of them. Buddy pulled the driver from behind the wheel while the car was still running. Pender was sitting up front and stopped the vehicle but did not get out. The other two sat frozen in the back seat. The parkway was at a standstill. Onlookers from both sidewalks stood awestruck as Buddy smashed his right fist into the driver's face, spinning him around and down in the middle of the street. Then Buddy straddled the belly-down driver, grabbed two handfuls of hair and slammed his face into the pavement.

As he was about to slam the driver's face into the street a second time, he begged, "No! Please, stop. I'm sorry. I'm sorry."

Buddy released his hold on the driver and dropped him to the pavement. He walked over to the driver's door, leaned in and asked Paul Pender, "How 'bout it, Champ? You wanna go a few rounds?"

Pender replied, "I'm sorry that happened, Buddy. Just let me get him, and we'll be on our way. I don't want any more trouble with you."

Buddy advised Pender, "If he can't back it up, then he should keep his mouth shut. Otherwise, this is what happens."

Pender looked down at his friend laid out in the middle of the street. He nodded to McLean, and Buddy walked away.

Back in the nightclub, one of Buddy's friends was approached by an older patron. "McLean is the most impressive man I've ever seen. You saw how Paul Pender, a pro boxer, just melted. McLean didn't do a thing until that driver acted like an asshole."

"Yeah, he won't fight unless he has to."

"Plus, that baby face must fool a lot of guys."

"He doesn't like that kind of talk, but yeah, it's true. I've heard a lot of people say that. Any man who is about to fight Buddy probably looks into those young, blue eyes and thinks he can't be that tough. Then imagine how the guy tries to comprehend the explosion set upon him when the fighting starts. Rapid-fire knuckles from rock-hard fists, nonstop."

"I've never heard anyone say it like that before."

"You have to understand, I've seen that explosion more than a few times. And when it happens, it happens damn fast."

"Oh, wow. Well, do you think it would be okay to say hi and buy him a drink?"

"Sure. Go ahead. He's a great guy. I'll take one, too, if you don't mind."

"Coming right up."

*September 30, 1956*

On a Sunday afternoon, a massive powerlifting street brawler walked into Jumbo's, a Teele Square barroom in Somerville. Jumbos is the mascot name for Tufts University athletic teams. The bar was located near the Tufts campus. It was frequented by people who worked at and attended the university, as well as by Somerville residents who lived in the Teele Square area. Buddy was meeting a few friends at Jumbo's after a game of two-hand touch football at Tufts' field.

Buddy was the first to arrive. He walked into the normally lively bar and found it crowded, but silent. The bartender saw Buddy enter the barroom and he came right over to him.

"Hi, Mike," said Buddy to the bartender.

"Buddy, how are you?"

"I'm good. How are you?"

"Ah, all right. Hey, you see the monster sitting in the middle there by himself?"

"Yeah, what about him?"

"You know him?"

"No, never seen him before. Big bastard, though."

"Yeah, huge, and he's been talking loud and tough since he came in here. Nobody wants to walk up to the bar. He already pushed one guy into a table. He's looking for more trouble, and I think he's going to stiff me on the tab, too."

"You want me to take care of this, Mike?"

"Yeah, but can you take him outside?"

"Sure, Mike. You just get a bunch of frosty mugs ready for me and my pals. They'll be along shortly."

"You got it, Buddy. On the house."

"What's his name?"

"Dangerous Dan."

Buddy laughed.

"That's what he told me."

The big man finished his last gulp of brew and was about to order another cold one when he received a hard tap on the back of his shoulder. The man turned with an ugly look to see a hard-staring McLean.

"What the fuck do you want?"

"You're sitting in my seat. Get up."

"Are you shitting me? Say this is a bad joke right now, beg for my forgiveness, and I won't have to fuck you up."

"Let's go outside and settle it."

"Yeah, fuckin' let's."

As Buddy and Dangerous Dan walked toward the door, someone in the bar yelled out, "Hey, Buddy McLean's going to fight."

The big man wondered about the statement and the rush of customers pouring out onto the street. Once outside, several more people yelled out to the neighborhood that, "Buddy McLean is fighting, right now!"

Buddy's friends pulled up and got out of their cars. Bill Cunningham called to Buddy, "What, beating the shit out of the other team isn't enough for one day?"

"This guy's asking for it," replied Buddy.

One of them asked, "Buddy, should I get him a priest?"

"Who the fuck are you, some kind of local hero?" asked Dangerous Dan.

"Some of the folks around here might feel that way."

"Well, their hero is about to take a fuckin' ass whuppin'. And there's a shitload of people that are going to see it happen. I'll let you back down if you want."

Buddy smiled at the big man and said, "I never back down."

"It's your funeral."

As the two men circled one another, a huge crowd from the busy square rushed to the scene. The fire station across the square emptied as if they were answering a call for an inferno. The firemen pushed through the crowd for the opportunity to witness Buddy McLean in a fistfight. Before one punch was thrown, an enormous circle of three hundred men, women, and children had formed around the two fighters. Dangerous Dan began to wonder, *Who the fuck is this guy?*

McLean went straight at the big man, ducked a right cross and delivered six blistering body shots. Buddy followed with a looping

127

left hook to the man's jaw. He staggered back, and McLean closed in. But Dangerous Dan was not badly hurt. He lunged for Buddy and tied him up. He was eight inches taller than Buddy and outweighed him by more than one hundred pounds. Buddy was struggling to get loose as Dan bear hugged him and threw Buddy onto the hood of a parked car. Buddy rolled off the hood and resumed his attack. Buddy crowded Dangerous Dan and kept thumping his rib cage. Dan bear-hugged Buddy under his arms again and lifted him high off the sidewalk. As he was starting to toss Buddy, McLean clapped the big man's ears. He immediately dropped Buddy, and McLean began firing body shots again.

Dangerous Dan's ears were ringing and he was gasping for air. He grabbed McLean by the shoulders and kneed him in the solar plexus and then to the face, but Buddy kept punching. McLean delivered a hard, right uppercut to Dan's chin and a left hook to his jaw. That combination staggered the big man again. This time, Dan went back a step off the sidewalk, and the unsteady landing rolled his ankle. Grimacing in pain, Dangerous Dan momentarily lost his concentration and Buddy uncorked a lightning right cross, breaking Dan's nose. Dan covered his face, and Buddy resumed hammering his body. With a perfect left hook, Buddy cracked one of the man's ribs. Dan pushed McLean back and yelled, "Enough! You can have your damn seat."

Buddy replied, "That's good. Let's go have a beer."

The two shook hands and walked back toward the bar while the crowd applauded and voiced their approval of how well Buddy had performed.

As the gathering began to disperse, Dan stopped Buddy and told him, "I'm going to pass on that beer."

"You sure? Not just one for the road?"

"No, thanks, really. I'm not feeling too good. I might have to go to the hospital."

"What's wrong?"

"I know my nose is broke, and I think you might have cracked a few ribs, and my ankle is killing me. Aw, fuck. My whole body is killing me. It feels like I got hit by a train."

"Yeah, but you're a big, young guy. You'll be okay in no time."

"Yeah, well, I'm sorry about giving you all that shit inside the bar, and I don't know who you are, but I never lost a fight until today. And all these people know you. And I should've picked up on that, but I guess it was a lesson learned the hard way."

"Where are you from?"

"Portland, up on Munjoy Hill."

"That's a tough neighborhood."

"Yeah, it is. But they don't have anyone like you."

"Well, thanks. You want a ride to the hospital?"

"Nah, I'll get there okay. Again, I'm sorry about all that shit, and will you give the bartender this for me?" He handed Buddy two twenty-dollar bills. "Tell him I'm sorry about being an asshole."

"All right. I think you have the potential to be a good man. Go take care of yourself."

They shook hands again and went their separate ways. As the big man was climbing into his car, a firefighter from across the street walked up and asked him, "What was it like, fighting Buddy McLean?"

"It was like being shot with machine gun bullets over my entire body. I wish one of you guys would've told me what I was getting into here."

"Would you have believed us?"

Dangerous Dan slowly shook his head and smiled. "Probably not."

"Looks can be deceiving."

*October 14, 1956*

On an unseasonably warm Sunday afternoon, Buddy McLean and John Canty were talking outside of Raymond Grande's business. A brightly dressed man named Antoine pulled up to the curb in a shiny white Oldsmobile with the convertible top down. He had a twelve-year-old boy with him, sitting in the passenger seat. Buddy and John watched the pair stroll into the pizza shop as Buddy's friend Bobby Blaisey was coming out. "What's Liberace doing in Somerville?" asked Bobby.

The three men had a good laugh, then Canty said, "That guy is a pedophile."

"What the fuck is that?" asked Blaisey.

"He diddles little kids," replied Canty.

"Why isn't he getting raped in prison?" asked a steaming McLean.

"Nobody wants to file a complaint because he pays off the kids and their families. Plus, the boys are scared, and the families are embarrassed."

"Jesus, John, that shit has to stop."

Canty looked at his friend for a moment, then told Buddy, "He lives at the top of Moreland Street. But we think he commits his crimes in that car. He calls it "The Club House."

Buddy nodded to John and told Bobby, "Let's go."

The next morning, Canty was dispatched to see about a car found in the Mystic River. It was Antoine's Oldsmobile. The previous night it was shifted into neutral and rolled down the steep hill, then across Mystic Avenue, then across a patch of grass, and then into the water.

Antoine was standing on the shoreline, stamping his feet and crying.

Buddy pulled up to the scene with Bobby Blaisey and yelled out, "What's up?"

John pointed to the ruined convertible being pulled from the river.

Buddy shouted out, "The Club House is closed."

Antoine squeaked, "You bastards."

Buddy smiled and got out of his car. But then, with dead eyes, Buddy walked up to Antoine and said, "You knock off the shit with those little kids, or you're going to be floating down that river."

Antoine was horrified. He did not say a word.

# Organizing the Winter Hill Gang

*August 22, 1957*

Buddy's best friend, Joe McDonald, decided to leave Somerville for a while. This was to avoid being arrested for a couple of robberies where he was the prime suspect. Instead of sitting in a prison cell, waiting for a trial to begin, Joe decided it was more appealing to see the country, specifically Florida. Before heading out, Joe Mac called his good friend Buddy McLean to come by his house. "I'm going to be gone for a spell. I'd like you to take over my numbers and shylock business. What do you think?"

Joe McDonald

"You show me what to do, and I'll run it for you."

"Great. This will be a major load off my mind, knowing the business is in good hands. We're going to be partners, and you'll be making some decent money."

"All right, Joe. That sounds good. And you won't have to worry, I'll take care of everything."

"That's why I chose you. You're the one guy I knew I could trust, and nobody's going to fuck with you. I won't have to worry about someone else trying to move in on me."

They both nodded, smiled, and shook hands. On the walk home, Buddy thought: *After what he did for me, how could I ever turn him down? I wouldn't. I'm going to return the favor. I'm going to help him with this. If I can maintain the same amount of money he's currently making, he'll be happy. But I might be able to expand it. I'll get this organized and make a lot of money for both of us.*

Within a couple of months, Buddy more than tripled the amount of betting stations Joe had previously controlled. He did this by soliciting friends who managed three social clubs: the Baltimore Post, the VFW, and the Italian-American Club. These people were only too happy to come on board. Soon he had all the barber shops on Winter Hill and East Somerville placing bets through Joe McDonald's book. He also picked up the bowling alley and a neighborhood pool hall. The business quickly flourished. Then, a few months later, three bar owners on lower Broadway approached Buddy.

Mike Khoury stated, "Buddy, we want to be with you."

"I thought you guys are with the Angiulos."

"We are, but the McLaughlins are trying to muscle in. It's a mess. Someone's going to get hurt."

"The Angiulos know about this?"

"Yes, but they're not helping us. The Hughes brothers have been showing up and making threats, and pushing people around."

"All right, you guys are with me now. Tell the Angiulos. And the next time the Hughes boys show up, tell them, too."

"The Angiulos are not going to like this."

"You want me to speak with them?"

"Yes."

"All right, I will."

The owners of State Spa, Whalen's, and The Cozy nodded to Buddy.

To not get overwhelmed or disorganized, Buddy hired a few trustworthy friends to help oversee specific locations. Buddy personally collected the profits each weekend. He spent about four hours making sure the pay ins and payouts were accurate. He subtracted the total going to the house and the overseer. Then after reaching the bottom line, Buddy split Joe Mac's and his share, which was fifty-fifty.

*This is easy money. I can't understand why so many people gamble. It's not for me. I would not want to depend on luck to take home money.* Buddy was earning a lot of money from honest, hard, physical labor. He began accumulating much more with his growing illegal enterprise.

The loan-sharking business was run right out of his house. Buddy kept cash and individual index cards in a locked tin box tucked away in the closet of the master bedroom. Any transactions, loans, or payoffs made throughout the day were recorded on a pad of paper. When he got home at night, Buddy transferred the documentations to the index cards along with any cash received. Buddy's bookkeeping skills were precise.

However, he did not push to increase this method for accumulating funds. Buddy did not care for chasing people down to collect late payments. He felt empathy for many of them. Most loan sharks would threaten or rough up delinquent customers. Buddy was more apt to reason with a man who owed him money. He maintained a line of two-way communication and respect when dealing with a late payment. His style made people feel bad about being late. He was well-liked and feared at the same time. So were his friends.

# Becoming a Crime Boss

*December 7, 1957*

Al Boudreau, a then seventeen-year-old Somerville product from Magoun Square, finally met Buddy McLean. Al and his friend Johnny Racioppi were drinking beers in State Spa. Buddy walked into the barroom with a few of his friends. They greeted everyone and sat down at a table near the back.

A few minutes later, Buddy walked up to the boys and introduced himself. Al winced a bit when he felt the strength of Buddy's handshake. Buddy then asked the boys, "Hey, fellas, would you mind doing me a favor?"

"Sure, what do you want us to do?" responded Al.

"Run up to White Tower and get a bunch of cheeseburgers. We're going to feed the whole bar. There's about two dozen in here, including you two. We'll get fifty."

"All right, Buddy, anything else?"

"No, I'm going to call it in, so they'll be ready when you get there. We're going to get French fries and onion rings, too. Hey, Mike, do you have any ketchup in here?"

"No, I don't," answered Mike Khoury.

"All right, I'm going to add four bottles of ketchup to the order," he said to the boys. "You guys finish your beers, then head on up."

He handed Al a one-hundred-dollar bill. "This should cover it, and if you bring it back hot, you get to keep the change."

The boys swigged their beers and hurried out the door.

*January 4, 1958*

Buddy and his pals showed up at the Winter Hill bowling alley, where Al and Johnny were working as pinsetters. Buddy greeted the boys, then he and his pals began bowling.

Johnny wasn't very fast at setting pins, and Billy Winn, who was with Buddy, started to get agitated. "You better get moving, kid, or you're going home with a swollen ankle."

"Fuck him," murmured Johnny to Al, and he proceeded to move slower.

All of a sudden, Billy hummed an underhand fastball at Johnny. Johnny barely jumped out of the way.

"That guy is fuckin' crazy," exclaimed Johnny to Al.

"Then you better get moving, like he said."

"Yeah, no shit."

*January 10, 1958*

Two Somerville men were sitting in Khoury's State Spa, having a few beers. One asked the other, "Did you meet with McLean yet?"

"I did. I went up to his house after work."

"What did he say?"

"He said he'd give me another week to pay him back."

"Wow, he wasn't mad?"

"Not really, it was more like he was disappointed."

"What?"

"Yeah, no shit. I thought he might break my nose or something, but he just told me to pay him next week."

"Wow."

"Yeah, he's such a nice guy, you don't want to let him down."

"Of course, there's that constant reminder that he's the toughest guy around, and you really shouldn't get on his bad side."

"Yeah, that too."

*February 1, 1958*

The Angiulo brothers, Jerry is second from the right.

Tempers began to flare up, and, before things got out of control, Buddy called for a meeting with the Angiulo brothers. They were the Mafia bosses of, not only Boston, but all of Eastern Massachusetts. They operated out of the North End. The Angiulos had never met McLean but were aware of his reputation as a tremendous street fighter. The Angiulo brothers were smart in that they did not react to a difficult situation without thinking it through. They were willing to at least listen to what McLean had to say.

The North End men also knew that McLean had earlier worked with their boss, Raymond Patriarca, of Providence, Rhode Island. Buddy and a few of his friends had put together a few truck hijackings and sold the stolen goods directly to the

New England mob boss. Although it agitated him, the North End boss, Jerry Angiulo, let it pass, knowing it was a bad idea to aggravate his boss.

Buddy welcomed the Angiulo group as they entered the meeting place Buddy had set up in Somerville at State Spa. It had recently been a North End bookmaking branch.

"Hi, fellas. Come on in. Let's sit over here. Can I get you guys some drinks?"

Four Angiulo brothers and three of their associates proceeded toward a long table at the back of the smokey, quiet, nondescript barroom. Buddy introduced the Mafia to his friends, Tommy Ballou, John Hurley, and Russ Nicholson, who were sitting at the bar. Howie Winter and Sal Sperlinga, a successful Somerville bookmaker and friend to Buddy and Howie, joined the men at the table.

After everyone settled into their seats and had their drinks served, Buddy began the conference. "I'm representing my friend Joe McDonald. He is out of town right now, and he asked me to watch over his business. He told me that you were reasonable men and that if we came to an agreement we would be able to help each other in the future."

"Tell us what you want to do," responded Jerry Angiulo.

Buddy opened and spread a map of Somerville and surrounding cities on the table. With a marker and a yardstick, Buddy drew a line straight through the middle of Somerville. "Winter Hill and lower Broadway is Joe McDonald's, everything else belongs to Sal. The only exception is Union Square, that's going to go to Joe Mac."

"Where does that leave us?" asked Jerry.

"You guys leave Somerville for us only, and, you have my word, we won't be looking to expand into any other area that you now control."

"Why the fuck would I agree to this?" exploded Jerry.

"As things stand right now, I have all these Somerville bookmakers wanting to join me and Sal. The McLaughlins are trying to muscle in on them, and they feel like you're not backing them like you should. There's a lot of confusion and arguments over who controls what area. You don't need this headache. Let me take it, and the McLaughlins will know that we're friends. And that should get them to back off."

"You want to take on those fuckin' animals?"

"I'll work it out with them."

"If I agree to this, then I'm out at least five to six grand a month."

"Yeah, but I'm going to be dealing with the McLaughlins. They're crazy, you just said so yourself. That alone deserves a good payday."

"That's still a shitload of money I'm leaving behind. People will take it as sign of weakness. I can't have that."

"You're not weak at all, Mr. Angiulo. You're a smart businessman who increased the number of his associates with capable, honest men. You're paying a lot of money for people who will make your business stronger."

"How does my business get stronger here?"

"We will be ready to help you with any problems that might come up."

"You mean adding muscle to my business?"

"Yes, but in other ways, too. We can always talk about other business ventures."

"Like hijacks?"

Buddy smiled. "That could be one of them."

Jerry Angiulo stared hard into the eyes of Buddy McLean. After a long moment, he nodded in agreement.

To give the Angiulos something to go home with, Buddy offered, "How about any large bets that we can't handle, we'll lay off to you."

"Yes, if you'll be the collector on those large bets."

"Of course, we'll take care of that."

"Anything else, Mr. McLean?"

"Call me Buddy. Yeah, if you guys need help in collecting outstanding debts or anything else that might come up, we'll be ready to work at a fifty percent split."

"Like partners."

"Yeah, partners."

Jerry motioned his head toward Illario Zaninno, the Mafia's enforcer and bill collector. He sat quietly at the table as the two leaders were finishing their conversation.

"I have a bill collector."

"Yeah, you do, and I understand he's good." Buddy nodded toward Zaninno.

Zaninno nodded back.

"But you know what they say."

"What do they say?" asked Jerry.

"There's power in numbers. And you just picked up some good guys in case you ever need them."

Buddy stood up and offered his hand to Jerry. The Mafia boss stood and obliged.

"So now you're moving up in the world," stated Angiulo.

"Yeah, well, it still belongs to Joe Mac."

"Send him my best regards."

"I will."

On the ride back to the North End, Mike Angiulo stated to his brother, "He's not a bad guy. He's trying to work with us."

"Yeah, he seems okay," replied Jerry. "We'll see what happens with those fuckin' McLaughlins."

"What do you mean?"
"They'll try to get McLean to go with them."
"You think so?"
"Count on it."

# The Business Grows

*March 23, 1958*

Raymond Patriarca, the boss of New England's Mafia, thought very highly of Buddy. "He's a smart kid and you can trust him—a real sweet guy."

Patriarca was secretly recorded in his Providence, Rhode Island, office by the FBI while talking about Buddy McLean.

Raymond Patriarca

When the rest of Boston's higher profile gangsters caught wind of Buddy McLean's negotiating skills, they asked to meet with him. He met with several of them at the Capitol Bar in

Somerville. They were trying to get a feel for what this young up-and-comer was all about. Some were looking for assistance in dealing with the North End, the McLaughlins, or other difficult people. "We'll pay you to represent us, or, maybe, you'd let us join you."

Buddy responded with, "Look, I'm already busy enough. I don't have time to represent you, plus I promised the Angiulos that I would stay in Somerville."

"Geez, we were hoping you could help us. If we can't collect, the McLaughlins or the North End will be trying to muscle in on our territory."

Buddy thought for a moment, then offered, "How about hiring a few of my friends to be your collectors. They're very reliable, and they would be representing me."

"So, we would be able to use your name."

"Yeah, that's right, but only as a collector."

"What's it going to cost?"

"My guys keep half of what they collect."

"Wow, that's a big chunk."

"It is, but they're damn good, and I have to get paid for lending them out. I'll take my share from their half."

An older Jewish bookmaker spoke up first, "Okay, Buddy, it sounds good to me. I'm in."

The rest of the men looked at each other and nodded in agreement. They were in, too.

Buddy's men were put to work immediately. Before sending them out, he met with his collectors and instructed them to, "Be friendly, but firm. You have to show respect but get right to the point. Keep on track and let them know you're there to help them settle up. If that doesn't work, let them know you're going to be telling me what happened. If you still don't get a payment started, then I'll go see them."

## Friday, April 4, 1958

The first collection was made on a cold afternoon outside the United States Post Office Garage in South Boston. The conversation went smoothly.

"Herm Newton, how are you?"

"Good. Who the hell are you?"

"Tommy Ballou. Nice to meet you."

"What the fuck do you want?"

"Buddy McLean asked me to talk to you."

"Buddy McLean? You know him?"

"Yeah, he's a good friend of mine."

"What does he want from me?"

"He wants me to help you get a payment plan going with your gambling debt."

"Oh, Jesus, am I going to get a pounding?"

"No. He's a nice guy, as long you're up front with him and we work something out."

"All right, what've I got to do?"

"We're going to set up a weekly payment plan with you that works for both sides."

"Okay."

The collections were made on Friday afternoons, payday for most people at the time. Buddy's men drove throughout Boston gathering debts. It was a nice part-time job for Tommy, John Hurley, Russ Nicholson, and Billy Winn. Nicholson often made his collections while wearing his MDC police uniform. He would finish his shift with the MDC, then drive straight to work for Buddy. The deadbeats were prewarned by the bookmakers to be available for the men.

When they finished making their rounds, the men dropped off the client's share of the recovered cash, and then

they headed back to Somerville to meet with their boss in a
Winter Hill barroom. After receiving his roll of cash for just
being Buddy McLean, he would "Set up the house," and then
be on his way.

# Buddy McLean and the Somerville Police

*July 4, 1958*

Many Somerville police officers revered Buddy McLean. Several were interested in being associated with the Winter Hill man. Sometimes, McLean could use his connections with them to avoid arrests and further his illegal affairs.

Buddy and a few of his friends were drinking inside the 318 Club. Tommy Ballou walked in with a box of fireworks.

"Buddy, take a look at this."

"Wow, barrel bombs. We can have some fun with these. Let's go outside."

He brought his friends out the side door onto Marshall Street and selected a barrel bomb from the box of explosives. Buddy lit the fuse and lofted the barrel bomb high in the air above the treetops down Marshall Street toward Joe McDonald's house. Kaboom! No response. Buddy repeated the toss twice more with hopes that Joe Mac, who had recently slipped into town, would come rushing out to the street.

"His car is right there," stated Buddy.

"Maybe he's a heavy sleeper," suggested John Hurley.

"Or he's on a bender," suggested Tommy.

"Maybe he's trying to have sex with his wife. Any of you young punks considered that?" added Russ Nicholson.

They all had a good laugh as Buddy responded, "Maybe he took off with a different car. One more try." Then he lit and launched one more barrel bomb down the street.

Instead of Joe Mac, a cranky old-timer across from Joe stormed out onto his front porch and started yelling, swearing, and threatening Buddy and his friends. "You fuckin' punks better get the fuck out of here or I'm going to kick your fuckin' asses!"

With that, Russ Nicholson drew his MDC police-issued revolver and fired a round into the old man's Cadillac.

"That's it, I'm calling the cops."

The geezer ran into his house, locked the door, and called the Somerville Police Department. The pranksters hightailed it back to the bar, laughing all the way. Tommy hid the goods under a table in one of the booths while Russ placed his gun behind the bar. The boys resumed their drinking. A few minutes later, two Somerville police officers strolled into the club and walked up to Buddy.

"We got a call. You shot up somebody's car."

"Not me. I'm a Boy Scout."

The club exploded into a fit of uncontrolled laughter. One guy laughed so hard he started vomiting on the floor, to which Buddy asked, "Am I in trouble for that, too?"

Even the cops could no longer contain themselves. When composure returned, one of the officers informed Buddy, "Just come down to the station tomorrow and take care of it, will you?"

"All right, boys. I'll take a ride by. Hey, before you go, let me buy you both a drink. Fourth of July, you guys deserve to celebrate, too."

The cops looked at each other and shrugged. They nodded to Buddy and bellied up to the bar.

*July 8, 1958*

Buddy walked into the Somerville Police Station to answer a complaint for disturbing the peace. He was standing in the lobby, chatting with a few officers, when the man behind the desk made a remark to the other cops about McLean.

"Why are you guys all so happy to see him?"

When nobody responded, he continued, "This guy's no big deal. Don't be givin' him the red carpet. He's no fuckin' saint. He needs to spend some time in a cell or take a few lumps on his fuckin' head. That'll straighten him out."

Buddy turned and stared hard at the desk cop as one fellow officer cautioned him to "Knock it off, John. You're messing with the wrong guy."

The desk cop ignored the warning and hurled his next insult. "Let him try something. I'll introduce him to my nightstick."

"He'll take that club and ram it up your ass, John."

The cop walked around to the front of the desk twirling the club in his hand as he taunted Buddy. "Come on, tough guy, you want to try me? Let's see what you got."

Buddy was squared up with the cop who was standing fifteen feet away from him. The cop felt a sudden surge of uncertainty when he observed the standard prefight look on McLean's face. Buddy sprinted straight at the cop. The cop was shocked that McLean was coming right at him, but he was ready. He took a hard swing at Buddy's head, but the furious McLean blocked him at the wrist with his foreman and slammed the cop into the desk. The club went flying back off the wall as Buddy swarmed the desk cop, who was sprawled on the floor. He proceeded to grab the cop by the front of his shirt and fired a straight right punch onto his left cheekbone.

As he hovered over him, Buddy held tight to the man's shirt collar, his right fist ready to launch again. "Do you want to try that again, or have you had enough?"

"Enough, let me go, McLean. I shouldn't have done that, but you can't hit a cop," was the solemn reply.

"You started it. You got what you deserved."

The other cops stood by but did nothing and said nothing. They all agreed later that their colleague had asked for it, but, more importantly, they did not want to have Buddy McLean mad at them. McLean was not arrested, and the complaint of disturbing the peace was eventually dismissed.

## August 9, 1958

Buddy and Jean met some friends late on a Saturday night at the Baltimore Post, a social club in Somerville. They were having a few drinks and enjoying a good time when two Somerville police officers entered the club to clear everyone out after the last call. One of the cops, a patrolman named Bill "Red" Bavin, approached Buddy. Bavin was an egotistical, envious watcher of McLean. He said to Buddy, "Let's go, McLean. Bar's closed. Give me your drink."

Bavin, who was a few inches taller and twenty-five pounds heavier, reached to pull the drink from Buddy's hand. Buddy moved his hand holding the nearly full glass away from Bavin and placed his empty hand on Bavin's chest.

"You don't fuckin' touch me, McLean. You want to get arrested?"

"I'm not doing anything wrong here, Bavin. I'm finishing my drink that I paid for."

"You're wrong! I said the bar's closed. Now hand me the drink and get the fuck out of here before I take you in, and I'm not going to say it again."

Buddy ignored Bavin's order. He stepped back and finished off his gin and orange juice.

"Here you go, asshole."

He went to hand Bavin the empty glass. Bavin grabbed Buddy's left wrist with his left hand and attempted to pull Buddy's left arm behind his back to handcuff him. As he handed Jean the glass in his right hand, Buddy stiffened his left arm so that Bavin could not move it. Bavin was not only angry, he was also embarrassed that he could not budge McLean's arm. With his friends looking on, and Bavin getting redder by the second, Buddy rotated his wrist against Bavin's left thumb, releasing the hold and established his own crushing grip on Bavin's wrist. Bavin pulled his nightstick from its holster. "You have to be a tough guy, McLean?"

Before he could raise the club, Buddy pulled Bavin toward him and fired a straight right shot to the patrolman's left jawline. Red Bavin went down with a loud thud. John Canty, the second Somerville police officer on the scene, hustled over to the commotion. Canty had been friendly with the McLeans for many years and, while he examined the semiconscious Bavin, he asked Buddy, "What the hell just happened here?"

"I was just finishing my drink, and this guy tried to take it away."

"So you knocked him out for that?"

"No. When I didn't give him the drink, he tried to handcuff me and take a swing with his club."

"Oh, well, then I want you and Jean to leave right now."

"I'm taking my time, John. He started with me," explained Buddy.

"If you don't leave now, you'll be arrested when he comes to," promised Canty.

"Fine. Let's go, Jeannie."

"Thank Christ," said Jean.

"Never a dull moment with him, Jean," offered her friend Pat Sperlinga.

"Yeah, try living with him," she responded.

The McLeans left the Post and began their drive home. Cruising down Broadway past Foss Park, Buddy spotted the blue lights in his rearview mirror flying over the top of Winter Hill. "They're coming after us, hang on tight." Buddy gunned the accelerator of his Chevy Impala to make it to their Otis Street apartment before the cops could pull them over. As he pulled the car to the side of the street, Buddy instructed Jean, "Tell them I'm not home."

He ran into the house and hid in their bedroom. Two patrol cars stopped in front of 6 Otis Street. Red Bavin was the first cop up the stairs, banging on the door.

"Get out here, McLean! You're under arrest!" screamed the jaw-swollen Bavin.

Jean opened the door and stepped outside. She was standing on the top step at the front door with her arms folded. "He's not here. He went out with some of his friends."

"Don't give me that shit. Let me in. I know he's in there," demanded Bavin.

John Canty intervened and said, "You wait out here, Red. I'll go in and get him."

Jean allowed Canty to enter the dwelling. After a quick check, Canty "determined" that Buddy was not home. He walked out front to the porch and stated, "She's right. He's not in there."

Canty, Bavin, and a third patrolman started down the steps. When they were on the sidewalk, Bavin turned around and hollered at Jean so that everyone in the neighborhood could hear, "You tell that fuckin' son of a bitch, cowardly husband of yours that the next time I see him I'm not going to arrest him.

I'm going to kick his fuckin' ass up and down Broadway in front of all his tough fuckin' cronies."

Suddenly, Bavin's eyes bulged wide and his mouth dropped open.

The next day, Jean laughed as she recapped the previous night's events with her friend Pat Sperlinga. "Nutso comes flying out of the house and does a Superman dive past me and lands on top of Bavin between the other two cops. Bavin fell to his back, and Buddy was sitting on his chest and punching him in the face. The other two cops pulled Buddy off him, but not before he gave Bavin a good pounding. Canty told us to go in the house and he'd talk to us later."

"They didn't arrest him?"

"No, but he'll probably have to go to court."

## December 7, 1958

Buddy was in the back room of the 318 Club, a Somerville bar and nightclub, near the top of Winter Hill. At that time, he was running Joe McDonald's bookmaking and loan-sharking interests. It was a Sunday evening and Buddy was sitting at a large table with Russ Nicholson and John Hurley. They were tallying the take from the afternoon professional football games. He was balancing the payouts versus pay ins when a Somerville jeweler was let into the back room. Tommy Ballou followed the jeweler up to the table. The jeweler removed his hat.

"How you doing, Buddy?"

"Hi Frank. What's going on?"

"I have a problem, Buddy."

Buddy put down the money and waited for Frank to continue. He stood in front of Buddy, looking down at the hat he held in his hands.

"What's the problem, Frank?" asked Buddy.

"I don't have the money to pay back what I owe you," Frank replied softly.

Buddy looked over at Russ and asked, "How much does he owe us?"

"Five thousand."

Buddy winced, then asked the jeweler, "What do you want to do, Frank?"

Frank shrugged his shoulders and raised his eyebrows. "Buddy, I'll do whatever you want me to. I don't want to have you or Joe mad at me. That's the last thing I would ever want."

"Well, let's come up with a solution so Joe and I won't have to get pissed off."

All the men in the room had a nice chuckle, which lightened the mood.

Tommy Ballou spoke up, "Frank, you've got insurance on your place, right?"

"Yes, I do."

Buddy immediately knew where Tommy was going with his question. He asked the jeweler, "Have you ever been robbed, Frank?"

"No, I haven't."

Buddy looked him in the eye and nodded. He did not say a word.

The jeweler broke the silence with, "If I got robbed, I could collect on the insurance and pay you back what I owe. Plus, there's over a hundred-grand worth of merchandise in there. What do you think, Buddy?"

"I'll let you know, Frank. Let me think about this first."

"Sure thing, Buddy. Let me know. I'll be around."

When Frank left the room, Buddy conferred with his friends. "That's a bright and busy area. If we rob the place, someone might see us coming or going."

John Hurley asked, "What do you want to do then?"

"We could have our friends in blue step in for us."

"What? That's a bold move, Buddy. It might backfire on us."

"Nah, we'll pick out a few guys who we know would go along with it. They'll pay us to open the back door for them. They go in and rob the joint. Of course, this happens after we go in first and do a little bargain shopping for ourselves."

"Wow. You think they'll go for it?"

"Sure, why not? They'd be taking care of some Christmas shopping. We'll charge them a couple hundred apiece to walk in and grab some stuff. Then, just after they leave, we set off the alarm. They'll walk around to the front of the building and answer the call."

Tommy spoke up, "That's a great idea. I say, let's do it."

They all nodded in agreement.

*December 22, 1958*

Buddy got the keys from the jeweler and handed them to Ballou and Hurley, who drove over to the business and opened the back door for two of Somerville's finest. This was after Ballou and Hurley had set aside a large amount of jewelry for Buddy and the rest of their group.

When the pilfering was complete, the Winter Hill men went outside and broke the front plate glass window, which set off the alarm. The call was answered by the same cops who had just robbed the place.

Buddy was out with his wife and a few friends when it all went down. He retrieved the money owed from the jeweler through his insurance company, plus some cash from the cops. Then, after he selected a few items for Jean, Buddy sold off his share of the stolen jewelry to a dealer in downtown Boston.

# A Fine Irish Neighbor

*May 1, 1959*

Buddy and Jean purchased their first house and moved their family to Snow Terrace, off Jaques Street in the Winter Hill area of Somerville. Right away, Buddy made an impression on the other families in the neighborhood.

3 Snow Terrace

On a Friday evening, Buddy walked into his house and called to his daughter, "Lea, come outside, I have something to show you."

Lea came running. "What is it, Daddy?"

She pushed through the screen door to the front porch, where Buddy was standing.

A huge cardboard box was standing out on the terrace in front of their home.

"Look what fell off the back of someone's truck," he said with a big smile. "Let's go check it out."

Lea's eyes bulged, and she covered her mouth as she gasped. It was a box for a refrigerator, and it was filled to the top with one hundred brand new Barbie Dolls. It had all the accessories (clothes, houses, compartments, cars) that came with the dolls.

Buddy told his daughter to, "Keep the ones you like, then share with the other little girls in the neighborhood."

"I will, Daddy. Thank you. I love you."

She jumped into Buddy's arms, squeezed his neck, and smothered his face with kisses.

The next day, Buddy backed his big box truck into the terrace. He jumped out and walked to the back of the truck and lifted the rear door. Then he called Jimmy and Michael out of the house and had them deliver live lobsters to the front doors of dozens of neighbors. The neighborhood was buzzing as many folks came outside to see what the commotion was. At one point, Michael began chasing Lea and her friends around the neighborhood with a big live lobster in his hands. Buddy kept pulling the containers off the back of his truck. He reminded Jimmy and Michael to, "Be polite and respectful, and don't take any money from the neighbors."

"This is fun, Dad," exclaimed Michael as he grabbed another container and ran off.

The neighbors were receptive to Buddy's generosity. As the boys were delivering the lobsters, one neighbor said to the other, "This guy is great, ain't he?"

"He sure is. I can't wait to see what he brings us next week."

A month later, Buddy staggered into the house looking like he gained twenty pounds. His face was turning red and he was bulging out of his rain jacket. Jean asked him, "What the hell happened to you?"

Buddy replied, "Help me, Jeannie, I can't get this jacket off."

She unzipped and pulled off his jacket. "Oh my god, are you crazy?"

Buddy was wearing about fifty different colored tee shirts. He and his pals grabbed the shirts off some truck in Boston. It took Jean a while to get the shirts off. "You're lucky you didn't suffocate, you crazy bastard. What are you going to do with all these shirts?"

"I'll keep ten and have the boys give the rest out in the neighborhood."

Buddy also took care of Joe McDonald's loan-shark operation from his new home. Some of the neighbors became clients. One neighbor came to the house to speak with Buddy about being late with his payment. He only owed Buddy fifteen dollars, but he asked, "Can I have another week to pay you back? I missed a day's pay to take my kid to the hospital. Then I had to go out and buy food for the house."

Buddy was sitting at the table in the kitchen looking at the man across from him but not saying anything. Then he looked at his wife and said, "Jeannie, go upstairs and get my tin box, would you?"

She went up and grabbed the box, then brought it down and put it on the table in front of Buddy. The neighbor didn't know what was going to happen. He was scared.

Buddy opened the box and pulled out a twenty-dollar bill. He handed it to the man and said, "Pay me back as soon as you can."

Relief appeared all over his face. "Oh shit. Thank you, Buddy. I wasn't expecting this. Thank you."

"All right, now you pay me back as soon as you can. And make sure I'm at the top of your list."

"I will, Buddy. Thanks again."

After the neighbor left, Jean told Buddy, "I could run this better than you. You're too easy. Everyone is going to find out and they'll think they won't have to pay you back."

"Listen, I'll give a guy one chance to get caught up. Then if he doesn't pay up, I'll shut him down, and if it gets out that he's a deadbeat he'll never get another loan around here. Nobody wants to be known as a deadbeat. That's almost as bad as being a rat."

"I guess you're right, but I wouldn't loan out too much money unless they put up some collateral."

"Maybe you *would* be better at this than me."

They both had a nice laugh.

# Buddy's In-Laws

*June 6, 1959*

Jean McLean's youngest brother, Tommy Kelley, was born in 1938. He was said to be one of Somerville's greatest basketball players. Known for playing tenacious defense and running the offense with precision passing, he kept his teammates in constant motion around the hoop. Tommy led his teams to many victories in leagues and tournaments throughout Boston and well beyond.

Jean was very proud and protective of Tommy. She made it clear that, "Nobody better touch a hair on his head." People who knew the McLeans were more afraid of Jean than of Buddy.

Even Buddy once spoke of Jean to his friends, "She's not only tough, but she's crazy, too."

Jean wanted Buddy to let Tommy drive his beautiful, white Chevy Impala convertible to a dance with some friends. Buddy agreed, but added, "I need the car back by ten o'clock tomorrow morning. I have an important meeting."

"No problem, Buddy. It'll be here," said Tommy.

After the dance, Tommy, his date, and their friends spent the rest of the night and into the morning at Revere Beach. Finally, Tommy realized to his friends, "Oh shit, I lost track of the time. I have to get the car back to Buddy."

He hurried everybody home to Somerville. After dropping off his date and friends, Tommy headed toward the McLean home on Snow Terrace.

Driving slowly down Jaques Street with the top of the convertible down, Tommy passed several neighbors who alarmingly asked him, "Where've you been?"

Another warned, "Tommy, you're a dead man!"

Panic-stricken, Tommy parked the car at the corner of Snow Terrace and Jaques Street and hustled up to the house. His sister, Jean, met him at the front door. "Where the hell have you been? Buddy's going nuts. He's down the street. Just bring him the car right now and take off. I told him not to hit you, but you know how he is. Now go."

Tommy sprinted back to the Chevy, hopped in and continued down Jaques Street. One hundred yards away, at the corner of Jaques and Bond Street, the toughest man alive was sitting on a street curb, a large, rolled-up, brown paper bag next to him. As he spotted his Impala driving toward him, Buddy grabbed the paper bag and sprung to his feet. "Where have you been?" bellowed the furious McLean.

Tommy pulled the vehicle to the side of the road and parked it, roughly fifty feet away from his storming brother-in-law. He ejected himself from the driver's seat with the engine running. Tommy yelled to his brother-in-law, "I'm sorry, Buddy," and began running back toward Snow Terrace. He figured his sister would save his hide if Buddy chased him. The irate McLean was running late for his meeting, so he slid into his car and drove away. Tommy stayed away from Buddy for two weeks to let him cool off. Buddy, however, loved Tommy and he soon forgot about the late return of his car. He began to let Tommy drive the vehicle every weekend.

## July 17, 1959

On a Friday night, Buddy was going to the Alibi Club with some friends. He made plans with Tommy to drop him off, then pick him up at closing time. While Buddy was at the Alibi, Tommy met up with his girlfriend and took her to a movie. After spending time with his girl, Tommy drove her home and then went to get Buddy.

Buddy and a Somerville friend, a good-sized man named John Devine, were walking out of the Alibi as Tommy pulled up. Buddy and John slid into the car and Tommy drove off.

"There's a lot of traffic here, Buddy," stated Tommy.

"Yeah, it's all the bars emptying out and the people coming back from Boston," replied Buddy.

"I'll try to get around all this," he said as he turned right onto a side street.

"Tommy, this is a one-way street. Turn around and go back."

Tommy tried to turn the vehicle around as another car came straight toward the Somerville boys. Tommy pulled back to the side of the road to let them pass by. Instead, the vehicle pulled over right in front of Buddy's Impala, blocking their way.

"Looks like trouble, Buddy," said John Devine from the back seat.

Four sailors got out of the car. Buddy pressed firmly on Tommy's chest and said, "No matter what happens, don't get out of the car."

Without saying another word, Buddy was out of the automobile and marching fast toward the driver of the other vehicle. The sailor started to say something about Tommy's driving skills, but Buddy drilled a right fist to the man's chin and knocked him back onto the hood of his car. The sailor who sat behind the driver was the next one to get it. Just after he smashed the driver, sailor number two called Buddy a "Motherfucker."

Buddy uncorked a four-punch combination on sailor number two that sent him to the sidewalk, unconscious. The third sailor was about to jump on Buddy's back but was grabbed at the back of his collar by John Devine, who whipped him around and tossed number three against the wall of a brick house. The fourth sailor came around the back of the car and took a swing at Buddy. But the street-savvy McLean saw it coming out of the corner of his left eye and ducked. As he dipped under the punch, Buddy drove his left shoulder into number four's solar plexus and slammed him into the side of the car. Buddy quickly straightened up and pinned number four with his left hand and fired five right cannonballs to his face. End of fight.

Number one was not quite done. He came off the hood with the intention of getting back into the brawl, but Devine was still holding number three. Big John flung number three into number one as Buddy closed in. The powerful McLean belted each sailor with what he referred to as "One for the road." The Somerville boys walked back to Buddy's Chevy and slipped in. Buddy said to Tommy, "Let's go. I'm hungry."

Not believing what he had just witnessed, Tommy did not know what to say, so he said nothing. Buddy and John were not talking until Buddy spoke up, "All those white uniforms looked like bowling pins."

"Yeah, and you rolled a nice string there," replied Devine, to which they all had a good laugh.

After dropping off Big John, the brothers-in-law returned to the McLean house, where Jean was playing cards with her mother and sisters in the living room. Before they got out of the car, Buddy advised Tommy, "Don't mention anything about what just happened to anyone."

"No one?"

"Right. No one."

"Why not? That was tremendous."

"All it does is bring more trouble my way. I don't need it. And besides that, if your mother or your sisters find out, they're not going to let you hang out with me. You know what I mean?"

"Yeah, you're right."

"All right. Let's go eat."

When they walked into the house, Buddy immediately asked, "Who's hungry?"

Everybody was, and Buddy quietly went to the kitchen and made BLT sandwiches.

## August 8, 1959

On a warm Saturday evening, Buddy fought the New England Golden Gloves heavyweight champ Herbie Bolduc, Jr., who was a Charlestown tough guy who had beaten up a Teamster friend of Buddy's. The much younger and larger Townie had plenty of incentive to take on Buddy McLean. First was the fact that, almost a decade earlier, the twenty-year-old McLean had clobbered Herbie Bolduc Sr., who had also won a few heavyweight titles in the Navy as well as some Golden Gloves tournaments. Second, Buddy McLean was then twenty-nine years old and, although still in great shape, was a family man more than a fighter.

They fought at a lumberyard in Charlestown. Before the fight began, Herbie Jr. yelled at Buddy and proclaimed, "I'm going to make you pay for what you did to my father."

"Your old man thought he was tough, too. Let's see if you're any better," responded McLean.

"Oh, man, I'm really going to enjoy this."

They squared off in the middle of the yard. A decent-sized crowd of men were watching, including Bernie McLaughlin, the Charlestown gang leader and a great street fighter himself. The match was basically five minutes of unremitting toe-to-toe punching. Young Bolduc's fists found Buddy's face repeatedly. Buddy was using his bread-and-butter strategy of attacking the body.

Buddy's face was bloody and swollen, but he did not let up. When he sensed that Bolduc was tiring, the Somerville punching machine shifted into overdrive. He increased the speed and power of his frenzied blows to swing the momentum in his favor. McLean wore down the powerful Bolduc and pounded him into an upright but defenseless position. Bolduc was unconscious, but still standing. McLean's eyes were swollen nearly shut, and he could not see that Bolduc was defeated. He continued punching Bolduc after he had staggered back against a stacked pile of wood. Buddy grabbed Bolduc's shirt at the chest and fired a straight right blast to his face. The punch made two disturbingly ugly, cracking sounds. The first was the sound of bones breaking in Bolduc's face; his left cheekbone and nose were crushed. The second sound was the back of Bolduc's head bouncing off a wall of stacked wood.

The totally captivated audience immediately let out a loud, united moan of shock. Russ Nicholson and Tommy Ballou stepped in and pulled Buddy away.

The fifty people who watched the fight could not accept as reality what had just happened. They had observed Buddy McLean withstand considerable damage to his face, yet he did not go down or even take a step back. He had sent another Bolduc to the emergency room.

During the fight, Bernie McLaughlin remained quiet and neutral. He did not root for either man. Afterward, he walked up to Buddy, shook his hand, and said, "Nice fight, McLean. You've got great hands, and I've never seen anyone take a punch better than that."

Bernie McLaughlin

"Thanks," replied Buddy.

"You should probably get yourself to the hospital. Those eyes don't look too good."

"Nah, I'll be all right. What brings you down here?"

"I was over at Driscoll's having a beer when someone mentioned you two were going to duke it out. So, I figured since I hadn't seen a good fight in a while, I'd take a ride over. And I'll tell you, it wasn't disappointing."

"Well, I'm happy you had a good time. Wish I could say the same. The kid was tough, tougher than his old man."

"Not tough enough."

"Not today."

"I'll see you around."

"All right, see you."

The two shook hands and went their separate ways.

Buddy disregarded the need for medical attention. He drove himself home, walked into his house and sat down in his living room chair. He put his head back and closed his eyes. A few minutes later, his relaxation was interrupted.

His young sister-in-law, Mary Kelley, walked into the room and gasped, "Oh my God, Buddy, what happened?"

"Not now, Mary," Buddy calmly replied.

"No, Buddy, please, you need to get to the hospital."

"Just go out to the kitchen and bring me a beer and an ice pack."

Without another word, Mary left Buddy to fill the ice pack and get him his beer. She instinctively knew not to rile him. As she went out to the kitchen, Mary thought about her brother-in-law: *I don't need to see that temper of his. He kicked that stool right out from under Jean the other night 'cause she hadn't paid the milkman. He's so nice and quiet. Where does that temper come from, and why is he always fighting? He's so generous and helpful to everyone. It doesn't make sense. It must be the people he associates with—troublemakers. Or if he's drinking, it could be the Irish in him.*

Mary returned to the living room and handed Buddy the ice pack, then placed the beer on the table next to him. She sat on the sofa nearby.

"Do you need anything else, Buddy?"

"No."

"Can I ask you something?"

"What?"

"Why do you keep doing this?"

A long sigh, and then, "I don't know, I really don't go out looking for it. It comes to me. There are so many punks out there. They don't respect people. It's rude behavior, I can't stand it."

"I understand what you're saying, but you fight so often, and you can't possibly enjoy the way you feel right now."

"It looks pretty bad?"

"Yes, it does."

"You ought to see the other guy."

They both had a nice laugh, then Mary finished with, "I just don't want to see you ruin that handsome face or have something worse happen. You have a lot of people who depend on you. I wish you would be more careful. Can't you do that?"

"Mary, I appreciate your concern, and I wish things could change, I really do. But this is how it's going to go for now. Now, would you mind getting me another beer?"

After a deep sigh, Mary answered, "Sure, Buddy, coming right up.

# The Friends of Buddy McLean

## Tommy Ballou

*April 8, 1960*

Buddy was not the only tough guy getting into scrapes and scuffles around Somerville and Boston. Bar fights and street brawls were as common as pickup basketball games. Oftentimes, Buddy attempted to be a peacemaker, but he was not always successful.

On a Friday night, Buddy was in Whalen's, a pub/eatery on lower Broadway in Somerville. He was at the bar having drinks with Tommy Ballou and a few other friends when he noticed Tommy's usual, jovial mood suddenly go sour.

"What's the matter?" asked Buddy.

"You see that fuckin' guy who just sat down with the sharp lookin' dame over by the front window?" responded Tommy.

"Yeah, what about him?"

"That son of a bitch owes me money. He keeps telling me, 'I'll pay you when I get it.' And now, here he is, acting like a big shot."

"Don't start in here. Take care of it tomorrow."

"No, Buddy. I've used your name a couple times with him. But he keeps making excuses. And now look at him over there, he thinks he's Rock Hudson. I'll take him outside."

Looking through the window, Buddy noticed a young boy standing on the sidewalk.

He told Ballou, "Hold back for a minute," and he went outside.

Buddy walked up to the boy and asked, "Hey kid. It's late, what are you doing out here?"

"I'm trying to sell the rest of my papers," replied the boy.

The boy looked about nine or ten years old, about the same age as Buddy's son, Jimmy, who was at home and in bed.

"How many more do you have?" asked Buddy.

"About ten," stated the boy.

"I'm buying all of them, and I want you to go straight home." He handed the kid a five-dollar bill for two dollars' worth of the *Evening American* and reminded the youth, "No hanging around. Get home."

The boy responded, "Sure thing, Mr. McLean. Thanks a lot!"

Buddy grabbed the newspapers and headed back into Whalen's. Once inside, he began handing out papers to the customers. When he came to the couple sitting at the table in front of the window with the last of the papers, he placed the newspaper on their table and told the man, "My friend at the bar needs to speak with you outside."

The man looked over at the scowling Ballou and refused to move from his seat. "I'm not talking to him now. We're having dinner here."

Just then, Buddy noticed through the window the young boy still standing on the sidewalk. He excused himself from the couple and motioned to Tommy to wait, then he hustled back outside.

"I told you to get home. Why are you still here?"

"I'm waiting for my pal across the street to sell his papers."

Buddy hollered, "Hey kid," and motioned to the youngster hawking newspapers in front of Khoury's State Spa to cross over. When the youth complied, Buddy grabbed the kid's remaining papers and gave him five dollars. Then he ordered both boys to leave. Buddy reentered Whalen's and left the newspapers on a table by the door. On his way back to the bar, Buddy glanced over at the couple sitting by the window, now ordering their dinner. By the time he walked back to Ballou, his friend was seething.

"I'm going to wallop him."

"Yeah, just don't mess up the joint. Take it outside. I already told him you want to talk to him."

"What'd he say?"

"He won't budge."

"We'll see about that." And without another word, Ballou marched up to the table.

"Excuse me, ma'am. I need to speak with your date outside for a minute."

The man interjected, "We're eating dinner here, Ballou. Get lost."

"Outside, right now," snarled Tommy.

"Scah-roo, Ballou," responded the man, who snickered at his own rhyme.

171

With that, Tommy pulled the dinner table away from the couple, came back to the flabbergasted deadbeat, grabbed him by his lapels, pulled him out of his seat, and violently pushed him through the plate glass window out onto the sidewalk. The woman and several others screamed as Tommy stepped through the now open frame. Buddy rushed to the scene as Tommy pulled the laid-out bloody deadbeat up from the sidewalk with one hand while holding a shard of the broken glass against his throat with the other.

"Tommy, don't," cautioned Buddy.

"Buddy, just watch my back. This bum is about to settle his debt with me and pay for the window."

"We have to go. They're calling the cops."

"We'll leave, right after he empties his wallet."

Tommy maintained his grip on the man's lapel while holding the shard to his throat. Fifty people looked on in hushed silence except for the sobbing, sharp-looking date as the shaking man frantically reached for his wallet and handed it to Tommy. Tommy opened the wallet and took the cash.

"This is barely enough to pay for the window," growled Tommy.

He handed the cash to Buddy and told him to give it to the restaurant's owner. Then he instructed the bloody deadbeat to, "Meet me at the Capitol Bar tomorrow and pay up, and don't make me come looking for you."

"I won't. I'll be there with the money. I promise. I don't want any more problems."

Tommy released the man and looked to the woman and to everyone else in the establishment. "I'm sorry this had to happen in front of you, ma'am. And folks, I'm sorry about ruining your dinners and your night out."

No one spoke a word except Buddy, advising Tommy, "Come on, let's go. I'll come back tomorrow and straighten this out."

"Okay, I'm coming. Just one more thing." He turned to the woman and said, "Darling, you should get rid of this bum. He's a loser. A sharp-looking dame like you shouldn't be wasting her time with a guy like this. By the way, what are you doing next Friday?"

The deadbeat's date had a horrified look on her face and was unable to speak. Tommy nodded, smiled, and said, "Okay. Well then, you think about it. I'll see you around. I got to run." The sounds of the sirens from the Somerville Police cruisers were getting closer.

The incident generated some new Winter Hill folklore. One table with six diners began with, "Who the hell was that guy with Buddy McLean?"

"That's Tommy Ballou, he's a Townie psychopath who goes nowhere without a longshoreman's hook holstered to his belt or a loaded pistol in his pocket. Most of the time he carries both, and he won't hesitate to use either one."

"He's a killer?" asked one of the women.

"No one knows for sure."

A man at the next table spoke up. "Tommy shot a man when he was sixteen."

"Oh my, why?"

"A guy was robbing the clerk's office on the Charlestown docks. Tommy happened to be walking into the office when it happened, and he was packin'. The bosses were so happy with Tommy shooting the robber that he went from scalawag to longshoreman overnight."

"Holy shit! And then he went into the union at sixteen?" asked another man.

"Yes, but it brought him good luck and bad luck at the same time."

"What do you mean?"

"Well, it was good luck that he got into the ILA at such a young age, but it was horrible, how he had to deal with the jealousy down there. Instead of being happy for the kid who was trying to make a living and take care of his mother, they hated his guts."

"It gets pretty hairy down there?"

"It gets fuckin' life-threatening."

"How did he become friends with Buddy McLean?"

"They met down there. They've been friends and partners in crime ever since."

# John Hurley

*October 3, 1941*

Buddy met John Hurley when they were both eleven years old. The two had just finished a football game at Foss Park and leaned over the water bubbler at the same time to have a drink. The collision of both foreheads led to a fistfight. An older gentleman working at the park broke up the scuffle and made the boys shake hands. He told them, "It's better to be friends than enemies, fellas."

As the boys shook hands, they smiled and agreed the old-timer was right. John's family had recently moved to Somerville from Charlestown. Buddy invited John to ride bikes with him around Somerville to gain knowledge of the area. He introduced

Hurley to many people as they pedaled their way throughout the city.

Buddy and John became great friends. They ended up working together and associating with one another daily. Hurley was wiry, quick, and strong. He was an excellent boxer, having learned the craft from his father, who fought in and around the clubs and gyms of Boston. John was a hardworking teenager in the Teamsters Union and, later, the ship docks alongside Buddy.

## May 8, 1988

Over a cup of coffee at a Somerville Dunkin' Donuts, Hurley told Buddy's son Michael, "You had this unbelievable tough, athletic kid who was friendly and respectful to everyone. He was not your typical Somerville smart-ass. He was the kind of kid who'd help an old lady carry her groceries. He'd go around helping people shovel their cars out of the snow and not take any money. I can't tell you how many times I saw him stick up for kids getting picked on. The more I hung around with him, the more I wanted to be like him."

"You know what, he had me and my brother doing things like that when we were young."

"Yeah, I can see him doing that with you and Jimmy."

"What else did you guys do back then?"

"Well, when we were about fifteen, we were working or playing sports together. I tried like hell to keep up with him. I couldn't do it. He was too strong, too fast, and he kept it going all day. He never knew it, but he was doing me a huge favor the whole time. By me trying to stay with him, it made me better than I would have been on my own. He encouraged me to keep pushing when we were unloading freight in those trailers that were hot as ovens, baking in the sun all day. He'd say, 'Come on, keep going. We're going to get rich.' I'm not embarrassed to say that I looked forward to having him praise me when I did well at work or in a game. We were the same age, but other than my parents, there was no one I loved or respected more than your father."

In his deep, cigarette-smoked gravelly voice, John Hurley finished by telling Michael, "Your dad is the best friend I ever had. When we were young, he was my role model. Yeah, we did some things we shouldn't have. But we did a lot more good things than bad, and it was because your father saw to it. He kept things balanced. We grew up in a tough neighborhood, during hard times. We stuck together. I would do anything for him, and he for me."

# Howie Winter

## 1942

Howie and his family moved from West Roxbury to Somerville when he was thirteen. He met Buddy McLean on the first day at his new home. Buddy introduced Howie to all his friends, and the new kid was welcomed into the group.

Soon, they were working, playing sports, and hanging out together. Howie was a year older, but Buddy was the leader and the guy everyone looked up to. When it came to confrontations, however, and there were many, Howie was the guy who tried to settle things.

## November 18, 1949

One night at a club in Boston, Buddy and his friends were involved in a big brawl with a bunch of college football players.

The Somerville boys were outnumbered and outsized, but they were holding their own against the team. Then the Boston police burst through the front door. Howie grabbed Buddy by the back of his collar and hollered, "Buddy, let's go. The cops are here!"

Howie pulled as hard as he could, but he could not remove his friend from the melee. Then Howie looked over Buddy's shoulder and saw that he had a big lineman wrapped in a headlock and was upper-cutting him to the face.

Howie pleaded, "Come on. We're going to get arrested."

"I'm not done with this guy yet. He suckered me. You had enough, big boy?"

"Yuh, yuh, yeah," huffed the lineman.

Buddy released the lineman, and he dropped to the floor. The Somerville boys escaped out the back door. They drove to an all-night diner, where they had breakfast and began rehashing the evening's events.

"That was a fuckin' great fight, boys. I love you guys," an elated Russ Nicholson bellowed.

"Yeah, Russ, you're fuckin' okay in my book, too," replied John Hurley.

Billy Winn chimed in, "Big Nic, you fought fuckin' great. I saw you toss one of them over the bar, and another one into a fuckin' wall. Then you pulled another one off Buddy's back and Buddy turns around and knocks the fuckin' guy out."

"I had him right where I wanted him, but thanks anyway, Russ," said Buddy.

They all began laughing.

"Hey, no problem. Hey, how many knockouts did you have in there anyway?"

Buddy thought for a moment. "Maybe six or seven, it was going so fast. I think I knocked out one guy twice."

They all laughed.

"How the fuck did that happen?" asked Hurley as the friends calmed down.

"I hit him good in the beginning, and his eyes rolled back and down he went. But I guess it wasn't good enough because he came back for more later on."

They all laughed again.

"Look at Howie over there—not a scratch on him," claimed Billy.

"Don't even fuckin' go there, Billy. I fight smarter than all you guys. I pick my spots and pop them. It's the first rule in boxing: hit and don't get hit," responded Howie. "Besides that, if it wasn't for me, you guys would be locked up right now."

"You're right. You got us out of there just in time. Thanks, H," piped in John.

"The voice of reason, that's what I like about you, Howie. You're a good guy to have around. Billy gets us into a fight, and you pull us out of it," stated Buddy.

"How did I get us into the fight?"

Howie interrupted, "Oh, that wasn't you who went over to their table and began pouring their beer into your mug?"

"That was a good one, you have to admit. Those guys had no sense of humor."

"I say, next time we fuckin' leave you home," responded Howie.

"You're not serious about that, right?"

"I tell you what. Instead of me or Buddy paying for the meal, as usual, you pick the bill up this time, and maybe all will be forgiven," answered Howie.

"All right, boys. It's on me," replied Billy.

Buddy looked over at Howie. They both smiled and nodded.

Years later, when Buddy began expanding the Winter Hill Gang, Howie proved to his friend that he was reliable and trustworthy. With that trust, Howie gained considerable responsibility.

# Russ Nicholson

Russ Nicholson was a tall, handsome chap from East Somerville. Buddy met him when they were both students at Northeastern Junior High School. Russ was a happy-go-lucky, fun-loving character who excelled in athletics. Russ did not work with Buddy for the Teamsters or down at the docks. Their friendship was formed through playing sports together and socializing with mutual pals.

When he was seventeen, Russ aspired to buy himself a car. He did not earn a lot of money at the time, so he decided to curtail his social life to save up enough cash.

When Buddy started seeing less of Russ, he asked him one day, "Hey, pal, how you doing? I haven't seen you in a while. Where've you been hiding?"

"Aw, I've been trying to make some extra money, so I can buy a car."

"Yeah, how's that going?"

"Slow but sure, but I still have a ways to go."

"Oh yeah? Well, why don't you take a ride with me," urged Buddy.

"Where to?"

"Not far, I'll show you some cars you might like."

"I'm not ready to buy one yet."

"Hey, it doesn't hurt to look. Let's go."

Buddy drove Russ to a used car dealership in nearby Medford. After browsing the automobiles on the lot, Buddy asked Russ, "See anything you like?"

Russ answered Buddy, "That Buick is kind of nice."

"Let's talk to the guy inside."

"I don't have enough money saved yet."

"We'll just see what he has to say."

Buddy walked the salesman over to the Buick and began inquiring about it. After listening to the man's sales pitch, Buddy asked if he could drive the vehicle to his mechanic for an inspection. The salesman got the keys, and Buddy had Russ drive the three of them to Fay's Transportation in Somerville. Russ was getting nervous, but he followed Buddy's lead.

Once they arrived at Fay's, Buddy asked his friend Vinny Murphy to have a look at the car. When he finished a thorough going-over, Vinny gave the vehicle a thumbs-up approval. On the ride back to Medford, Buddy, sitting in the back seat, began negotiating with the salesman, who was sitting in the front passenger seat. Russ was sweating so much he had trouble holding on to the steering wheel.

Buddy told the salesman, "I agree with you. It's a nice car. But we don't have a lot of money to spend here, so give us a break."

The salesman responded, "Listen, you two seem like nice kids. But I have a wife at home that I take care of, and the cars aren't exactly flying out of here."

"That's my point. You can give us a nice deal on the car, and you'll still make a decent profit on it."

"Now how the hell do you know that?"

"Hey, I know how it works, you leave a little room for guys like me who, when they get a nice deal, they tell all their friends about this place. Plus, when the time comes that Russ or I need a new car, who do you think we're going to go to?"

The salesman massaged his forehead as he slowly shook it. He did not know what to say to Buddy.

Finally, Buddy told the man, "Look, we're going to pay cash for a car today. Do you want to take your wife out to dinner tonight?"

The salesman looked at the seventeen-year-old McLean and responded, "Kid, you should be selling cars. You'd make a fortune. Let's go inside and fill out the papers."

On the way into the office, Russ whispered to Buddy, "What are you doing? I told you, I don't have the money."

"Don't worry about it, I'm going to lend you the money. You can pay me back as you get it."

Russ stopped on a dime and gasped for a breath of air. Then the wide, teary-eyed Nicholson grabbed his friend in a bear hug and lifted him a foot and a half in the air and kissed him on the cheek. "Thank you, Buddy. Thank you! I can't believe you just did that. Oh my God, wait till I tell my parents. They're going to love you, too. Oh my God, thank you."

From that moment on, Russ Nicholson was a fiercely loyal friend to Buddy. "Big Nic," as Buddy called him, went on to become a decorated MDC police officer. His friendship with Buddy never wavered.

Russ spent a half dozen years assisting Buddy with a few illegal activities while he was on the force. Big Nic was even known to collect bookmaking debts while dressed in his police uniform. It eventually caught up to him, and Russ retired before getting fired. That way, he would still be able to qualify for a small pension from the MDC.

# Sal Sperlinga

Buddy and Sal met through playing sports in Somerville. Sal was a decent athlete, but his reputation was built on his strength and toughness. He was considered by many to be the second-best fighter in Somerville.

Though Buddy and Sal never fought each other, they often put on the boxing gloves. Many times they wrestled—on a mat at the YMCA, on grass, on sand at the beach, or in the Foss Park swimming pool.

One afternoon, Sal arrived home after sparring with Buddy. He walked into the kitchen to fill an ice pack. His brother Bobby was sitting at the table eating a sandwich. Bobby looked up to see his brother's face.

"What the fuck happened to you?"

"Buddy."

"Again. Don't you ever beat him?"

"No."

"And you keep going back for more?"

"Listen, I get my shots in. I hit as hard as he does."

"Then what's the problem?"

"He's faster, and he lasts longer."

"Is it worth getting banged up?"

"Of course it is—it's a great workout, and he keeps me sharp."

"Sharp for what?"

"Sharp for my line of work, dopey."

"Oh, all right, if you say so."

At the time, Sal was working at a Boston bar in Kenmore Square called the Rathskeller. He was the head bouncer. The bar was frequented by college students from throughout Boston. On one night, Sal had a problem with a few Boston University hockey players. Though he handled the situation, the players promised they would be back with reinforcement. Sal mentioned this to Buddy, and his friend asked, "You want me to back you up?"

"Sure, if you don't mind."

"I'd be glad to."

The night the six BU hockey players showed up at the bar, Sal was standing at the door with Buddy by his side.

"You guys are not getting in," Sal told them.

"Fuck you!" said the biggest player.

Sal pushed the player back, and that moved the whole group out to the sidewalk. Buddy followed Sal. The punches started flying. The BU boys were pounded and tossed around like rag dolls. In less than one minute the hockey players were done.

As they slowly gathered each other, one said to the rest, "I'm never going in there again."

With Buddy, Sal, and a crowd of people watching the hockey players limp and carry one of them away, Sal asked Buddy, "You want a job?"

"Nah, but I could go for a beer."

Later on, Sal went into the bookmaking business. He eventually became very prominent. Like Buddy, Sal was extremely generous, well-liked, respected, and feared throughout Somerville.

Sal's wife, Pat, and Jean McLean were good friends. They often told Buddy and Sal that they had to go to a wedding shower or a baby shower. Then they and a few other women would go out dancing instead. The men never found out, and the women laughed about it every time.

# Typical Days in Somerville and Lea

## 1960

While driving a truck for the Teamsters and for his own business, Buddy took advantage of the opportunity to load and unload his truck. His thought was, this is a great way to get a workout and get paid at the same time. Plus, he worked much faster than the other men, and he knew that working with a sense of urgency kept his bosses and customers happy. Sometimes he would put on a heavy sweat suit, jog down to the local bowling alley on Broadway and roll a few strings. People wondered, but nobody ever laughed. Other times, Buddy could be seen jogging around Foss Park with his two German shepherds, Cindy and Smokey, right behind him. He also enjoyed running the track at nearby Tufts University. His boys, Jimmy and Michael, would pedal their bicycles as fast as they could, racing their dad around the track. Other days, his daughter, Lea, would run the track with him. He gave the five-year-old a quarter every time she finished a lap.

Lea was born in 1956. Buddy was so ecstatic about having a daughter that he threw a huge party at a club on Broadway that lasted an entire weekend. "My little princess," he'd call her. He loved to cuddle with Lea and teach her to sing his favorite songs.

*May 1, 1960*

On a bright Sunday afternoon, Buddy told his daughter, "Lea, come take a walk with me."

"Okay, Daddy, where are we going?"

"I have to do a few errands. Let's go."

"All right, Daddy."

Father and daughter walked together up Broadway from Temple Street over the top of Winter Hill. Lea was looking inside the windows of the buildings along the way. Buddy was humming his favorite song and waving to the drivers beeping their horns to him on Broadway. As Buddy was humming, Lea asked him, "What is that song, Daddy?"

"It's called," and he sang, "'Unforgettable, that's what you are.'"

"Will you teach me that song?"

"Sure."

And as they continued down the hill toward Ball Square, Buddy began teaching Lea the words to Nat King Cole's famous song. Before they realized it, Buddy and Lea were standing in front of the DAV hall. There was an outdoor payphone there, and Buddy made a couple of quick calls. Lea was getting tired of standing around, so Buddy lifted her on his shoulders. She began singing "Unforgettable." Buddy smiled as he dialed his last call. When he finished the call, Buddy brought Lea inside the hall and sat her on a barstool. He bought her a Coke and a bag of chips. He talked to some men at the bar, but he never left her side. One of the men gave Buddy a big roll of money with elastics around it. He stuffed the cash in his front pocket and, after Lea finished her snack, they said goodbye to everyone and left.

During the walk back up Broadway, Buddy asked Lea, "How's your dancing lessons going, dear?"

"Good, Daddy. I can tap dance now. Watch me."

Lea began tapping away on the sidewalk for her father. He stood there watching with a big smile on his face.

The two continued the walk back up Winter Hill. A minute later, Buddy asked Lea, "Would you like to go to the drive-in movies tonight?"

"Yes! Can I sit up front with you again?"

"Of course. That's your spot, right next to me, forever."

"I love you, Daddy."

"I love you, too, hon."

Soon enough, they were back over the top of Winter Hill. This time, they stopped at the Capitol Bar on the other side of the hill. Inside the Capitol, there were a lot of men drinking, and it was very loud. "Hey, Buddy's here!" boomed one of the men.

Although the place was packed, Buddy had no problem getting Lea a seat at the bar. A big bunch gathered around Buddy to greet him, but he never left Lea's side. He told his friends, "This little girl is a tap dancer," and he lifted her up and onto the bar. "You show them, Lea." A space was cleared out and wiped down for Lea, then she tap-danced for everyone there. His friends got a big kick out of it, but Lea could see tears in her father's eyes, and a big smile on his face. He loved it. When she finished her dance, Buddy gave Lea a big hug and a kiss. All the men in the bar were hooting, hollering, whistling, and clapping. Then a man walked up to Buddy and gave him a big roll of money with elastics around it. He put that roll in his other front pocket and said goodbye to all his friends. Then, Buddy and his daughter walked out the front door, heading for home, hand in hand.

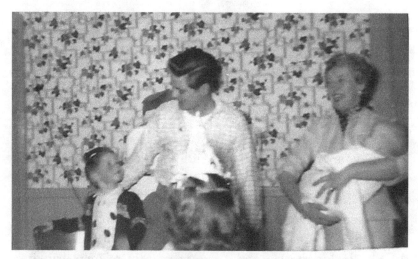

Buddy with Lea. Mother-in-law, Veronica Kelley
holding baby Kellie.

# Michael McLean

Buddy with Michael

*May 2, 1960*

Some days, Buddy left home for work before sunrise and returned after his children were in bed. It bothered him when he was unable to spend time with his children.

On this Monday morning, Buddy stayed around the house a little late. He walked into Michael's room and told him, "I'm driving you today. Hurry up and get dressed. And wear your sneakers."

"Okay, Dad."

Michael dressed quickly and called to his father, "I'm ready."

"Did you do your push-ups and pull-ups?"

"I'll do them right now."

"Meet me outside when you're done."

After completing his exercises, Michael ran out of the house without eating breakfast or saying goodbye to his mother. He jumped into the front seat of Buddy's car and off they went.

Buddy warned his son, "Don't tell your mother."

"Why, where are we going?"

"You're coming with me to work today."

"Wow, this is going to be great!"

"Yeah, it's going to be fun, but you do exactly what I tell you, all the time. You got that?"

"I got it."

"And make sure you are respectful and polite to everyone I introduce you to. Look them in the eye and give them a good, strong handshake."

"I know, Dad. I will."

Once they arrived at a South Boston pier, Buddy introduced Michael to a few of his friends and coworkers. Then Buddy positioned two big trucks backed up to each other. There was a steel plate between the two ends connecting the trucks. He handed Michael a wide push broom and told him, "You keep sweeping the ice off the plate so I won't slip."

Buddy put on a pair of leather work gloves and began unloading frozen fish from one truck and loading it onto his. He was moving fast, picking up heavy frozen haddock, carrying or dragging it, and neatly stacking the load. Michael kept sweeping the steel plate every time his father crossed over. "That's it, Michael, you're doing real good. Keep it up."

When the truck was loaded and packed with ice, Buddy locked it up. Then he told his son, "Let's go eat." They sat down in a diner and enjoyed a fresh, hot breakfast.

As they were eating, Buddy began to speak about his family. "Michael, it is very important to stick together and look out for one another. Never forget that. When a family sticks together, they can accomplish a lot."

"Yeah, like what?"

"Like how about you, me, and Jimmy having our own trucking business? We'd have our own fleet, and we could make a lot of money working together."

"I would do that."

"Good, we might do that someday, or something else. But always remember, stay together."

When the meal was finished, they walked outside and climbed into Buddy's truck. They drove off to deliver the fish to a big market in New York City. After making the delivery, Buddy drove to the South Street Seaport and picked up something else and drove it back to Boston.

On the ride back, Buddy reminded Michael, "Don't tell your mother, or we'll never be able to do this again." Michael nodded. "And we're not going to do this very often. It's more important that you get a good education. You understand?"

"Yup. That sure was fun, though."

"Yeah, it was."

* * *

*A family gathering in 2012*

Buddy and Michael in Gloucester, Massachusetts

Jean asked her son, "How often did he bring you to his work?"

"A few times, Ma."

Jean rolled her eyes and slowly shook her head. "Jesus Christ, I wonder what else he had you kids doing."

Michael smiled. He thought about teasing his mother with a wild, made-up story, but then decided not to get her upset. "You know, Ma, Dad was famous for being the toughest guy around, and all that other shit, but we never knew about it. We never saw him fight."

"Yeah, he tried to keep you kids away from all that."

"Sometimes he would come home with a torn shirt with blood on it or a few bruises on his face, but he wouldn't talk about it. He'd sit in his chair in the living room with blood on his knuckles and rest his eyes. I'd go in and ask him, 'Dad, are we going to the drive-in tonight?'

'Not tonight, Michael.'"

Jean added, "Yeah, I remember that. I would walk in, take one look at him and say, 'Aw, no, Buddy. Not again.'"

Michael nodded, "He'd just put his head back in that chair and close his eyes. You knew he didn't want to talk. I'd go outside and play with my friends. Then, a few minutes later, he'd get up and find us outside. He told us he changed his mind and to get ready for the drive-in. He hated to disappoint us. Some nights, I remember, we had ten kids packed into his big convertible. Ma bought us sub sandwiches up at Leone's and off we'd go. She never went to the drive-in with us. She liked to go to bingo instead."

Everyone in the room laughed.

"You're damn right I did," added Jean.

"A lot of times, Dad brought his friend 'Little Nicky' with us. They used to work out together. They ran for miles around Tufts' track. Dad and Nicky would sit up in the front seat with Lea and they'd split a six-pack during the movie. None of us could drink beer, but he'd buy us Cokes or a Richie's Slush before the movie started."

"Those were fun times," chimed in Lea. "But I don't remember Jimmy going with us that much."

"He went, but not all the time. If he wasn't with us, he was probably with some girl or studying in his room."

"Yeah, he was a genius. He was always on the principal's list."

"Yeah, and I was in the principal's office."

"Ha! What did Dad say?"

"He got mad, but then he'd tell me to do the right thing and try my hardest. I tried to listen to him, because I never wanted to disappoint him."

Jean added, "You turned out okay. You all did. Your father was always proud of all you kids."

# Smart as a Whip

*May 5, 1960*

After wrapping up a union meeting, several Teamsters stood outside the building, conversing and smoking cigars. It was a cool Friday afternoon. The Teamsters were in a jovial mood as they were looking forward to the weekend. Just then, a loud triple honk rang out from a tractor-trailer. The men all looked and waved back to Buddy McLean cruising through Sullivan Square.

One man stated, "There goes the toughest man in Boston."

Billy McCarthy

Teamster President Billy McCarthy added, "And the smartest."

"What do you mean, 'smartest'?"

"Think about all the shit he has going on. He never gets caught, he doesn't show off, he keeps his mouth shut, and he lives like a regular guy. He's smart."

"Oh, all right, street-smart. I thought you meant he has a high IQ or something."

"Yeah, well, he probably has that, too."

"You think so, Billy?"

"Yes, he has a natural ability to think fast. Also, when he likes doing something, he learns everything there is to know about it."

"Like what?" asked another Teamster.

"He is so good at backing forty-foot trailers into tight alleys or tricky loading docks that people will often stop whatever they're doing just to watch him complete what looks like an impossible task."

"No one else can do that?"

"Not on the first try or without help."

Local 25 Secretary Arthur O'Rourke chimed in. "Billy's right. I was with Buddy one time, out in Worcester. He had to back up to a loading dock down a tight alley off a narrow street. I asked him if he wanted me to get out and direct him. He told me, 'No, I'll be okay.' And sure enough, he did it on the first try."

"How did he do that?"

"I asked him. He said, 'You always pull up alongside the spot you're going to back into and take a good look at it. Study it. Then drive forward enough to clear the rear of the trailer from the turn you are about to make. As you pull forward, start to turn the tractor toward the opposite side of the street, bringing that front corner bumper as far over as possible without hitting anything. Sometimes you might have to pull up onto the sidewalk. This will shorten the blind spots. Then back it in real slow, keeping an eye on that lead rear corner. Bring it back as close as you can without scraping the building or whatever it is that you're trying to get around.'"

"He makes it sound easy."

"I told him that, and he said, 'It becomes easy, after you have done it enough.' And you know what? Billy and I were two of the guys who taught him that. Now, he's better than all of us."

# Endless Physical Conditioning

*June 12, 1960*

Martin "Pushka" Murphy was a childhood friend of Buddy's. He went on to become a captain in the Massachusetts State Police. Though they went their separate ways when it came to abiding by the law, the two remained friends. The pals worked out together at the Somerville YMCA many times.

At a cookout with many troopers in attendance, someone brought up the name Buddy McLean. Another trooper mentioned that Murphy was good friends with McLean. Murphy overheard the beginning of the conversation as he was sitting down to join the group.

"You guys want to ask me about Buddy McLean?"

"Yeah," piped in one trooper, "what do you know about all those hijacks and the other shit he does?"

"Nothing. He never talks about it, and I never ask him. It's an understanding we have. That's why we're still friends. It's been that way since we were kids, and it's never going to change."

"What about that tough guy reputation? Is it all true?"

"Yes, absolutely. That part is all true; he's the toughest guy I've ever met. No one is even close to him."

"No one?"

"That's right. No one."

"I heard he's not that big. What makes him so good?"

"It's all because of his fitness routine—he works out all the time."

"A lot of guys work out on a regular basis. What's he do different?"

"He goes at it longer and harder than anyone."

"You've seen him work out?"

"Many times. We've trained together for years."

"So, what exactly is it that he does?"

"He's able to make his body work beyond the point of fatigue. Somehow, he can generate a second burst of energy, you know what I mean? He gets a second wind. Then there comes a third, fourth, fifth burst, and so on. He constantly challenges himself physically, and he has the discipline and courage to endure it. I don't know of anyone, including Marciano, who can push himself to that level."

"He trains harder than Rocky did? That's impossible."

"A typical McLean workout is much longer and more strenuous than a professional boxer's. He punches the heavy bag as hard and as fast as he can. He bends the bag in half, and oftentimes, he tears the canvass or snaps the S hook above it. I've seen it happen. He smashes that bag like it's his worst enemy. And he does five-minute rounds, two minutes beyond the boxer. Instead of taking a one-minute rest between rounds, Buddy drops down and does fifty push-ups. Then he'll take a sip of water and do another five minutes on the bag, followed by twenty pull-ups. After a half-dozen rounds on each circuit, twelve rounds altogether, he's done. Then he'll rest for a few minutes while he's drinking a quart of water."

"Are you shitting me?"

"No, and what's even more incredible is that he usually does this without wearing hand wraps or gloves."

The troopers were silent as they slowly shook their heads.

Then one of them asked, "Why does he do that, Marty?"

"The strategy is to toughen his hands and knuckles because he's not going to wear gloves in a street fight. So, it's good practice."

The men remained quiet for a moment, sipping their beers and comprehending what Murphy had told them. But he was not finished.

"Most of you guys, even if you could do that much of a workout, you'd be done for the day and ready to go home and take a nap. McLean however, is only halfway done."

"No fuckin' way, Marty. I'd have to see this. Nobody can keep going like that."

"You guys asked me, and I'm telling you. You can come down to the Y and see for yourselves."

Another trooper asked, "What else does he do, Marty?"

"He'll go in the sauna for a little while, and then he'll take a light swim, or a quick shower. That gears him up for the second half of his workout."

"And what does that mean?"

"Weightlifting. And that is also a long, drawn-out process."

"What happens in the weight room?"

"Well, I'll give you an example. He sets two hundred pounds of weights on a squat rack. Then he bangs out twenty squats. After that, he takes the same two hundred pounds and does a set of ten perfect standing military presses over his head before returning to the squats. After completing five sets of each exercise, he moves to a different station."

"Holy shit, and he does this on a consistent basis?"

"During the cold months, Buddy usually does a total-body weightlifting workout five to seven days a week. Most fitness experts would consider this to be overtraining and declare McLean to be insane. On the other hand, he's built like chiseled granite, and he's never injured himself in training. He eats whatever and whenever he wants, and he drinks—gin or beer. And through all this training, he's never lost in the hundreds of fights he's been in."

# The German Shepherds

*June 12, 1960*

Buddy loved dogs. The family had several. The two German shepherds, Cindy and Smokey, were the most memorable. Buddy kept a lot of cash in the house, and he figured the big dogs would be a deterrent for someone looking to break in when he was not home. Starting them as pups, Buddy trained the shepherds to protect his kids and the house. No one came near the house unless the dogs were locked up.

After Buddy thought the shepherds were trained adequately, he decided to put them to a test. He walked his kids and a few of their friends down to a lower Broadway movie theater. The dogs walked behind them. Buddy bought the kids tickets for the movie and sent them in with money for drinks and snacks. He instructed the shepherds to sit outside the theater and not let the kids leave. Buddy crossed to the other side of the street and watched. Sure enough, a minute later, Jimmy walked out of the theater. Cindy immediately trotted over to him and nose-pushed him back toward the entrance. Smokey was barking and trying to push Jimmy also. Buddy waved to Jimmy and gave him a thumbs-up, signaling that everything went according to the plan. Jimmy went back into the theater, the dogs returned to their posts, and Buddy ventured over to Khoury's State Spa to have a few beers with his friends.

*June 18, 1960*

One Saturday afternoon, Buddy was in Mike Khoury's barroom having a few beers with some of his pals while his daughter, Lea, and her friends were across the street at the movie theatre. Tommy Ballou walked in. "I saw your wolves outside the movie and figured you'd be here," he announced to Buddy in front of the packed barroom.

"Hey Barrel-Chest, how are you? Come over here and have a few cold beers with me," invited Buddy.

Tommy made his way through the crowd, shaking hands, giving hugs, and receiving slaps on his wide, thick back along the way. When he finally bellied up to the bar, there was an ice-cold mug of Michelob waiting for him. Tommy grabbed the mug and clanked it against Buddy's. Then he poured five big, steady gulps down his throat and slammed the empty mug down on the bar. In his loud, clear, Bostonian pronunciation, Tommy asked Buddy, as well as everyone else in the room, "You know how they say a dog is man's best friend?"

"Yeah," agreed Buddy.

"Do you know how to prove that statement to be true?"

"How?"

"You take your wife and you take your dog and you throw them both in the trunk of your car. Then you slam it shut and leave them there. Then you come back an hour later, open the trunk and see which one is happy to see you."

*July 9, 1960*

Jean complained to Buddy that, "You are the only person who can control Smokey. He loves you, but I don't know about the rest of us. He only wants to be with you, and you are the only one he listens to. When you're not home, there's no telling what that damn dog is going to do. He bit the mailman, the milkman, the paperboy, and, now, everybody is afraid to come up to the house."

"I had that fence put up for him, just keep him in the yard. And when someone comes by, put Smokey in the cellar."

"I tried to do that the other day. I didn't want him going after my mother. I grabbed him by the collar and dragged him over to the cellar door. That no good bastard growled and showed his teeth at me."

"What did you do?"

"I grabbed a frying pan and smashed it on his head and pushed him down the stairs."

"Jesus Christ!"

"And another thing, Smokey climbed over the fence and chased a guy who was reading the electric meters in the neighborhood."

"Damn, it's a wonder he didn't rip his stomach open on the top of the fence. What are we going to do?"

"Get rid of him."

"No, he's good protection."

"Yeah, but he's a nutcase. Remember last week, you went out for a run and you didn't want to bring the dogs because it was too hot out?"

"Yeah, Smokey caught up to me down near the park. How did he get out?"

"He was going crazy in the house trying to get out. Then he ran up the stairs to the front bedroom and pushed the air conditioner out the window. He got out onto the roof of the front porch, jumped down to the stairs, and onto the sidewalk. Then he took off like a bat out of hell, chasing after you down the street."

Buddy shook his head in disbelief.

"My brothers put the air conditioner back in for me. Yeah, the dog is psycho, you should get rid of him."

Eventually he did.

# Getting to Know Buddy

*July 10, 1960*

Jean was cleaning up after a Sunday dinner one late afternoon. Her mother and a couple of sisters were in the kitchen helping. Buddy was in the living room, watching baseball on the television.

"My God," Jean started, "he could eat all day long."

"It's a good thing he works out so hard, or else he'd be chubby," said Mary.

"Yeah, like Jackie Gleason," added their mother.

They all laughed. Then Jean added, "He likes everything: Italian, Portuguese, boiled dinners, Chinese food, steak, chicken, seafood, lamb. Anything I put in front of him is gone in no time."

"He's big on fruits and vegetables, too," added Joan.

"Yeah, and he likes to start his mornings with a mixture of raw eggs and wheat germ. Yuck. He's not so strict with the kids, but he insists that they drink eggnog."

Mary exclaimed, "Jean, you make great eggnog. And your home-cooked meals are delicious. No wonder he married you."

"Please. He married me because I have a great body."

Dinner would be waiting for Buddy when he arrived home from his long workday. He would sit in the kitchen and eat, some nights as late as eleven o'clock. Jean sat at the table, chatting with Buddy. The children were long since put to bed. The conversation was mainly family-related and pertained to their daily routines.

When Buddy finished eating, the couple cleaned Buddy's dishes as well as the pots and pans—Jean washed, Buddy dried. Then they went upstairs, got ready for bed and settled in for the night. At the crack of dawn, Buddy would be up and ready to do it all again.

Buddy stayed away from most junk food, but a special treat for the McLean family might be a stroll down to the local ice cream stand or a ten-minute drive to Everett for a Richie's Slush. He was mainly a weekend drinker. He liked gin with orange juice. On hot summer days, Buddy enjoyed ice-cold beers.

*July 15, 1960*

Howie Winter

Howie Winter felt that Buddy was an outstanding truck driver and even better behind the wheel of an automobile. "He should have been a professional race-car driver," Howie said to a few friends over dinner at the Mount Vernon Restaurant. "Buddy can drive a car balanced on two wheels and stay that way as long as he pleases. When he's driving an eighteen-wheeler, it's like he's cruising along in a Cadillac—smooth. And he gets where he's going faster than anyone I know. He's a little crazy, too. One time, Buddy and Bobby Mahoney were driving down the Mass Pike in a tractor-trailer behind some other guys we knew in their rig. As Bobby drove the truck, Buddy sat in the passenger seat studying the truck in front of them. Now both trucks were cruising along at about sixty miles per hour when Buddy rolled down his window and slowly crawled out onto the step.

"Bobby screamed at him, 'Are you crazy? What the hell are you doing?'

"Buddy told him, 'Relax. Just do what I tell you. Don't slow down.'

"'My God, are you nuts? What do you want me to do?'

"'Pull up real close to them. I'm going to jump on to their back step.'

"So Bobby pulled up real close behind the lead truck. Then Buddy maneuvered his way around the front side fender so that he was standing on the front bumper when Bobby closed the gap to within three feet. Then Buddy jumped to the back step of the trailer and he climbed to the roof. Bobby pulled alongside the other guys as Buddy, with a big smile on his face, walked the length of the roof of the trailer and lightly dropped to the top of the tractor. Bobby could hardly contain himself as he watched Buddy slide down the windshield and scare the shit out of the guys in the other rig.

"Sometimes, the truckers will get together and bet on who will be the first one to arrive back in Boston. Buddy loves that. He's out there tearing down the turnpike at over one hundred miles per hour, and of course he pulls into the combine well before the others."

"I understand he's a great worker, too," quipped one man. "I heard no one can keep up with him on the loading docks."

"Yeah, his daily work ethic is something to see—maximum effort, all day, every day. He takes pride in his work, too, whether it's unloading or loading a trailer. The freight is always arraigned in perfect alignment. Everybody marvels at how focused and methodical he works. He builds strong, tight walls from floor to ceiling in his trailers."

Another man spoke up, "Yeah, he taught me how to load trailers."

"What'd he tell you?"

"You place the heaviest boxes on the floor. It'll save your back, and it's a good start to building a wall. The medium boxes go in the middle, and the lighter boxes on the top as you build the wall. The wall should be flat and tight with fillers (smaller packages behind the wall and some wedged into the wall) strategically placed into the wall. This will keep the wall strong and tight and prevent the freight from shifting when the shipment is on the road."

Howie added, "That's right, in a forty-foot trailer, there could be up to twenty ten-foot by eight-foot walls. This work is physically taxing. Two men, loading a trailer together, and moving right along, can finish the job in about two hours. Working by himself, Buddy always closes his doors in less than two hours. And one time an industrial engineer watched Buddy loading a forty-foot trailer. His recommendation was that Buddy's performance should be filmed and documented as the standard procedure to complete such a task."

# Standing Up for the Teamsters

*July 18, 1960*

On a trip to Albany, New York, Buddy and Howie encountered a confrontation with a local mobster. They were delivering seafood for their business, Travelers Transportation. When they backed up to the dock, a large Italian man approached the pair.

"Are you boys just dropping off, or are you taking something out, too?"

"We're doing both, why?" asked Buddy.

"You have to pay me fifty dollars for the outgoing freight," smiled the big man.

"What for?" wondered Buddy.

"It's an export fee."

"Are you kidding me?"

"I'm very serious."

"Does everyone else pay that?"

"Yes, absolutely."

"What happens if we don't pay?"

"Oh, you don't want to know about that."

"Yeah, I do."

"If you don't pay me, you're going to have some bad luck."

"That's impossible. I'm Irish."

"Suit yourself. But you've been warned."

Buddy looked at the man as he walked away to collect from the other drivers. *Who the hell is that guy? And why is everybody paying him? Something is wrong here.* Buddy and Howie continued their work. They unloaded the seafood and loaded bananas.

When they finished loading their trailer, Buddy asked one of the dockworkers, "What do you know about that guy going around looking for an export fee?"

The dockworker told Buddy, "He's a local mob boss, and he does shakedowns on every driver in the terminal."

Buddy wondered, "Does everyone pay the fee?"

"They all pay, one way or the other. And you don't want to see the other," claimed the dockworker.

Buddy looked over at Howie. His friend responded, "Let him try something. He'll regret it."

The dockworker slowly shook his head and walked away.

After loading their freight, Buddy and Howie took a lunch break in the terminal's diner. When they returned, Buddy noticed, "Howie, look, two of our tires are flat."

"I guess that's the bad luck we were going to have."

"Yup, the guy who tried to shake us."

"Where's that fat fuck? We'll make him pay for this."

The dock foreman told the Somerville men, "He and his men are long gone, fellas. They punctured your tires as soon as you guys went into the diner."

"And you let him get away with that?" steamed Howie.

"Hey, you don't get it. I have to live here. They're fuckin' dangerous. You pay, or you get hurt, simple as that. You guys got off easy. Now, I'll help you guys get new tires, but I'm staying out of it. You don't know what these guys are like. They're fuckin' animals."

Buddy and Howie looked at each other. Then Buddy answered, "You don't know what we're like. Let's get the tires."

As Buddy and Howie were getting ready to leave, Howie seethed, "I hate letting them get away with this. I think we should go find them."

"Relax. Next time we'll be ready, and we'll get them.

## *August 1, 1960*

On a Monday morning, Travelers Transportation had another delivery going to Albany. Buddy and Howie set off from Boston at sunrise with a couple of baseball bats and a loaded pistol in the cab. They arrived in the Albany trucking terminal four hours later. It was the busiest time of day at the terminal. Buddy backed up to the dock, and the pair began unloading their freight. About an hour into their work, the mob boss and three of his henchmen approached.

The boss greeted the pair with, "Hey, it's the boys from Boston. Too bad about them tires. Now you owe me for the last time you were here and for today."

Buddy coolly replied, "We're not paying you a dime, but you owe us for the tires, and you better pay us, right now."

The boss laughed and said, "You dumb Irish fucks, you're in way over your head, and you can't fuckin' see it."

Buddy told the boss, "That's how you see it. I see that you just made the biggest mistake of your life."

The boss paused for a moment. He was caught off guard by the lean, medium-height McLean not caving in to his intimidation tactic. He swallowed and responded, "All right, I'm tired of talking to you." He looked toward his men and told them, "Make this little fuck pay us—bust him up."

The goons surrounded Buddy. Howie stepped up with a baseball bat in his hands and the pistol in his belt. "All of you can fight him, but only one at a time."

The boss ordered his biggest man, "Rocco, flatten this guy."

"My pleasure, boss."

"Then, you two, beat the shit out of Mickey Mantle over there."

"No," interrupted Buddy, "I'm fighting all three."

"That's fine with me," chuckled the boss.

Rocco had eight inches in height and over one hundred pounds of body weight on Buddy. He was about to raise his hands and shove Buddy back into a stack of boxes. The stoic-faced McLean stood with his left foot slightly forward, his left big toe pointed directly at the closing-in thug. Buddy's right foot was pointed forty-five degrees off center. His balance was perfect. A dozen truckers watched from a distance. When Rocco was within one step, Buddy pushed off his right foot and fired a right cross that connected perfectly with the big man's forward-moving chin. The bullet punch stopped Rocco dead in tracks. He immediately became confused and scared. He had never been hit by a punch so fast, so powerful, and so accurate. The big man was a bully, not a fighter, and he wanted nothing to do with McLean. He looked over at his boss, who was just as stunned. Buddy gave him no quarter. He moved forward in a slight crouch and pivoted his hips right as he walloped a left hook into Rocco's ribs. Buddy recoiled as Rocco sagged to his right, then banged a second hook, this time to Rocco's jaw. Another right hand smashed into his neck, just under his right jawline. Five seconds in, Rocco was holding his neck and gasping for air as he staggered back.

A larger crowd of truckers and dockworkers began to close in at the scene.

The mob boss hollered to another one of his men, "Bruno! Get in there and help your fuckin' brother!"

Buddy turned to Rocco's brother, Bruno, who was a little smaller. He reluctantly moved toward McLean. As the smaller brother brought up his hands, Buddy blasted the wind out of him with a straight right into his solar plexus. A left hook to the ribs and a right uppercut to the chin finished Bruno.

"Holy shit. Who is that guy?" asked one of the stunned onlookers.

"I don't know, but this is fuckin' great."

"Yeah, it sure is."

The mob boss suddenly moved into a state of panic. As a large audience of truckers assembled to watch the commotion, he knew he was losing his grip on the terminal and was helpless to stop the probable outcome.

As Buddy marched toward him, the boss reached into his front pocket. "Hold on a second."

Howie was ready. As the boss reached, Howie swung. The blow to the arm dropped the boss to his knees. Before Buddy confronted the boss, he slap-left-hooked the third enforcer on his right ear, seating him on the cement floor.

The boss stammered to McLean, "I, I was going for my billfold. I'm going to pay you back for the tires. No tricks. I don't carry a piece."

Buddy demanded, "I want all of your wallets, right now. And turn your pockets out, too. Make sure you're empty, or I'll start hitting again."

The gangsters complied. Buddy instructed one of the drivers to collect all the personal items the men were carrying. The driver brought everything to Buddy. He took the cash and driver's licenses, then tossed the wallets aside. He walked back to the boss, grabbed him by the collar, and pulled a huge wad of cash from his jacket pocket. Then he poked his right index finger between the boss's eyes. "The game's over. I know who you are and where you live. I better not hear about you starting any more trouble around here again. You got that?"

The boss did not answer. *Boom!* Buddy blasted his right fist, crushing the man's nose.

"Okay, it's over," replied the boss as he held his blood-gushing snout.

The deflated mobsters assembled and meekly slipped toward the steps leading to where their automobile was parked. Before they could make their exit, Buddy ordered, "Hold on a minute."

Buddy had Howie gather the truckers into a circle while he kept an eye on the gangsters. He told the truck drivers in front of their former extortionists, "Nobody has to pay these guys anymore. In fact, they owe you. If you don't get your money back by the next time I come out here, let me know." Buddy gave the mobsters one last hard look, then walked away. Howie gave one trucker a wad of cash he took from the mobsters and told him to divide it equally. He kept more than enough for Buddy and himself.

The truckers immediately spread the word of Buddy McLean's stand and assault on the Albany gang. He became an overnight hero to Teamsters up and down the East Coast.

*September 12, 1960*

Jimmy Hoffa

Jimmy Hoffa, the Teamsters national president, found out and called into Local 25. He spoke with Billy McCarthy. "You tell Buddy McLean that I'm grateful and I'm proud of him. And if he needs anything to get ahold of me."

"Well, you're coming to the banquet in two weeks. He's going to be there. You'll get to tell him yourself."

"All right, good, I'll look forward to that."

Hoffa, a union thug himself, had dealings with mobsters on several occasions. He was aware of the adversity and danger that Teamster truckers often faced when confronted by mobsters.

*September 24, 1960*

Buddy and Jean attended the Local 25 banquet where Hoffa was one of the guest speakers. When they walked into the function hall in Boston, Buddy's friend Arthur O'Rourke, the Local 25 treasurer, approached Hoffa to let him know, "The McLeans are here."

"You'll have to excuse me, gentlemen," stated Hoffa as he abruptly ended his cocktail conversation with John Collins, the mayor of Boston, and Foster Furcolo, the governor of Massachusetts. He hurried across the room to greet and hug Buddy and Jean. Left standing in the middle of the room, Furcolo asked Collins, "Who the hell is Hoffa all giddy about? Some star athlete?"

"No, that's Buddy McLean. You ever hear of him?"

"Yeah, I have. Holy shit. That's really him? The state troopers have talked about him many times. Truck driver, real tough guy, lawbreaker. Problem is, they all seem to have a high regard for him."

"That's true," replied the mayor. "And so does every cop in Boston. What do you say we go over and meet him?"

"I'm right behind you," stated the governor.

Pat Sperlinga, Jean McLean and Arthur O'Rourke
at Local 25 banquet

# Gaining More Friends and Associates

*October 3, 1960*

During a meeting at his Prince Street office in the North End, Mafia boss Jerry Angiulo related to his brothers and associates what he knew about Buddy.

"Boss, we heard McLean is an FBI informant."

"Whoever said that is a fuckin' idiot," replied Angiulo.

"Boss, he's got friends everywhere. No one ever bothers him. It might be true."

"Shut up and listen. He's respected, loved, and feared, all at the same time. That's the way it is. You met him. You know what he's like."

"Yeah, he comes across like he's a nice guy, but he's building a fuckin' army over there. He could be getting ready to make a move."

"He's got fuckin' Somerville, Boston, MDC and state cops all kissing his ass. In their eyes, he's fuckin' Robin Hood. Now the fuckin' FBI is on the fuckin' bandwagon. That's true. They're giving him updates all the time. But he's not giving them shit. Raymond (Patriarca) told me."

"Then why are the Feds helping him, Boss?"

"Because they hate the McLaughlins, and they want to shut 'em down. It's that simple."

"All right, but where does McLean fit in with all this?"

"I'm not sure yet, but they might want McLean running Charlestown."

"Instead of us?"

"Yeah, why not? It's mostly Irish. He works there, and everybody likes him. They might be trying to make some money with him. Who knows?"

"Yeah, but McLean fuckin' told us he wouldn't move out of Somerville. You don't think he'd go back on his word?"

"He wouldn't, but he might put one of his friends down there."

"What are we going to do?"

"Right now, nothing. Just watch."

"Shouldn't we let the McLaughlins know?"

"Fuck no! What are you? Stupid? I fuckin' hate those assholes. They've been grabbing up sections all over Boston for a long time, and they're always looking to get more. They'd love to have our sections, too. We'd all be better off without them around. Punchy says he's going to run the FBI out of Boston. Let him hang himself."

*October 5, 1960*

The McLaughlin brothers, Bernie, Georgie, Ed
"Punchy"

Over lunch one afternoon with his brother Bernie, Eddie McLaughlin stated, "I'm getting a bad feeling about McLean."

"What's the problem?"

"He's getting stronger every week. Some of our customers are driving over to Somerville to bet with him instead of with us."

"You know this for a fact?"

"Fiddler told me."

"Who told him?"

"Some guys on the dock."

"Hmm, that could become a problem. He's got a shitload of friends, too," added Bernie.

"What do you think we should do?"

"Do you have any info we can use against him?"

"I can't think of anything. How about you?"

"No, he's pretty clean. He's a family man, plus he's got a shitload of cops on his side."

Eddie thought for a moment, then responded, "Yeah, but he still likes to fight, and he's hounded by broads everywhere he goes. We might be able to use something like that against him."

Bernie contemplated, then responded, "Or we could recruit him."

# The Pitch

Buddy and Jean sat with the McLaughlin brothers at the Alibi Club. Buddy listened intently to every word Punchy and Bernie had to say.

"You come in with us, you'll have more money than you know what to do with," boasted Eddie.

"If you join with us, it makes both of us stronger, and there will be no boss. It'll be partners," piped in Bernie.

"We'll push the fuckin' Mafia right out of Boston. I got connections down in New York. They'll back us. Angiulo, and Patriarca, they'll be gone. It'll be just us and New York, whenever we need them," continued Eddie.

While this conversation was taking place, Jean remained composed and mainly uninterested in the business proposition that was being made. She made small talk with the youngest McLaughlin brother, George. After a few drinks, she tired of listening to him boast about his female conquests. She later told her mother, "He asked me to dance. Buddy told me to, 'Go ahead.' He's a little guy, shorter than me. He thinks he's God's gift to women, for Christ sake. Give me a break. The more he drank, the less he made any sense. I couldn't wait to get out of there."

Meanwhile, Buddy remained focused on what Eddie and Bernie were saying.

After the McLaughlins finished their sales pitch, Bernie asked Buddy, "What do you think?"

"This is Joe McDonald's business, I'm just looking after it for him right now. Nothing happens without his okay."

"You also made it a lot bigger," responded Eddie.

"And I also made an agreement with the Angiulos that I wouldn't expand out of Somerville. I intend to keep my word on that. Now you guys want to take over everything that the North End controls, and you think you're going to close out the FBI in Boston. I don't see that ever happening. You're looking to start a war you can't win. I say you form an alliance with me, Joe Mac, and the North End, and everybody pays the FBI to look the other way. That way everyone makes money, everybody gets along, and nobody gets hurt. What's wrong with that?"

"So you're not coming with us?" asked Eddie.

"Not the way you want to do it. If you change your mind or come up with another idea, let me know."

Bernie understood Buddy's position. He replied, "You're probably right. We'll have to rethink about all this and I'll get back to you. In the meantime, you should think about what Eddie said. If you join with us, we will become one hell of an Irish clan."

"Yeah, we would. But it would take a lot of planning and organizing, as well as a good amount of negotiating and probably some bloodshed. Besides, I'd rather work with Angiulo, not against him. I think that, for right now, we should just be friendly neighbors. In the meantime, I'll be thinking about all this and I'll talk with Joe. If we come up with something new, I'll let you know."

Eddie quickly asked, "What about Charlestown bettors going over to Somerville?"

"I understand your concern. A few of my guys are from Charlestown, plus I work two jobs here. It was inevitable that this would happen. I'm not trying to steal your customers. They came to me. I think that most of your customers who are now with me live in Somerville. If I have any guys from Charlestown wanting to bet with me, I'll send them back to you."

Eddie huffed a long sigh and got up and walked away from the table.

Buddy and Jean got up to leave. Bernie stood up, looked Buddy in the eye, shook his hand, and said, "We'll do it your way for now."

"Thanks, Bernie, I'll talk with you again."

Bernie kissed Jean on the cheek and said, "It was nice to meet you, ma'am. Thanks for coming down here tonight. I hope to see you both again soon."

They left the Alibi and headed back to Somerville.

On the drive home, Buddy asked Jean, "What'd you think of them?"

"I wouldn't trust them for a second, especially the big fat one."

"Punchy. Yeah, you're right. What about the other two?"

"The little one's a drunk. He must be living off his brothers. The other one, Bernie, he seemed okay. He's the smartest of the bunch, and he's a gentleman. But that Punchy, he's the leader. They're going listen to him, and I don't like him at all."

"Right again. How the heck did you get so smart?"

"Listen, you didn't marry a dummy."

"Nope, I married a smart, gorgeous woman. A great mother, wonderful cook..."

"Listen, if you think you're getting on top of me tonight, you are dead wrong."

"Wow."

# The Following Day

Buddy met with some friends at the Capitol Bar. They were eager to find out about the previous night's meeting.

John Hurley asked Buddy, "So how did it go last night?"

"Well, it went back and forth for a while, then finally I said no thanks."

"How did that go over with Punchy?"

"He didn't like it. He just walked away. He's not a very friendly guy. What's his problem anyway?"

"He's a bully who's used to getting his way. He's cheap as hell, too. He was probably beside himself pissed that he spent the evening buying you two drinks and appetizers and then had nothing to show for it. Plus, the fact that you were, I'm sure, pleasant but firm. It placed Punchy in uncharted waters. No one ever tells him how things are going to go."

"He wants us to help him push the Mafia out of Boston. At the same time, he thinks he can shut down the FBI. He's off his rocker if he thinks that is ever going to happen."

"Yeah, well, all that aside, you'd be smart to keep an eye on him. He's not one to be trusted."

At the same time in Charlestown, Punchy met with his men at Driscoll's Bar.

As he ambled over to a table with a dozen of his men waiting, Stevie Hughes asked Punchy, "Well, are they with us?"

"No."

"What happened?"

"McLean said no."

"No to everything?"

"Right. No to everything."

"Shit. Now what?"

"I'll figure it out. For now, it's business as usual."

"Yeah, but McLean is getting stronger. He's got connections all over Boston, plus the Mafia likes him. He might come after us. Did you think about that?"

"Nah. He'll stay in Somerville."

"Not true. His men are helping the Angiulos and the Bennetts and a few others with collecting. Next thing you know, there'll be more gangs looking for his help. And then some of our guys may want to join him."

The normally self-assured Punchy became confused and agitated. "Don't bother me with that shit right now. I need time to think about it. Bernie, let's get out of here. I want to talk to you about all this."

"All right, in a minute," replied Bernie. "Listen, fellas, we're still in good shape here. We haven't lost anything. McLean said he'd be willing to sit down another time and talk with us. He's not a bad guy. We still might be able to work something out. Let's not throw in the towel. We'll talk to him again. I'll see you guys later."

Outside Driscoll's, the McLaughlin brothers slid into Bernie's automobile. As they pulled away from the curb, Punchy asked Bernie, "Do you think McLean is going to try and push us out of business?"

"I don't think it's his intention to."

"What the fuck does that mean?"

"It means he's telling you the truth, that he wants to stay in Somerville."

"Yeah, what about all that shit we heard in the bar? Do you believe it?"

"It could be accurate. We'll have to consider it. In the meantime, you should knock off your fuckin' bragging and quit telling people you're going to wipe out the Mafia and the FBI. That's how you lose friends, not gain them. It's no wonder people are talking about joining McLean. He's fair and honest, and you, well, you know what you are."

"Fuck you. I'll put a fuckin' hit out on McLean."

"What for, being a good guy? Here you go talking nonsense again. You'll get us all killed for talking like that."

"You're making him sound like a fuckin' hero."

"He's got friends everywhere, you fuckin' idiot. Local 25 and the ILA, they love him. So do all the cops and the FBI. Now, thanks to you, he's going to have the Mafia and everyone else in Boston kissing his ass. And if you try to whack him, chances are good he'll take the fuckin' gun and ram it down your hit man's throat. Have you ever seen this guy fight?"

"No, but I heard about him."

"Yeah, well, it's all true."

"What should we do then?"

"Nothing with him, for now. Just be patient. Concentrate on our territory, no need to expand right now. Pay attention to our boys, maybe give them a little more money. It'll keep them happy and loyal to us. If they do something good or bring in more cash, toss them a bonus or a gift."

"A fuckin' gift! Have you gone soft? What gift do you want me to buy?"

"I don't know. You could buy them a night in Scollay Square. Get them all laid."

"You're fuckin' crazy, plus most of our guys are married anyway."

"That never slowed you down, Punch."

"Fuck you."

As they drove off in the car, Eddie McLaughlin suddenly had feelings of anger, hate, and fear toward Buddy McLean. *What am I going to do with this guy? It's impossible to scare or intimidate him. Fight him? That's the last thing I want to do. But if I don't do something, I'm gonna lose my clout in Charlestown.*

# Punchy's Opportunity

*October 14, 1960*

Six days after Buddy had rejected the offer to work with the McLaughlins, he was involved in a massive barroom brawl at the Stork Club in Charlestown. During this free-for-all, Buddy was hit in the mouth with a flying beer bottle and had his eyeteeth knocked out. He was furious. He picked up his teeth and stormed out of the club.

The next day he saw an Asian Somerville dentist named Dr. Moy, whose office was in Powder House Square, close to Tufts University. Dr. Moy could repair Buddy's mouth to look as good as new. It cost Buddy a lot of money and pride. He craved to get even. Jean joked that, "All he wants for Christmas is his two front teeth."

"Yeah, okay, it ain't funny."

When he received details of the brawl, Eddie McLaughlin came up with an idea: *I'll tell everyone it was Ditso who threw the bottle, then McLean will want to fight him.* Richie "Ditso" Doherty was a fast, tough boxer from Charlestown. He was part of the fracas, but did not fight Buddy, nor did he throw the bottle at him. He was an inch shorter and fifteen pounds lighter than Buddy, but Punchy figured Doherty's skill and speed would be more than enough to take care of McLean.

Ditso met with Punchy. "Sure, Ed, I'll take the fight. Just don't tell anyone that I didn't throw the bottle, because then McLean won't have a reason to fight me."

"Yeah, no problem. Do you think you can take him?"

"I'll beat him. You can put money on it. He's not a boxer, he's just a banger. I'll cut him up real good for ya."

"That's just what I wanted to hear."

# The Big Fight

*November 2, 1960*

The big fight was scheduled to happen a month after the fiasco at the Stork Club. Buddy needed time to let his teeth heal as well as his wrist, which he injured during the brawl. After it was set, Buddy received a riling phone call from Eddie. "Yeah, McLean, that Doherty kid is real good. Everybody in Charlestown says he's a killer and he's going to box your ears. It's not too late to back out."

"You don't know me very well. I would never back out of a fight."

"I'm just thinking, you have those young kids at home, you don't need to get your face messed up, embarrass your kids and yourself. You don't need that shit. I can talk to Doherty and call the whole thing off."

"First and foremost, what kind of a lesson would my kids be learning if I didn't fight? Second, how would I look in front of all my friends? Third, do you really think that for one minute I would let Doherty off the hook for knocking out my teeth? I don't care how tough he is, I'm going to fight him."

"A lot of people are betting against you. You want to wager a bet on yourself?"

"What are the odds?"

"Even."

"I'm the underdog, and it's even."

"Take it or leave it."

"Two thousand on me."

"Good, it's a bet."

Punchy smiled and nodded as he hung up the phone. *That's my boy. You're taking the bait, hook, line, and sinker.*

The two weeks leading up to the fight generated great interest in Somerville and Charlestown. The fight was going to take place on a football field in Charlestown. The field was known as the Oilys, named for the oil trucks that were parked on it during World War II. It was located adjacent to the ship docks under the Tobin Bridge.

## November 20, 1960

On the day of the fight, a cool, sunny Sunday afternoon, Buddy McLean drove to Charlestown with Joe McDonald and a few other friends. Joe Mac was risking arrest for outstanding warrants, but he wanted to be there for Buddy. When they arrived at the field, the Winter Hill boys were pleased to see roughly three hundred supporters from the Highlands. They were not so happy to see a couple thousand Townies thirsting for Somerville blood. Punchy McLaughlin and a dozen of his soldiers were standing with Ditso Doherty in the middle of the field.

Buddy's friend John Hurley came running over to the McLean group to inform them, "Those fuckin' McLaughlins are all packing heat over there. The Hughes brothers are saying they're going to kill Buddy if he wins the fight."

Joe McDonald interjected and said, "Don't worry about those bums. They're not going to do anything. We're going to be fine."

Hurley asked Buddy, "What the fuck's Joe Mac got, a couple machine guns in the trunk of his car?"

"I wouldn't doubt it. There's nobody like him, and the McLaughlins are definitely aware of that," replied Buddy.

Buddy and Ditso met on the fifty-yard line. "How do you want to do this, McLean?"

"It's your field. You make the rules."

"Everything is in except for kicking."

"Fine with me," responded Buddy.

The heralded battle finally commenced. Doherty was effective right from the get-go. His stick-and-move combinations had the Charlestown fans on their feet and rooting for the hometown boy. Doherty's punches, however, were not hard enough to keep McLean from closing in and slamming Ditso's body with hooks and short uppercuts. He was unable to slip the body shots. Buddy began pounding Doherty's arms when he tried to protect his ribs from the thunderous body shots. The Charlestown fans sat down when Buddy uncorked a right-hand fastball into Ditso's mouth, loosening up four of his teeth and sitting the Charlestown fighter on his butt.

"Aww, fuck," muttered Doherty as he slowly got up. On his way to standing, the Townie scooped a handful of dry dirt, spit out a mouthful of blood, then moved toward Buddy. He slipped Buddy's next right cross and threw the dirt in his eyes. Doherty got a headlock on McLean and started throwing uppercuts to Buddy's face. The Charlestown throng came to life again, but it was short-lived. Buddy lifted Doherty's legs and slammed him to the ground. This gave him time to wipe his eyes and clear his vision. While the Townie was on the ground, Buddy scooped up some dirt himself. After he was certain Doherty's hands were empty, Buddy dropped his handful and let loose his final assault, a four-punch combo that ended with a straight right cannonball between Ditso's eyes. The punch was so good it knocked Doherty out for twenty minutes, and he missed the action that followed.

Just after Richie Doherty's brothers ran on the field to aid their unconscious sibling, a Charlestown hulk named Butchie Quinn stormed out of the stands.

"I'm next, McLean."

"Who the hell are you?" asked Buddy as Quinn marched toward him.

"I'm the guy who's going to fuckin' knock you into next week."

McLean responded, "I don't know you. I don't have a beef with you. What's your problem?"

Butchie told Buddy, "You ain't coming to Charlestown to beat up a smaller kid and go home that easy."

While Butchie was taunting Buddy, Joe Mac asked John Hurley, "Who the hell is that guy?"

"That's Butchie Quinn. He's home on leave from the Navy, and, as far as I know, he's not affiliated with the McLaughlins."

Joe called out to Buddy, "Hey champ. Put him away."

"All right, looks like we've got ourselves a fight, big boy."

Quinn pulled off his tee shirt, revealing his massive muscular physique and strutted toward Buddy. As he was loosening his neck and shoulders, Quinn informed Buddy, "You're in over your head, McLean. I'm the Navy's heavyweight champ. You should call yourself an ambulance."

The men began to circle each other.

"An ambulance. Wow, you must be real good. Maybe I need a hearse," replied Buddy.

With that Quinn popped Buddy's head back with a quick jab. The Townie followed with a right cross that grazed the right side of Buddy's scalp. McLean had slipped outside of Quinn's right fist as he was delivering his own right hand straight into the sailor's solar plexus.

"Uhhh," gasped Quinn as the wind was knocked out of him.

Buddy continued with a left hook to the ribs, a short right uppercut to the liver, and then another left hook to Quinn's right kidney. The fourth punch buckled Butchie's right knee, and his right hand dropped. Quinn started to say something as Buddy went for the knockout. A right cross to the nose with a jaw-breaking left hook had Butchie leaning back on his heels, his eyes looking up at the sky. Buddy fired his body forward by pushing hard off his right foot. A right hand to the chin ended it. Quinn was spread-eagle on his back, lights out—a ten-second knockout. Buddy walked about three yards to the sleeping behemoth. He observed that Quinn's nose was crushed, blood streaming from each nostril. His jaw and chin were disfigured. Buddy later claimed the last right hand to Butchie's chin was the best punch he ever threw. McLean waved to the McLaughlins and hollered out, "This guy needs an ambulance, fast!"

The cheering Somerville crowd rushed onto the field and crushed Buddy. They congratulated him with hugs, handshakes, and pats on the back. Then they hoisted him up on their shoulders and began hooting and hollering as they marched and carried him off the field.

The rowdy Highlanders showed complete disregard for the hometown crowd, though they were vastly outnumbered. Before the Somerville men moved toward their cars, Joe McDonald hollered over to the McLaughlins, "Anyone else want to fight him?"

The Townie's mentor, Steve Hughes Sr., shouted back, "That's it for now."

Following Joe Mac's orders, the proud and keyed up Highlander clan exited the field together in tight formation, making it to their vehicles. Joe McDonald was alert to the possibility of Townie repercussions. Buddy was riding in Joe Mac's car. They were the last to leave. Before leaving, Buddy walked up to Punchy and said, "You owe me two grand."

The off guard and embarrassed McLaughlin answered, "I don't have it on me."

"I showed up with my money," Buddy said as he pulled a roll of cash from his front pocket.

The McLaughlin gang stood silent. Bernie slowly shook his head in disgust.

"I don't have it on me. I'll send it up the Capitol Bar tomorrow. Okay?"

"Yeah, sure, and no charge for that big bastard."

Bernie smirked.

The rest of the gang remained silent, watching, as Buddy and Joe walked away. They drove back to Somerville for a celebration on Winter Hill.

*Winter Hill In The 1960's*

Broadway Winter Hill

The next morning, Eddie had one of his men drive the money up to McLean's hangout, the Capitol Bar. Sitting with his brothers in a diner, Eddie lamented, "McLean's going to be the most popular guy in Charlestown now. A fuckin' truck-driving longshoreman from Somerville walks into our neighborhood, ignores us, and then fuckin' obliterates the best fighters we have. Even lifelong Townies are taking a shine to him."

"What are you gonna do?" asked younger brother George McLaughlin.

"I have to take the wind out of his sail."

"How?"

"I don't know yet."

# The DeAngelis Fight

In 1960, Edward "Punchy" McLaughlin was said to be the most powerful nonmafia gangster in New England. With the results from the fights at the Oilys, Buddy McLean damaged the gangster's reputation and ego. The "Big Potato" on Bunker Hill was desperate to slow down the "Rising Star" from Winter Hill.

Punchy McLaughlin decided to try again. This time he managed to instigate one of the most memorable bar fights ever seen in the city of Boston. It was the night Buddy McLean went at it with a well-known Greater Boston area boxer named Joe DeAngelis. A tall, strong, highly skilled heavyweight who, in 1947, won the national Golden Gloves tournament with a decision over the great Rocky Marciano. DeAngelis had no doubt that he could handle the smaller, lighter, less talented McLean. Many others were of the same opinion, for it was widely agreed that DeAngelis was the best pure boxer Marciano had ever faced, including his years as a professional.

Punchy was trying to recruit DeAngelis to come work with the McLaughlins. DeAngelis had been thinking about it. Over a few drinks in the Alibi one evening, Punchy mentioned, "We'd love to have you with us."

Boxing poster

"Yeah, I'm still thinking about it."

"Yeah, those shitheads over in Somerville are trying to move in on our territory."

"I didn't know that."

"Yeah, McLean thinks he's the toughest guy in Boston and that he can go anywhere and just do as he pleases."

"He's the toughest guy in Boston?"

"That's what he thinks, and so do a lot of other people around here."

"He hasn't fought me yet."

"That's true."

The next afternoon, Punchy drove over to the Charlestown docks. He had the Hughes brothers, Stevie and Connie, with him. They spotted Buddy leaving work with a few of his friends.

"Hey McLean, I need to tell you something."

"What's up?"

"Joe DeAngelis wants to fight you."

"The boxer?"

"Yup, the one and only."

"What's his problem with me?"

"Nothing really. He just heard a lot of people talking about how tough you are, and he doesn't want anyone thinking you're better than him. He asked me to set up a challenge. What do you say? Will you fight him?"

"Gee, Punch. You're just itching to see me lose one, aren't you?"

"I'm just relaying the message. You don't have to fight him. I mean you're pretty damn good, but this guy's the best. If you want to back down, it's no big deal. I'll tell him you said no."

Buddy looked at John Hurley and Tommy Ballou. They both had grave looks of concern on their faces but said nothing. Buddy turned back to Punchy and replied, "I told you before, I never back down. I'll fight him. Go ahead and set it up."

As Buddy and his friends continued to their cars, Hurley mentioned, "Buddy, DeAngelis is a fuckin' headhunter. He's a fuckin' sharpshooting, dangerous motherfucker with those knuckles. He fuckin' beat Marciano, for Christ sake."

Buddy looked straight ahead and said, "Then it should be a good fight."

A week before the fight, Buddy stopped into the Capitol Bar on Winter Hill. The room was packed with friends. They all greeted and welcomed him.

Tommy Ballou walked over to Buddy, put his arm around him, and told his friend, "Punchy's got a lot of money riding on DeAngelis for next week."

"Yeah, well I'm going to make him regret that."

"That's good, but you should also know that DeAngelis has been training, and they say he's looking real sharp."

"I train all the time. I'm ready. Don't worry about it."

"I know that, but this guy's unbelievable, plus he's five inches taller than you and maybe forty pounds heavier."

The room was silent. All eyes were on Buddy. He looked around at his friends, then he finally spoke, "Have I ever let you guys down before?"

"Of course not. We just don't want to see you . . ."

"Listen. DeAngelis is going to have better hands than me, no doubt about it. But he doesn't train as hard as I do. No one does. I'm going to wear him down, then take him out. Now if you don't think I can do this, then you shouldn't bet on me. But if you believe in me, then bet all you can."

After a couple seconds of silence, Tommy yelled out, "Fuck yeah! Buddy's going to fuckin' kill him!"

The room shook as all the men in unison boomed, "Yyyeahh!"

### January 27, 1961

The fight took place at the Alibi Club in Charlestown. Buddy arrived at the club twenty minutes before the prearranged time. He had Howie Winter, Tommy Ballou, Russ Nicholson, Billy Winn, and John Hurley with him.

They entered the smoke-filled, loud, and rowdy main room. It was jam-packed, mostly with men from all corners of Boston who were anticipating Buddy McLean's first defeat.

"McLean is here!" shouted one man. Applause, whistles, greetings, and encouragements surrounded the Winter Hill men. The loud shouts came from Teamsters, longshoremen, and Somerville men who were there to support Buddy. The DeAngelis side of the room became quiet as they intently studied the shorter, leaner, handsome, and unobtrusive McLean.

"He looks like he's in high school," mentioned one DeAngelis supporter.

The floor was cleared of tables and chairs to provide ample space for the two hitters. Joe DeAngelis was standing at the bar with his brother and a few friends. Punchy and George

McLaughlin were also with the DeAngelis group. Big Joe snapped down his third shot of whiskey and turned to find Buddy. McLean was standing in the middle of the cleared area loosening his neck and shoulders. He was wearing a white T-shirt tucked in to his light gray khaki work pants held snugly by a black leather belt. A pair of white sneakers, double knotted, completed Buddy's fighting attire.

DeAngelis approached the clearing. He had on a black undershirt, a pair of black pants, with a belt, and a pair of black sneakers.

The crowd of two hundred onlookers closed the circle to about a twenty-foot diameter. They became deathly quiet. DeAngelis and McLean had never spoken to or even seen each other until this moment.

"You ready?" asked Joe as he lifted one leg then the other to wipe the dust from the bottom of his sneakers.

"Yup," answered Buddy.

"Let's begin the lesson."

Wasting no time, Buddy came right at DeAngelis. Joe caught Buddy on the way in with a perfect one-two that straightened him. Buddy moved back a step, then slid to his left a step and then to his right. Buddy crouched a bit, then rushed DeAngelis. Joe pinpointed a jolting straight jab between Buddy's eyes that buckled his knees and dazed him. Buddy backed off to clear his head. DeAngelis continued forward with stiff measuring jabs and a hard cross to McLean's left eye, which immediately began to swell. Buddy attempted to tie up DeAngelis, but Joe parried him and launched another blast to Buddy's left eye that cracked the socket. The punch sent Buddy back a step, and it gave Joe room to set up a nasty four-punch combination that put Buddy on the floor. The DeAngelis contingent was delighted to see their man perform so quickly and precisely.

They cheered loudly, and a man in the crowd yelled, "Finish that fuckin' mick, Joe."

Some of Buddy's friends began to get watery eyes. Their hero was taking a shellacking. But even with a quickly swelling left eye, McLean was back up in less than a second and game to continue.

DeAngelis had a six-inch reach advantage, and he used it effectively. When McLean was within firing range, DeAngelis connected full force with tremendous combinations to Buddy's head and face. The accuracy and power of these punches was something Buddy had never experienced. At this point, not even two minutes into the fight, DeAngelis thought he had the match well in hand.

"Had enough?" asked DeAngelis as the two circled one another.

"You're pretty good Joe, but I'm not even warmed up yet," replied McLean as he charged DeAngelis.

Joe sidestepped the rush and countered with a hard-left hook to the side of Buddy's head. Buddy turned to face straight up with Joe and got nailed with a perfect one-two, square in the middle of his face. Down again went McLean.

Punchy McLaughlin burst out with a girly giggle, then composed himself enough to growl, "Yyyahaa."

McLean pushed himself back upright. Now bleeding from his mouth, nose, and left eyebrow, Buddy tucked his chin, clinched his teeth, kept his hands high and started back in on DeAngelis. Joe fired a jab at Buddy's face. Anticipating the punch, McLean pushed the outside of Joe's left wrist inward with his open right hand. This opened the left side of Joe's rib cage, and Buddy shot a hard, straight left jab to the body, cracking a rib. DeAngelis bent enough for McLean to launch a hard, straight right into his mouth. Blood began to pour. Everyone in the crowd, including

Buddy's friends, were shocked that McLean could land two damaging blows on the master boxer. DeAngelis became furious.

"That's it, McLean. I'm going to fuckin' ruin your face," shouted DeAngelis.

"Let's go, you big bastard. You don't scare me."

McLean's words inspired many in the crowd of onlookers to secretly root for him. His Somerville pals were pushed over the top.

"Get him, Buddy."

"Knock him the fuck out."

At the same time, Buddy pushed through a terrible beating as he kept trying to nullify Joe's big reach advantage. Every time Buddy pressed forward, DeAngelis had a combination ready for him. If there was one glimmer of hope for Buddy, it was that Joe was starting to breathe heavily.

Buddy was knocked down twice more. Each time, the DeAngelis fans cheered loudly. Each time, Buddy got right up and charged forward, bringing shouts of encouragement from the Highlanders. Buddy covered as best he could and kept pounding Joe to his arms and body. DeAngelis fired back with everything he had, but McLean refused to slow down or back off. Then, the exhausted Joe DeAngelis sensed the inevitable; he could not stop Buddy McLean.

Eight minutes into the fight, DeAngelis faltered and McLean closed in. The Somerville man tore into big Joe and totally turned the momentum in his favor. McLean's friends erupted into deafening roars of elation as Buddy relentlessly pounded Joe back to a wall. The DeAngelis crowd stood horrified by what happened next. Joe's arms dangled at his sides and he would have crumbled to the floor except that McLean had a death grip on his throat and had Joe's body pinned to the wall. With buckled knees lowering his height, DeAngelis was now a straight-ahead, motionless target for McLean's right hand. The bombs came fast and furious. Joe's face was crushed. Blood splashed with each hit. The boxer's brother and his friends tried to stop the annihilation. They grabbed McLean from behind and pulled him away from DeAngelis. Buddy ripped himself from their grip as he turned and pushed them back. Then he bellowed, "Who wants to go next?"

Joe's brother, Mike, stepped toward McLean but was quickly pulled back. Buddy turned back to DeAngelis, who had slumped unconscious into a pool of his own blood.

The Somerville crowd was going berserk.

"Finish him, Buddy."

"Kill that motherfucker."

Standing over DeAngelis, Buddy hollered down, "Come on, Joe. Punchy's got a lot of money riding on you."

Punchy was nowhere to be seen. He had left the building when Buddy took control of the fight.

There was no response or movement from DeAngelis. A heel nudge to Joe's butt followed by, "Hey Joe? You had enough, Joe?"

Again, no movement. Mike DeAngelis pushed his way through the crowd until he was in front of Buddy. "That's it, McLean. It's over. What do you want, to kill him?"

"You and your friends weren't too worried about me in the beginning, were you?" asked the bloody and swollen McLean.

"You're right. But he's my brother, and he needs to go to the hospital. It's over. You won. You're the best. Now let me get him out of here."

A short look at Mike, and one final stare at his opponent, then, "All right, take him," replied Buddy as he walked away from Joe DeAngelis.

It was a dramatic, room-shaking performance from Buddy McLean. His jubilant friends were accustomed to a winning outcome, though this fight was his toughest yet. They mobbed the Somerville man.

The DeAngelis crowd was overwhelmed by a sense of shock from their underestimation of Buddy McLean. They were very concerned about the condition of their idol. They were not sure how they felt about McLean. They could not hate Buddy after watching him battle back and then tear apart the most talented boxer Boston had ever produced. Emotions of terror began building from the hostile Somerville celebration. The one hundred DeAngelis fans quietly and quickly left the building.

Most of the McLaughlin gang in attendance were deathly silent. Except Bernie McLaughlin, who worked his way through the crowd of Highlanders until he was in front of Buddy and shook his hand. "Nice going, McLean," offered Bernie. "I never saw anybody make a comeback like that before. Especially against DeAngelis. He was undefeated until tonight."

"Yeah, well, I may have beat him, but my head doesn't feel that way."

"Ha! Yeah, but you're a lot better off than him. Hey, you want to grab a beer?"

"No, I'm just going to go home and collapse. Thanks anyway."

"All right, I'll see you around, Buddy."

"Yeah, hey, where's your brother? He owes me some money."

"I don't know, but I'll see that you get it."

Buddy nodded. The Irishmen went their separate ways.

Joe DeAngelis was rushed to the emergency room. He was there for a while. After extensive medical treatment, Joe was released from Massachusetts General Hospital and never heard from again. The word spread fast throughout Boston. Buddy McLean destroyed a man who had once defeated Rocky Marciano. In the minds of many, he became a folk hero.

# Hard Knuckles, Soft Heart

*January 30, 1961*

1:00 a.m. The phone rang at the McLean house.

"Buddy, it's John Devine. Sorry to bother you at this hour, but I'm in Miami and I lost my wallet. Can you help me out?"

"Sure, how much do you need?"

"A thousand."

"All right. Give me about a half an hour. I'll wire it down to you through Western Union."

"Thank you, Buddy. I'll pay you back when I get home."

"That will be fine."

"The usual vig?"

"No vig. This an emergency."

"Okay. Thank you again, Buddy."

Sore and still healing from Joe DeAngelis's punches, Buddy walked out the door and into a New England blizzard that was starting to hit the Boston area. Buddy drove to South Station in Boston. He parked in front of the building and left the engine on. He ran inside to wire the money. Nobody was around; the city was a ghost town.

Buddy was back in his car in less than five minutes. He drove back through Downtown Boston and Charlestown to Somerville. The snow was piling up fast, but Buddy made it home in less than ten minutes because the streets were deserted, and he liked driving fast through the snow.

As he pulled the car to the curb, Buddy glanced at the rearview mirror and saw a shadow pop up in the backseat of his vehicle. He spun hard to his right and smashed his right forearm into the stranger's head, knocking him back into the rear seat. Buddy completed his turn, squaring his body to his attacker while positioning himself on his knees in the driver's seat. The man had a rusty screwdriver in his right hand. Buddy grabbed his right wrist and plowed his own right fist into the man's face. The man began crying and pleading with Buddy to stop. Buddy disarmed the man and ordered him not to move, and then he straightened his vehicle and parked it.

The furious McLean got out of the car and pulled the man out to the sidewalk.

"What are you doing in my car?"

"I had nowhere to go. They kicked me out of the train station. I just wanted to get warm in your car. I'm sorry. I fell asleep."

"What were you going to do with that screwdriver?"

Looking down at his feet, the man replied, "I was going to rob you."

Buddy looked at the man. He was wearing a US Navy peacoat. Buddy thought the man might be a veteran.

Buddy told him, "Get back in the car, and sit up front."

"Please, I'll just leave. I won't bother you again."

"Yeah, where are you going to go?"

"I don't know. I'll just head back to town."

"I'm not going to let you walk around in this storm."

"You're not going to get the cops on me, are you?"

"No, I'll find a place for you to stay tonight."

They drove through the storm again into Boston, where Buddy finally pulled up in front of a homeless shelter. They exited the car together and walked up to the front door. Buddy pounded on the front door. The night attendant opened the door, looked at the two of them, and told Buddy, "We're full."

Buddy waved a twenty-dollar bill at the man and said, "You can find room for one more."

The attendant answered, "All right. Come on in."

Before he left, Buddy put his hand on the homeless man's shoulder and told him, "Everybody has some bad luck. You're young enough to help yourself. This will get you started."

He handed the man five twenty-dollar bills. The man's eyes were filled with tears as he thanked the gent who, a half hour earlier, he intended to rob.

# Becoming Famous

*February 1, 1961*

After the fight with Joe DeAngelis, Buddy was known throughout Boston as the one man you did not bother. There were very few looking to challenge him.

During a lunch break with some coworkers, Mike DeAngelis answered a few questions about his brother's fight with McLean.

"So, Mike, what the hell happened that night?" asked Jim Leavitt.

"The impossible happened."

"Yeah, what was that?"

"I never thought I would see the day. I could not believe what was happening right in front of me. I did not think there was a man alive who could beat my brother, Joe, in a fight. McLean staged a miraculous comeback and nearly killed my brother. The one good thing was, he cooled off enough to let me get Joe out of there. Otherwise, I'm not sure what would have happened."

"McLean was that tough?"

Mike's response to Jim was, "Put it this way, if the three of us were walking along the sidewalk together and Buddy McLean came walking toward us, I would strongly suggest that we cross the street immediately."

Mike, Jim, and another man who was listening were all physically fit athletes. They sat in silence trying to comprehend Mike's statement.

The McLean legend continued to grow.

*March 26, 1961*

On a Sunday afternoon in the back room of the 318 Club, Buddy and Howie were about to conduct their bookmaking business. "How's it look today, Howie?"

"There's a few more winners coming in, but it's going to be a good day."

"Great. How are you doing?"

"I'm good. Hey, I heard you and a few of the boys were boxing at the Y this morning."

"Yeah, we had a bunch. You're welcome to join us."

"Thanks, I will. Who did you have today?"

"Sal, Tommy, John, Russ, Pushka, Bill Cunningham."

"Wow, that's a tough crew."

"Yeah, they're all good. Hey, I have to make a call. I'll be back in a few minutes."

"All right."

A minute after Buddy walked out of the room, Tommy Ballou walked in. "Hey, Howie. How are you?"

"Good, and you?"

"Fuckin' fantastic. I had an awesome workout with Buddy this morning."

"I heard. I'm going to start training again, too. Is Buddy still in tip-top shape?"

"Absolutely. He trains as hard as ever."

"He hasn't fought in a while."

"Not since the DeAngelis fight. Which is good, because he had to let those injuries heal. He's wearing a headgear, but, otherwise, he's as good as new now. And I'll tell you, everybody talks about that fight. Nobody wants to fight him now. It cost Punchy a lot of money, too."

"Yeah, I bet it did. You know, that fight not only made him famous, it added to our business. We're doing better every week."

"Really? Wow, that's great. I'm surprised the story of that fight wasn't on the news or at least on the sports page."

They both laughed. Then Tommy added, "You should have seen the crowd watching the sparring this morning—huge crowd."

"I'll bet Buddy didn't let them down."

"No, he didn't, but he lets us get our shots in, too. He's good to spar with. It's toe-to-toe banging, but he doesn't try for the knockout."

"That's smart. Everyone gets a good workout, but they don't get hurt. Plus, they sharpen their skills at the same time."

"Yup, you're right, H. Everybody enjoys it, plus it keeps you in shape and ready."

"I'm looking forward to working out with you guys."

# The Boston Strong Boy

*Memorial Day Weekend, 1961*

Though he was the embodiment of physical fitness, Buddy usually did not like to talk about his workouts or brag about his strength and endurance. However, there were times when he would perform feats of strength, which only added to his status.

On a Sunday afternoon cookout at the Sperlinga house in the Ten Hills neighborhood of Somerville, Buddy put on a little show. A young man, home on leave from the Marine Corps, walked up to Buddy and asked him, "Sal said you're 'The Push-up King.' Is that true?"

"I do them every day. You look like a push-up boy yourself. Am I right?"

"I can do push-ups all day long."

Buddy asked, "How about one-hand?"

The military man said, "No problem." And he got down and did ten on each hand.

"That's pretty good." Then Buddy called over to a friend of his, "Bobby, can you come over here for a minute?"

Bobby Sullivan was a big man, six feet four inches tall, and he weighed over two hundred pounds. Buddy got down in a push-up position, and then he told Bobby, "Sit on my back and lift your feet off the grass, and don't put them down."

Bobby did as he was told and crisscrossed his legs across Buddy's neck and shoulders. Then Buddy began doing pushups with Bobby on his back. The Marine's eyebrows rose as his eyes widened and his mouth opened. "Ho-ly shit," he murmured.

After he did about ten of them, Buddy switched into one hand push-ups, first the right, then the left, with Bobby Sullivan still sitting on his back. The Marine just stood there, not saying a word, as he began shaking his head in disbelief.

Tommy Ballou liked to brag, "I can lift a barstool by the very bottom of one leg, and only use one hand. Then, I'm going to raise it over my head."

He used to bet with other men in barrooms throughout Greater Boston on achieving this feat of strength and balance. Most men might get three legs off the floor. Very seldom did Tommy meet a man who could lift all four legs, never mind raise the stool over his head.

Ballou had a long run of winning wagers going until one afternoon at Mike Khoury's State Spa; he hoisted a stool up to chest level, at which point everybody in the bar began gasping and pointing behind Tommy. Ballou turned around to see Buddy McLean standing there with a big smile on his face, holding up two stools, one in each hand and the same height as Tommy. Ballou quickly remarked, "Yeah, I taught him how to do that. Now, put them down before you hurt yourself. And you're costing me a lot of money here."

One hot Saturday afternoon, Buddy and a few other pals walked into Coleman's on lower Broadway, Somerville, to wet their whistles after unloading a ship in Charlestown. There were a group of men sitting at the bar trying to catch a fly that was buzzing around them. The first one to catch the fly was going to receive a dollar from each of the other men.

Buddy asked if he could get in the contest.

"No. You're too damn fast. It won't be fair," replied a spokesman for the competitors.

"I'll only use my thumb and index finger, and I'll throw in five bucks if somebody else wins," replied Buddy.

"You're in," was the answer.

Buddy pulled up a stool and sat with the group waiting for his turn. When it came around to him, Buddy sat straight up on the stool with his hands positioned lightly on his thighs. As the fly zipped past the men toward him, Buddy's left hand snapped forward like a biting rattlesnake and plucked the fly out of the air with his finger and thumb.

He dropped the fly in the spokesman's beer mug and said, "Have some protein with your beer."

Then he laughed and threw a five-dollar bill down on the bar and said, "Next one's on me, boys."

Back home, Jean brought in the new Boston telephone directory that had just been delivered to their residence. A McLean tradition was about to happen. She placed the new one on a table under the phone and handed Buddy the old one. "Okay, muscle boy, let's see if you can still do it."

Buddy looked up from reading the newspaper and smiled at Jean. "My pleasure, dear."

He sat up in his chair and proceeded to rip the book into equal fourths. Jean rolled her eyes and slowly shook her head as she walked away.

Another time, he picked up the bathroom scale and squeezed it as hard as he could. The dial spun past the three-hundred-pound weight limit to almost four hundred pounds. When Buddy released the pressure, the scale would not go back to zero. "Nice going, nutjob. Now go buy me another one," said Jean as she tossed the broken scale into the trash.

# McLean Folklore

On a warm summer night in 2002, Paul Campbell was finishing up his voluntary groundskeeping job at MacArthur Park in Peabody, Massachusetts. The one-time National Basketball Association referee drove his tractor through the open gate and near a set of bleachers where a group of fathers were sitting.

One of the fathers mentioned to Campbell, "Nice job out there. You've got that field looking like Fenway."

"I don't know about that, but thanks anyway."

Another father mentioned to Campbell, "You don't even have a kid playing in this league right now, and you still help out."

"Yeah, what's wrong with that?"

"Nothing. We think it's great, but it's not very common around here."

"Well, it is from where I grew up."

"Where was that?"

"Somerville."

"Tough town," said one of the fathers.

"Toughest city anywhere, but it built character. If you did something stupid in Somerville, you'd get smacked by a couple of neighbors, then go home and get punched by your old man."

They all had a good laugh, then one of the dads asked Paul, "Did you ever hear of guy named Buddy McLean?"

"Of course, everyone in Somerville knows Buddy."

"Toughest guy there ever was?"

"That's what they say."

"Did you ever meet him?"

Campbell responded, "Yes, I was shooting hoops at the Somerville Y one day. I was probably eleven or twelve years old at the time. McLean and his friends were boxing at one end of the court. They were going at it like there was no tomorrow. No headgear, just toe to toe pounding. Nobody gave an inch. They were all fast, strong, and tough. After he was done sparring, Buddy McLean went upstairs and punched the heavy bag nonstop for twenty minutes. I swear, that bag would bend when he hit it. He talked to me before he went upstairs, and I'll never forget it."

"What did he say?" asked one of the fathers.

"I was shooting baskets. McLean and a few of his friends were sitting on a bench on the sideline. They had just finished their sparring, and some of them were getting ready to leave. My shot caromed off the rim, and the ball bounced toward those men. As I ran over to retrieve my ball, McLean scooped up the ball with one hand and began dribbling. As I got closer, he bounce-passed it to me. I said thanks, and he said, 'Come here, kid.' He had a nip bottle of gin in his other hand. As he opened the bottle, Buddy McLean said to me, 'You see this, kid? Never drink this. It's no good for you.' Then he swigged the shot. All his friends laughed, so I laughed with them."

And so did the men at MacArthur Park.

*Summer, 2010*

An elderly gentleman from Arlington, Massachusetts, walked onto a Peabody baseball diamond. The man was there to umpire a Babe Ruth League baseball game. One of the coaches was raking around home plate when the umpire arrived.

"Hi. How are ya?" asked the coach.

"I'm good. How are you?"

"Good, too. I don't think we've had you here before. Am I right?"

"That's right. I usually work the Medford, Somerville, Arlington leagues."

The coach looked up at the tall, fit, blue-eyed umpire who looked to be of Irish descent. The coach instantly remembered Paul Campbell's story from nine years earlier. He asked the umpire, "Do you live over there?"

"Yep. Arlington, my whole life."

"Did you ever hear of a guy named Buddy McLean?"

"I certainly have. There was nobody like him. I saw him one time, and my father met him another time."

"Really, how did it happen?"

"I remember like it was yesterday. It was a steamy hot Sunday morning in the summer, around 1956. My father and I were riding our brand-new bicycles around Fresh Pond in Cambridge. As we were pedaling along at a pretty good clip, a guy wearing a heavy sweat suit came running up behind us. He said, 'Good morning,' and blew right past us. My father recognized him immediately and told me, 'That's Buddy McLean.' He looked like Superman. I knew the name because he was already well-known throughout the Boston area as the toughest guy around.

"My father met McLean a few years later. My dad was a court officer in Cambridge, and McLean had some issue to attend to. He asked my dad for some advice. I'm not sure what it was about. When my father came home, he told me what happened. He said that Buddy McLean might be the toughest guy around, but that he is also the nicest, most polite person he ever met. He said McLean was wearing a suit that day, and he looked like a movie star. About a week later, my father received a letter in the mail. It was a simple note that said, 'Thanks for your help.' The note was unsigned and had a one-hundred-dollar bill folded inside."

*Summer, 2010*

Michael McLean met with three Charlestown men at their social club on Main Street. The men, who were getting on in years, wanted Michael to know what they knew and thought about his father.

Michael "Mickey" Murphy was a tough, hardworking Charlestown kid, twelve years younger than Buddy. He sought out work on the rough-and-tumble waterfront docks, where he learned early on that, "Closed mouths catch no flies." Also, "Never trust a man who doesn't drink."

Mickey told Buddy's son, "The first time I met your father, I was sixteen years old and looking for work at the trucking combine down in Southie. Your old man said, 'Let's see what you can do.' I didn't let him down, and he hired me twenty more times to help him unload and load freight. I loved working for your dad. He paid you that day, and he paid better than anyone else."

"Yeah, I remember, you were there a couple times when he brought me to work."

"Yeah, those were great days. You know, everyone knew how tough he was and not to screw with him. What a lot of people don't know was that he was a great guy, always polite and friendly, even to young kids like me. We all looked up to him because he was tough, but he never acted like it. Like I said, he paid better than the other drivers if you did the job like he told you to. He'd give you advice on where to find other work, or he'd buy you a meal. The nicest guy I ever met."

Jackie Mansfield, another Townie sitting at the table, chimed in, "One time I was loading lobsters onto Buddy's truck. He said, 'Make sure you only load the boxes that are lined up behind my truck. Don't take anyone else's.' With Buddy McLean, you do what he tells you. When I was done, the dock foreman offered me half a dozen lobsters for free. I told him thanks, but no thanks. The guy said, 'Take them. Everybody does.' Not me! I told him.

"The next day, I see your father, and he asks me why I didn't take the lobsters. I said, 'You told me not to.' Buddy said, 'Listen, if it is offered to you, then it is okay to take some home. Gee, Jackie, you are one honest kid, aren't you?'

"I smiled and nodded to him, but in my head I was thinking, only a meathead would screw with Buddy McLean."

The men at the table, and a few at the bar, all had a good laugh.

The third man sitting with Michael was Billy Coleman. He was another old but still tough Charlestown boxer who looked up to Buddy McLean. Billy worked as a bartender/bouncer at the rowdy Alibi Club.

"I saw Buddy fight more than a few times. He'd come into the club to have a few drinks with his pals. He was always friendly to me and he was a 'big duker' (good tipper). He didn't look for fights, but he didn't try to avoid them either (everyone chuckled). I thought it was kind of funny how, every once in a while, some fuckin' huge tough guy would come into the club looking to fight Buddy. They'd see the baby face, average-sized body—you couldn't appreciate his physique in street clothes. He had nice-combed light hair and a smooth, steady voice. He was not intimidating, especially to guys who outweighed him by a hundred pounds or more. When a challenge came his way, he'd smile and say, 'All right. Let's go outside.' Once he got you out on the sidewalk though, he was totally different. It was like *Dr. Jekyll and Mr. Hyde*."

The social club became deathly silent as every man intently listened. Then Michael asked, "What would happen, Billy?"

"He'd get this real serious, focused look on his face, and then, oh my God, he'd come at you like there was no tomorrow. The other guy would be totally caught off guard by the lightning punches coming one right after another. He was fuckin' strong too, unbelievable. And he could wrestle, fuckin' fantastic. I saw him get under and lift a big bastard and drive him into the wall. Ruined the guy. He was out before a referee could count to one. Then he goes back inside, goes into the men's room, washes up a little, and goes back to his seat with his friends like nothing happened—Jekyll and Hyde."

# Crime Pays

*June 3, 1961*

The Sperlinga brothers were sitting in Leone's on a Saturday afternoon. They were enjoying a couple of slices while they sat at the window looking out at busy Broadway. Suddenly Bobby exclaimed, "Hey, there goes Buddy McLean."

Sal looked up to see his friend wearing a sweat suit and sprinting up the hill. "Yup. Pretty fast, don't you think?"

"Yeah, what the hell's he doing?"

"Getting a workout in. He does that every day."

"Jesus, it's a wonder he can find the time."

"I know. He's busy as hell, always on the go."

"Doesn't he have, like, three jobs?"

"Yup, plus that little side business, which ain't so little now. I'd say he works between seventy and eighty hours a week."

"Wow, does he still hijack trailers, too?"

"Once in a while. Buddy is what you call an opportunist. If something good comes along, and it's a low risk, he'll grab it."

"He must be rolling in the dough."

"He's doing very well."

*June 5, 1961*

An opportunity came along. It was one of the gang's best and easiest paydays—a pair of trailers loaded with copper pipes.

Tommy Ballou boasted, "Grabbing those pipes was like taking candy from a baby. And I bet you the pipe company is crying right now."

## June 11, 1961

About a week later, another money-making prospect came along. In front of the Capitol Bar one afternoon, Buddy asked, "Howie, I got a chance to buy a couple slot and pinball machines. Where do you think I could put them?"

Howie thought for a minute, then replied, "How about right over there, at the Greeks? They're always busy. People can come in, get something to eat, and do a little gambling. It might work."

Buddy nodded, smiled, and said, "Not a bad idea, I'll go over and ask them." He walked over to the Winter Hill Grill and had a word with the owners. The Greeks liked Buddy and gave him the green light. The machines were installed and became an immediate success. They were hugely popular throughout Somerville. However, the gambling machines also presented a problem.

## June 19, 1961

On a Monday morning, after roll call, the Somerville chief of police called John Canty into his office.

"Hi, Chief, how are you?"

"I've been better, John. I have a problem I need you to take care of."

"Sure, Chief, what is it?"

"It's your friend McLean and those fuckin' slot machines of his. We're getting complaints from a bunch of restaurant owners throughout the city that their businesses have suffered since he put those machines in the Winter Hill Grill."

Canty smiled, "Do you want me to have him put machines in their restaurants, too?"

"Don't be a wiseass, John. I want you to talk to McLean. He's your friend. He has to get those damn things out of there."

"Gee, Chief. They've only been there for a week. You don't want to let him break even on his investment?"

"See if you can get him to move them to another location, preferably out of Somerville. Otherwise you're going to have to confiscate them."

"I'll talk to him, Chief."

The next day, John spoke with Buddy. "They're illegal to begin with, and you never got a permit or a waiver for them. Why don't you move the machines before we have to seize them?"

Buddy responded, "All right, John. I'll look for another place to put them, but it might take a while. That's too bad. We're doing real well at the Greeks. I don't know if you're aware, but a good amount of the money is being donated to people who need it."

"I'm sure that's all true. You don't have to convince me. But I have orders to follow. Try not to take too long, or the chief will be giving me shit about it."

Buddy nodded.

A week later, the chief reminded John that the machines were still in operation and that they had to go. Canty walked into the Greeks' restaurant and observed that the slot and pinball machine business was still booming. He talked to both the owner and his wife. "Listen, I'm warning you that if I return and find these machines have not been removed, I'm going to confiscate them."

The owner replied, "I don't want any trouble. Please, talk to Buddy."

Then Canty found Buddy just a few doors away getting a haircut at Tony the Barber's on Broadway. He reminded his friend, "Buddy, those machines have to go. The chief is getting a lot of grief from City Hall."

"I know. I know. I'm trying to find another place. Anywhere I go in Somerville, it's going to bring the same problem. I know a guy in Everett who might want to put them in his club. Then, if he doesn't take them, I was going to try the Angiulos or the McLaughlins."

"Yeah, well, if they're still at the Greeks next week, then I'm going to have to take them."

"All right. I'll do my best to get rid of them."

Another week went by and Canty received word that the machines were still active. Armed with a warrant and accompanied by four cops with a paddy wagon, Canty impounded the machines. As the seizure proceeded, the local newspaper rushed to the scene and photographed Canty supervising the removal.

John Canty, wearing suit

On the following Sunday, Canty ran into McLean as the two were walking into church.

"Nice picture in the paper, John," remarked Buddy.

"I warned you a few times to get those slots out of there," reminded John.

"Yeah, I know, don't worry about it. They became more of a headache than anything else."

"Those things were getting used all day long. You must have made pretty good dough."

"I had more coins than I knew what to do with."

"Piggy banks."

"They're all full now. The money bags were heavy, too. I was getting a workout every time I emptied the machines."

"Getting paid to work out. Not too shabby."

"Yeah," laughed Buddy. "You know, we could set up a gambling hall somewhere else."

"Yeah," chuckled John. "Great idea, but if you don't mind, I have to make sure it's okay with the chief."

"Okay. Let me know. Maybe he'll want to go in on it with us," replied Buddy.

"Yeah, maybe I should let you go talk to him."

"Just say the word and I'll do it."

"I'm sure you would," Canty said as the two blessed themselves with holy water.

In his mind, Buddy was certain—a gambling hall in Somerville would make a ton of money. *Next time I see Joe Mac, I'll have to run it by him.*

# Joe Mac's Affairs

Joe McDonald

*June 19, 1961*

Joe McDonald walked into a small country bank that had several millionaire clients who owned citrus farms in Florida. He was wearing a derby hat, eyeglasses, and a fake mustache. There were five people working in the bank: the president of the bank, his secretary, two tellers, and a security guard. There was a sheriff's station directly across the street from the bank. Joe Mac calmly walked up to the security guard and placed two black leather satchels on the floor in front of the guard. He proceeded to pull two pistols from his suit jacket and announced to everyone, "This is a robbery. Do what I tell you and nobody will get hurt."

He put one of his pistols away, then disarmed the security guard. Joe had the security guard pick up the satchels and walked him over to the tellers. He had all three sit on the floor. He then told the secretary, "Join the others over here, dear."

Joe Mac picked up his satchels and walked over to the bank manager. "Let's go," and nudged him by the arm. He marched the manager over to the front door and told him to, "Lock it."

The other four sat together on the floor behind the counter, facing directly in front of the safe. Then Joe Mac, in a calm, polite tone, instructed the manager to, "Empty the drawers into these satchels."

Finally, he walked the manager to the safe, where the bags were filled to the top with cash. The whole ordeal took less than five minutes. As he was leaving the bank, Joe spoke to the employees and told them, "I want you to know that I appreciate your cooperation."

He placed five thousand dollars on a table by the front door. Then he told them, "Folks, don't worry about this. It's not your money, and we all know the bank has insurance. I want you to split this money up amongst yourselves, but put all the blame on me. Then you can call for the sheriff or his deputy. I sent them both on a couple of wild-goose chases in opposite directions across town. You have a nice day now."

Joe Mac strolled out the front door. In the two satchels the total was over three hundred thousand dollars.

He drove five miles out of town to switch cars. He changed his clothes and added a wig, makeup, and women's glasses to disguise himself as an elderly woman. He stashed his bank robbing clothes in a suitcase and threw it in the high grass of a swamp. He placed the two satchels in the trunk of the second getaway car. Then Joe proceeded to drive leisurely north toward Boston.

* * *

Meanwhile, back in Somerville, Joe's Winter Hill bookmaking agency was rolling along. Buddy had Howie Winter overseeing the operation.

One afternoon, Buddy mentioned to Howie, "Joe is very happy with the way you run the books. I told him about the young up-and-comers you brought in. He likes that you're expanding the action."

"Yeah, it's working pretty well so far. I'm trying to stay on top of it."

"I think you're doing great. You're going to make us all rich."

"Thanks, Buddy."

"If you have any problems with the cops, the McLaughlins, or anyone else, you let me know."

"You know I will."

"And when Joe gets back, he's going to want to look at the books. Everything has to be perfect: no questions, no mistakes."

"The books are ready right now. Everything is up-to-date, no skimming, no deadbeats. We're looking good."

Buddy smiled and nodded. "That's what I like to hear. I knew you were the man for the job."

# Keeping Life in Balance

*June 26, 1961*

One afternoon, a Winter Hill neighbor walked over to Snow Terrace to ask Buddy for a favor.

"Hi, Buddy."

"Hi, Bob. How are you?"

"Can I talk to you for a minute?"

"Sure. Come in the house."

Buddy grabbed two beers from the refrigerator, and the men sat down at the kitchen table. "What's going on, Bob?"

"My brother got jumped and robbed the other night down in Charlestown. They beat him up real bad. He's in Mass General."

"Is he going to be okay?"

"Yeah, the doctors think so, but it's going to take a while."

"Do you know who did it?"

"Yeah, it was this three-piece band. They were playing that night at the Stork Club. My brother was in there. One of them saw his wallet. He carries a lot of cash. They got him outside in the alley."

Buddy took a sip of his beer. He looked Bob in the eye and asked, "Do you want me to do something about this?"

"I wouldn't normally ask for this, but, yes, I would like your help."

"Okay, give me about a week. I'll take care of it."

"Thanks, Buddy, but what will I owe you?"

"Don't worry about that. We'll settle up later."

The next day, at the Charlestown docks, Buddy approached John Hurley. "Hey John, I need a favor."

"What's up?"

"Find out what you can about the band that played at the Stork last Friday night."

"What do you want to know about them?"

"Names, addresses, relatives or friends of theirs, people who we might know."

"All right, what did they do?"

"They beat up and robbed a neighbor of mine."

"Okay, I'll get right on it."

The same day, Hurley gave Buddy the information he was looking for.

At the end of the week, Buddy called his Winter Hill neighbor to come by the house for a visit. When he arrived, Buddy was standing on his front porch waiting for him.

"Hi, Bob. Come on in." They walked to the kitchen and sat at the table, drinking a couple of beers. Buddy asked his neighbor, "How is your brother doing?"

"He's still in a lot of pain, but he's getting better. He should be back at work in a couple of weeks."

Buddy reached into his pocket and pulled out a huge roll of cash.

"This should make him feel a little better."

"Buddy, Holy Jesus! What the ... What about what I owe you?"

"I already took out my share. We're all set."

"Buddy, you're the greatest."

"Don't tell anyone. It's between you and me."

"I won't. I promise. Buddy, you're the best friend a guy could ever have. How did you get the money?"

"You don't need to know about that. I'll just say those guys were taught a lesson they'll never forget."

"Oh my God. Thank you, Buddy, from my whole family."

"You're welcome. Remember, it's just between us."

"Absolutely. You got it."

It remained a secret.

# Kellie Completes the Family

*June 28, 1961*

Buddy hired a Somerville man named Charlie Robinson to build an extension to his house on Snow Terrace. Jean was pregnant with their fourth child, so they had decided they needed more space. Buddy thought, *This will be a nice house to raise the kids in, plus it's a great neighborhood.* In August, Buddy and Jean celebrated the birth of a daughter they named Kellie. When Buddy brought his other three children to the hospital to visit their mom and meet their new sister, Jean was sitting in a chair holding Kellie. Her mother and sisters were crowded around her.

"Isn't she beautiful?" asked Jean.

"She's perfect," responded Buddy.

Lea pushed her way to the front. "I want to see my baby sister."

She stared at Kellie sleeping in her mother's arms.

"What do you think of your new sister, Lea?" asked Buddy.

"She's perfect."

Buddy felt, *I'm so lucky to have such a wonderful family.* He still attended mass on Sundays at Saint Benedict's Church. Oftentimes, after mass, Buddy would chat with his favorite priest, Father Hogan.

"Yeah, Father. I've been truly blessed with the best family a guy could have."

"That's wonderful, Buddy. Make sure you spend as much time as you can with them. That's the most important thing."

"I will, Father."

Unfortunately for Buddy, confrontations remained a part of his life.

# They Keep Coming

Paul Raymond

*August 26, 1961*

On a lively Saturday night at the crowded Somerville Italian-American Club, a young, swaggering Massachusetts state-Golden-Gloves light-heavyweight champ named Paul Raymond picked a fight with another Somerville man named Bobby DeSimone, who was an acquaintance of Buddy's. The beef was over a woman. However, Raymond's plan was to not only give DeSimone a boxing lesson, but intimidate everyone in the bar, including Buddy McLean.

Raymond was peppering DeSimone with flashy combinations, and his slick footwork left him untouched. Raymond maneuvered himself so that he was in front of Buddy, with DeSimone between them. Raymond drilled a straight right to the man's chin, knocking him back and into Buddy's arms. Buddy held the bemused man up, and, while turning to sit him down in a chair, Raymond popped a quick jab off Buddy's shoulder. He demanded that Buddy let the fight continue. "Don't be nursing him, McLean, I'm not done yet."

Buddy answered, "Just what I've been waiting for. Now it's my turn."

"Okay, big shot. I'm not afraid of you. Get ready to look like your fuckin' friend over there."

Instantly, the gathering of one hundred onlookers became unexpectedly excited to the point where huge commotions swelled within the crowd. Anticipation and predictions quickly circulated throughout the room.

"Raymond wants to fight Buddy," exclaimed one of Buddy's friends.

"That's a big mistake for McLean. Paul Raymond is unbeatable," stated one man who was with the Raymond clan and had never seen Buddy fight.

"Buddy will send Raymond to the hospital," chimed in another McLean friend.

"No way. Raymond's bigger, stronger, more skilled, plus he's a killer," answered the nonbeliever.

"You know what? After he knocks out Raymond, I'll let him know what you said."

The Paul Raymond backer became deathly silent.

The cocky Raymond waved Buddy out to the dance floor. Raymond shuffled and shadowboxed his way to the middle of the floor as Buddy moved toward him. Suddenly, Buddy charged him. Raymond tried to slip Buddy's rush but was not quick enough. Buddy grabbed Raymond's shoulders and rammed him into the bar. A barrage of punches followed. Paul Raymond threw none. Raymond attempted to spin away from the bar. Buddy got his hands into Raymond's armpits, lifted him and threw the taller, heavier boxer into a wall. The instant Raymond came off the wall, he was met with a cargo of sledgehammer blows to his head and face. In less than one minute, the fight was over. Raymond's face was turned into red mush. His friends were smart enough to immediately leave the club. Quickly and quietly, they escorted Paul Raymond out to their car and drove him to the emergency room at Somerville Hospital.

The next day, Paul Raymond sought out Buddy McLean. He found him at the Capitol Bar on Winter Hill. Buddy looked at Raymond, thinking he might be looking for another fight and said to him, "Let your face heal first. Then I'll give you a rematch."

"I never want to fight you again. I just wanted to apologize for what I said last night."

The two shook hands and never had another altercation.

# Family Man

## August 28, 1961

As he did every summer, Buddy rented a house near or on a beach for a week or two. This year, it was Hampton Beach in New Hampshire. *I love it here. Someday I'm going to buy a place, right on the water. Yup, I'm going to do it.*

Buddy with mother-in-law, Veronica Kelley at
Salisbury Beach. Michael and Lea are behind them.

The McLeans vacationed on Cape Cod, Massachusetts, also. They made day trips to Gloucester and Salisbury. A last-minute plan might be a ride to Revere or Nahant because they were only fifteen or twenty minutes from Somerville.

During the summer months, Buddy was constantly outside in the sun and always had a great tan. Even with his busy work schedule, Buddy might take a quick half hour now and then to lay out in the sun and maintain his tan.

One bright sunny day, Jean looked out her front window and saw Buddy laid out on the roof of his car wearing only his boxer shorts. She rolled her eyes, shook her head, and muttered, "I should've had him committed a long time ago."

Jimmy, Jean and Lea at Pleasure Island

Buddy and Jean brought their kids to amusement parks like Pleasure Island in Wakefield or Canobie Lake Park in Salem, New Hampshire. Sometimes Jean's mother and sisters would join the McLeans.

Jean's mother came by the house one Sunday evening.

"Where's Buddy and the kids?"

"He piled them and a bunch of neighbors' kids into the car and took them to the drive-in."

"He loves kids, doesn't he?"

"Yeah, and they love him, too. He's like a big kid himself."

"I saw him the other day. He was buying a big gang ice cream down at the store."

"That sounds like him. He takes them to the park, the beach, or to the pool. They love him."

With two boys and then two girls completing his offspring, Buddy felt, *This is great. Everything's coming together.* The rough-and-tumble, inner-city upbringing he endured no longer mattered to him. He wanted to concentrate on building a secure future for his family.

# A Desire to Change

Michael, Jimmy and Buddy at Salisbury Beach

*September 2, 1961*

Over breakfast in their kitchen on Saturday morning, Labor Day weekend, Buddy told Jean, "I've been thinking about a few things."

"What's that, hon?"

"I think I'd like to move us up to New Hampshire."

"Jesus Christ! Why the hell do you want to do that?"

"I love it up there. I think it would be good for the kids, too."

"What's wrong with right here?"

"It's crowded, it's busy, and it's noisy here. We could buy a nice piece of property up there, right on the ocean."

"I don't care for the ocean, you know that."

"Yeah, but the kids love it, and I think you would come to like it, too."

"My whole family lives here. I don't want to leave them."

"I bet your mother would come with us, and, the next thing you know, the rest of them would follow us up there."

"I doubt it. Besides that, what would you do for work?"

"Hampton is only an hour away, I can make that ride easy. On top of that, I'm thinking about different ideas for investing in real estate and maybe a business or two."

"What business?"

"Maybe a seafood joint on the beach, like Kelly's on Revere Beach and maybe a bar right next to it."

"So first you feed your customers, then you get them drunk?"

"Yeah, or the other way around. Either way, it doesn't matter."

They both had a good laugh.

"So, what do you think?"

"You can go if you want to, I'm staying here."

As Jean got up from the table, Buddy slowly shook his head. A sad smile appeared on his face: *Someday, I'm going to do it. No more hell-raising, no more crime, make an honest living. I'm going to get everyone and leave all this behind. We're going to stick together and build a new life. Strong. Healthy. Happy. It's going to be great.*

# Devastation

*Labor Day Weekend, September 3, 1961*

Out of nowhere, turmoil and violence descended on Buddy McLean like Japanese bombers attacking Pearl Harbor. He was handed a crisis that placed him at the forefront of a terrible, and now historic, gang war.

George McLaughlin

Two of Buddy's bookmaking associates, Billy Hickey and Red Lloyd, were having a good time with their wives, friends, and some Charlestown men in a cottage rented by Somerville loan shark Jimmy McGaffigan at Salisbury Beach, fifty miles north of Boston. During the party, George McLaughlin, the youngest brother of the Townie gangster family, drunkenly advanced on Bill Hickey's wife, Ann. An argument ensued, and McLaughlin received a savage beating from Buddy's men, Hickey and Lloyd. The pair loaded McLaughlin into their car and drove him to Anna Jaques Hospital in Newburyport, where they dropped Georgie on the front lawn. They drove back to Somerville and informed McLean of what happened.

Lloyd told Buddy, "Georgie grabbed Ann's tits. So, Billy pushed him back into the kitchen counter. Georgie picked up a glass and smashed it into Billy's face. I stepped in and pushed the little fuck back into the counter again. He picked up another glass and threw it at me, but he missed and it fuckin' hits Ann. By then, we'd both had enough. We both jumped on Georgie, wrestled him to the floor. Then he bites a chunk out of Billy's arm, so I smashed a whiskey bottle off his head. He was bleeding real bad, and he wasn't moving. We thought he was fuckin' dead."

"Then what happened?" asked Buddy.

"We rolled him up in the living room rug and loaded him into the back seat of Billy's car. Then we drove off looking for a good place to dump the body. As we're driving the back roads of Salisbury, the little fuck began to stir and moan. We were both shocked that he was still alive. We started to panic. We didn't know whether to finish him or save him. After a few minutes of figuring our next move, we thought that you wouldn't want Georgie dead. So, we drove to the nearest hospital and dumped him on the front lawn."

"He could've died on the lawn. Why didn't you take him inside?"

"We wanted to make a clean getaway. We didn't want to answer any questions or take a chance of getting pinched."

Buddy nodded slowly and said, "You guys were drunk, too?"

Red nodded and replied, "Yeah."

"I guess that explains why you were stupid. You should've brought him inside the hospital and told them what you told me. How's Ann? Is she okay?"

"She's got a black eye, but otherwise she's okay."

"What about McLaughlin?"

"We don't know. Like I said, we took off."

Buddy shook his head and said, "Jesus. All right, listen up real good. You guys have to leave the state right now."

"What?"

"Shut up and listen."

"You are going to sell the bar (the Capitol Bar on Winter Hill was co-owned by Hickey and Lloyd) and disappear. When Punchy and Bernie find out who put Georgie in the hospital, and they will find out, they're going to come after you two. And it won't end well. So, you two should leave, right now. I'll try to work something out with the McLaughlins."

Hickey and Lloyd nodded to Buddy in agreement. They left without hesitation. As he watched them walk away, Buddy thought, *Those idiots. This is going to come back to me, and they're not a bit grateful. I should've beat the shit out them.*

The partners hired a young Somerville lawyer named Frank Marchetti to handle their affairs, and they disappeared. Buddy called Marchetti the morning after Hickey and Lloyd took off and told Marchetti to meet him at the Capitol at eleven a.m. Marchetti arrived a few minutes early to ensure he did not agitate or disrespect Buddy, who was waiting for Marchetti in a booth and waved him over. Frank slid into the booth across from Buddy.

"Hi, Buddy. How are you?"

"Where's Red and Billy?" asked Buddy.

"I don't know," replied Frank.

"Yeah, you do."

"No, Buddy. I really don't know where they are."

"I'm only going to say it once. If you don't tell me where they are right now, I'm going to break both your arms and your legs."

"Buddy, please. I don't know where they are, and I would not want information like that to leak out. Their lives are at stake here."

Buddy stared long and hard at Marchetti. Then he responded, "You're okay, Frank. I just wanted to make sure you were a stand-up guy. Now listen, the McLaughlins might try to pull the same shit I just did. If that happens, you tell them to talk to me. Then you give me a heads-up."

Buddy reached forward to shake Marchetti's hand. Marchetti breathed a sigh of relief, nodded, and took Buddy's hand. Marchetti was visibly shaking as he asked Buddy, "So, are you going to be the new owner of the bar?"

"I don't know yet. I might. I don't want my name on it right now. I'll let you know whose name to put on it. I might end up selling the place to someone else. I don't really need another headache right now."

"Okay, Buddy. I won't say anything about that either. You let me know if I can help you with anything else."

"Just make sure all the paperwork is in order. And if anybody gives you a hard time, or comes snooping around, you tell me about it right away."

"Yes, sir, I will. And if you need me for anything else, let me know, too."

"I will Frank. Thanks."

As Marchetti left the barroom, Buddy thought, *He's a good guy. I like him. But, if I ever see Hickey and Lloyd again, I'm going to pound the shit out of them.*

Buddy began spreading the word around Somerville that Frank Marchetti was a good man and a fine lawyer. Marchetti's Powder House Square law business skyrocketed. Scores of

Somerville residents engaged Marchetti for legal work, claiming that Buddy McLean referred them. Years later, Marchetti retired a rich man and vociferously remained grateful to Buddy.

Almost two months passed without a word from the McLaughlins. Buddy went about his daily routine like nothing had happened. People from Somerville and Charlestown had been asking Buddy about the incident at Salisbury Beach. He kept his answer quick, simple, honest, and consistent. "I don't know much about it. I wasn't there."

"What about Red and Bill?"

"As far as I know, they left town. They didn't want to deal with the McLaughlins."

Finally, young George was discharged from the hospital. His brothers, Eddie and Bernie, decided it was time to talk to Buddy McLean. Bernie called Buddy to set up a meeting for the two of them to "straighten things out."

*October 28, 1961*

"Why don't you come by my house and we'll have a few beers?"

"This is not going to be a social visit," replied Bernie.

"Bernie, I understand why you're mad about all this, and I would be, too. I just hope we can work something out here."

"We'll see."

"How about tomorrow, around noon?"

"I'll be there," said Bernie.

# The Townies

After he ended his conversation with Bernie McLaughlin, Buddy called John Hurley and Tommy Ballou to come by his house. Both men lived in Charlestown and knew all the players. A few other close friends were invited.

When everyone was seated at the kitchen table, Buddy started with Hurley and said, "All right, tell me everything you know about these guys, and it doesn't matter if I already know what you have to say. I want to hear it again."

"All right. Edward 'Punchy' McLaughlin, early forties, six feet tall and weighing in at about two hundred seventy-five pounds. He's co-boss with his brother, Bernie. He's an ex-boxer, longshoreman, and debt collector. He has a reputation for shaking the hand and crushing every bone in it when he's collecting on a late payment. He has a huge ego, and he's a cheap bastard. He's a compulsive shoplifter, and he's been arrested for it several times. When it comes to crime, he's fuckin' good at it, real shrewd. He's also very good at manipulating people with threats, lies, half-truths, and exaggerations. He is definitely not to be trusted with anything he says or does.

"Bernie is the organizer of almost all the Charlestown rackets. He's a tough motherfucker and one of the most feared men around. He's also got a nasty Irish temper. He has a reputation for severe violence with deadbeats. I heard he carries in his left hand a fuckin' lead window sash rolled into a newspaper. Then, when he's shaking hands with an unsuspecting sucker who owes him money, *Bang!* A broken arm. His friends will say that McLaughlin doesn't need a sash and that his fists keep deadbeats in line.

"He's been arrested several times, mostly for assault. But, one time, he was shot in the back when he broke into a bar in Charlestown. After he recovered, he spent some time in the joint. He worked on the Charlestown docks as a longshoreman in his late teens and through his twenties. As the gang accumulated more money, he moved his family from their cold-water Townie flat to the new housing project on Mission Hill over in Roxbury. A few years later, he moved his family to a nice home in Melrose. He's still there right now. He's about forty years old, but he's still in great shape and he's real tough. He's got great hands. He's not as good as you, but he's a force to reckon with. One time he was in City Square with his little son, who just had an operation and had a big bandage over his eye. Five sailors come along and start giving the little kid some shit. Bernie went nuts and had all five of them laid out in less than a minute. Nasty Irish temper. You have to be careful with him—don't get on his bad side. On the other side, he's a straight shooter, and he'll treat you with respect, as long as you do the same with him."

Hurley continued, "Two of his brothers were both decorated heroes during World War II. Bernie named his two sons John and Charlie after his veteran brothers. The two soldiers were never involved in anything that their brothers were into."

Buddy nodded, as he listened intently.

"The other three brothers, Bernie, Eddie, and Georgie, run the family business. Not so much Georgie. They're New England's second most powerful criminal enterprise. Only the Mafia is ahead of them. But we've been gaining on them, and, believe me, they know it, and they don't fuckin' like it. They're loan sharks, bookmakers, and waterfront thieves. Somehow, they manage to skim hundreds of dollars every day from the toll booths on the Mystic River Bridge. They extort cash once a week from legitimate businesses throughout Charlestown, calling it 'protection payments.' They get a cut from booze distributors that make deliveries in Charlestown. They've got a shitload of Boston cops they pay to look the other way or handle minor violations. It's also pretty well known that they work as enforcers and assassins for a New York mobster family. I'm not sure which one, or maybe several."

Harold Hannon

Tommy chimed in, "They got this guy named Harold Hannon, from Everett. Fuckin' guy is a psychopath, likes to torture people before he kills them. Hannon's older than the rest of them. He's lean and homely as hell, worse than Phyllis Diller with a hangover. When he's working, he's quiet, devious, and dangerous. He mostly likes to work alone. Sometimes he uses a getaway driver or a lookout. He's very patient and prepared. He's good with a knife and better with a gun. He's friends with the old man Hughes, and he taught Stevie and Connie how to shoot. They're both sharpshooters, too.

"Hannon likes to go down to Scollay Square for prostitutes. That's the only way he's going to get laid. The McLaughlins pay Hannon to kill. That's all he does. They'll throw his name around occasionally to scare someone, but, most of the time, he's there, waiting to kill. Then he disappears. He doesn't hang around in Charlestown like the rest of them. Keeps to himself, kind of like Joe Mac. Now Georgie, that little sick fuck, he loves Hannon and his stories of mayhem. He wants to be like him. His brothers are grooming him. But he drinks a lot, and when he's tanked he gets violent, including with women. You can't trust him for a second. He's nutty, but his brothers love him, and they're going to want revenge."

"What about the Hughes brothers?" asked Buddy.

Connie Hughes                    Stevie Hughes

Tommy answered, "Stevie and Connie, a couple of hard-drinking, chubby Charlestown bullies who, one-on-one, can't fight a lick, but they're big, they intimidate, and they're always together. They spend a lot of time with Punchy. They watch his back or dish out beatings. They'll show up with baseball bats, but you know they're packing heat also. Punchy, too. Everyone in

Charlestown is afraid of them. Punchy knows this and, because of that fear, he gets whatever he wants. Both brothers are first-rate sharpshooters with a rifle. They learned the skill from their father, Steve Hughes Sr. Then Hannon started teaching them. The old man Hughes is a lifelong Charlestown criminal and he's a mentor to Punchy and Bernie."

"All right," Buddy responded, "Punchy's the boss, then Bernie must be number two."

"No, they're equal," answered Tommy. "But Bernie stays out of the spotlight. He's the only likeable one in the bunch. The rest of them are no good sons of bitches. As mean and tough as he is, Bernie always conducts himself as a gentleman, especially in front of women. When a professional athlete wants to place a bet on a game, he goes through Bernie, knowing that his identity and his bet is silent and safe. One night, Bernie was having drinks with Mickey Mantle at the Stork Club in Charlestown. The two were sitting at a table when a young, pretty waitress from Bunker Hill walked up and asked the Mick, 'Can I get you something Mr. Mantle?'

"'Yeah, I'd like it if you would suck on my dick,' says Mantle.

"In a split second, Bernie turns and fires a straight right punch into Mantle's chin, knocking him back and over his seat. Then Bernie gets up and grabs Mantle by his collar and drags him over to the stairway and pushes him down the fuckin' steps. This guy lives by his own set of rules and nobody tells him what to do. He's rough around the edges, but he'll never put up with a man disrespecting or mistreating a woman in front of him. And he's the best of them all at collecting money. He tells you that if you owe him money you better find him and pay up on time. If he has to come looking for you, you're going to get hurt. You need to be careful with him."

\* \* \*

At the same time, the McLaughlins were discussing the upcoming meeting with McLean.

Punchy asked Bernie, "You don't want me to go with you?"

"No. I'll handle it."

"He's a tough bastard. He might tell you to fuck off. Then what?"

Bernie acknowledged to his brother Eddie that, "Buddy McLean is the toughest guy I've ever seen, but I'm not afraid of him. I'll talk to him. I think I know him good enough to make him understand what must be done."

Eddie responded, "I hope you know him good enough to get us the right fuckin' payback."

The next day, Bernie drove to the McLean family home in the Winter Hill neighborhood of Somerville.

# The Sit-down

*October 29, 1961*

Buddy had Jean drive the kids and the dogs to her mother's apartment to ensure absolute silence in the house. Bernie arrived on time, and the two Irishmen shook hands and walked through to the back of the house.

"How's your brother doing?"

"Not that good. He's still got a ways to go."

"He'll be all right, though?"

"Yeah, eventually."

"Want a beer?"

"Yeah, sure."

"Have a seat."

Sitting at the kitchen table, sipping their beers, the two leaders stated their positions.

"Something has to be done, Buddy," demanded McLaughlin.

"What do you want?" asked McLean.

"I want them dead," McLaughlin stated emphatically.

"You're not getting my permission for that," responded McLean.

"I don't want your fuckin' permission. I want you to fuckin' help me set them up."

"That's not going to happen. First of all, I don't know where the hell they are. Second, Georgie was way out of line and had it coming. He hit a woman. You, of all people, would not let that go."

"That was an accident. He was trying to hit her husband."

"Georgie grabbed her tits. You wouldn't tolerate that behavior in any man. He was an asshole."

Bernie hesitated for a moment, then replied, "They almost fuckin' killed him. We're not going to let this go."

"Well, like I said, Hickey and Lloyd took off, and no one knows where they are."

"Then you better fuckin find them and turn them over to us."

"Your brother is still living. You're not going to kill them for giving Georgie a beating that he deserved. How about some money instead, pay for your troubles?"

"Listen real good, McLean. You don't tell us what's going to happen. We fuckin' tell you."

"You're wrong, Bernie. Nobody tells me what to do. And I never back down. You guys should let things cool off a little. Then maybe we can work something out. How about if I gave you a percentage of their bar?"

"Fuck that, and I'm way beyond cooling off. I need fuckin' revenge. Anything less than death makes us look weak. They have to fuckin' die, and you have to help."

Buddy slowly shook his head and said, "Go home, and think about it for a day or two. You might come up with another solution."

"There's nothing else to think about. You're telling me you won't give me those motherfuckers?"

"That's what I'm telling you. And none of this would have happened if it wasn't for your brother."

With that, McLaughlin slammed his beer can down on the table, aggressively slid back his chair, stood up, pointed at McLean and hollered, "Fuck you, and fuck all your friends, too!

This ain't over, not by a fuckin' long shot." Then he spit on the floor and stormed out of the house. Buddy remained seated in his kitchen, wondering, *How bad is this going to get?* He did not have to wait long to find out.

# No Turning Back

Late that same night, the barking of his two German shepherds awakened Buddy. Jean had been watching a late-night show in the living room. She got up to shut off the television set when she looked out the front window and noticed some men outside. The men had lifted the hood of the family car and were doing something to the engine. Jean thought they were going to steal it and she yelled upstairs, "Buddy. Get up. Someone's trying to steal the car."

With both dogs barking like they wanted to tear someone apart, Buddy sprang out of bed and bolted to the front window. Looking down from the upstairs window, he spotted two men lurking around his car and slowly closing the hood. He retreated from the window, grabbed a loaded pistol, sprinted down the stairs and burst out the front door. Three men were running around the corner onto Jaques Street when Buddy hit the pavement. He fired three shots straight up into the dark Somerville sky. They scampered away, heading toward Temple Street. The neighborhood was silent as Buddy walked back to his car and made a quick inspection of the vehicle his wife was going to use to drive their kids to school in the morning. In the darkness, everything seemed to be okay. *I wonder if the McLaughlins were screwing with the car.* He went back into the house to gather his thoughts.

*October 30, 1961*

At six a.m., Buddy answered a knock at his front door. His neighbor from across the terrace was shaking when he asked, "Buddy, can you come outside? I have to show you something."

"What is it, Tony?"

"I saw the hood of your car wasn't closed all the way. I went to lift it and close it."

A hard, intense look came across his face as Buddy followed Tony out to the street. When his neighbor slowly lifted the hood, Buddy saw the death trap—three sticks of dynamite strapped to the engine. He immediately knew what had to be done.

As the sun began to rise on Winter Hill, Snow Terrace was swarming with Somerville cops and detectives. While the police were investigating the previous night's gunshots, one neighbor let on about the dynamite. The cops called for a bomb specialist. Buddy ordered his family to move to the backyard and stay behind the house. Michael McLean separated from his mother and siblings to sneak a peek of the events out front. His eyes met his dad's as Buddy stood next to the car along with several Somerville police officers. There was a grim look on his father's face as he slowly shook his head at his son. Michael returned to the back staircase and sat with the rest of the McLean family until Buddy came for them.

Jean had called her mother to come to the house. When his mother-in-law arrived, Buddy placed the handgun in her pocketbook and told her to go home. She nervously walked past a dozen cops and on to her home at the Mystic Avenue projects.

The Somerville police detectives questioned Buddy about the previous night's incidents. "Who do you think booby-trapped your car?"

"I have no idea," answered Buddy.

"Well then, who were you shooting at?"

"I wasn't shooting at anybody."

"We've got a complaint of gunshots fired."

"It wasn't me."

The police looked at each other, shook their heads, rolled their eyes to the sky, and sighed. They did not push him any further. They packed up their equipment and took the dynamite away. Buddy walked back into his house.

He told his wife, "Jean, take the kids to school, then you and the baby go to your mother's. I'll come down there later. I'm not going to work today."

When his family left, Buddy contemplated his next move: *Those motherfuckers, they could have killed my whole family. There's no turning back now. I'm gonna have to kill them all. I have to plan this out. I wish I had Joe Mac with me right now. He'd know what to do. I have to think like him. I have to take care of that shit in court, too. Come on, think, God damn it, think!*

He was due to appear in court the next morning to answer for the first of two outstanding assault charges. Both of the charges were the result of incidents that had occurred in Somerville. The first was for a stabbing outside the White Tower Restaurant on Broadway across from Foss Park. Buddy had backed into a tight parking space on the street and bumped into the car behind him. Although there was no damage to either car, the fuming owner of the other vehicle rushed out to the sidewalk to confront McLean.

"You fuckin' moron. Where'd you learn how to drive? I swear, if there's a scratch on my car, I'm going to fuckin' kick your ass."

"You better think twice before you do something you're going to regret."

"Fuck you."

The young thug, who had been recently released from prison, charged at Buddy and tried to stab him with a fork. McLean disarmed and pinned him against his own car, then slapped him across the face. The punk spit in Buddy's face, so Buddy jammed the fork into his shoulder.

"Ahh, shit, you motherfucker. Pull it out. Pull it out now!"

"Fuck you, ya little punk. Pull it out yourself."

Buddy turned and walked into the restaurant, leaving the whimpering hooligan out on the sidewalk, leaning against his car.

When the police arrived, Buddy was sitting at the counter eating a hamburger. He explained to the cops what happened, and the staff at White Tower plus several customers concurred. Buddy was not arrested, but the ex-con wanted to file a complaint.

In court, the day after the dynamite discovery, Buddy received a continuance.

The second stroke of bad luck happened a week later at a sandwich shop on Mystic Avenue. Buddy and a friend named Alex "Bobo" Petricone walked into the shop as a fight broke out between two groups of teens. Buddy and Bobo broke up the fight and the kids took off. The place suffered significant damage. When the owner ran up from the basement, he saw Buddy and Bobo standing over his injured employee, the owner's son. The owner attacked Buddy with a long carving knife, but McLean physically controlled the man and threw him to the floor. Buddy held the man down and explained, "Hey, calm down. We had nothing to do with this. We came in to get a sandwich and there was a brawl going on, so we broke it up."

"Yeah, what about my boy there? What were you doing to him?"

"Helping the kid up. Ask him."

"They were, Pop. If these men didn't come in when they did, the place would've been ruined."

"Yeah, you might've threatened the kid to keep his mouth shut. I know you, McLean. You're always fighting and beating people up."

"Bobo, call the cops. This guy's not making any sense, and I really don't need this headache."

The owner continued to struggle with Buddy but remained planted on the floor until a Somerville squad car arrived. Although the owner's son corroborated Buddy's version, another complaint was filed.

A couple of weeks had passed before the meeting with Bernie McLaughlin, then the car bombing attempt. Buddy had to deal with the assault charges, but this failed mob hit had his mind spinning. The turmoil and stress took a toll on Buddy, but he showed no signs of fear or weakness. *It's too late to make peace. I'll have to kill them. That's all there is to it.* Buddy began to formulate his countermove.

# A Brazen Murder

*October 31, 1961*

Buddy called Alex "Bobo" Petricone and ordered him to his house. The two had to appear in court together several hours later for the incident on Mystic Avenue. Petricone did as he was told. Before leaving for court, Buddy called a Charlestown friend of Bernie McLaughlin's to set up a meeting with Bernie for later that day. After receiving a continuance, they left court around 11:00 a.m. Buddy had Bobo drive them to pick up Russ Nicholson at his house in Somerville. Nicholson was still working as an MDC cop but was a longtime and still-loyal friend to McLean.

Buddy planned his strategy. "Nic, you drive. Bobo, you sit in back and be lookout and backup."

Buddy sat up front in the passenger seat. He was wearing a Charlestown High School football jacket. They drove Bobo's car to Charlestown in search of Bernie McLaughlin. Around noon, they spotted Bernie's vehicle parked in City Square. Nicholson drove slowly past the car when Buddy saw Bernie leaving the Morning Glory Café. Nicholson drove past the diner and pulled over, fifty yards away. Buddy told his friends to stay put. Then he quickly and deliberately slid out of the car. He immediately flanked McLaughlin. Swift and quiet, Buddy walked up behind him, and, when there was two feet separating them, Buddy said, "Bernie."

The startled McLaughlin turned, and McLean told him, "We have to talk."

"Over here," replied Bernie.

Morning Glory Cafe

The two walked to the side of the building next to a cement pillar under the Mystic-Tobin Bridge, which spanned over City Square. Buddy looked Bernie in the eye and said, "This shit has to stop right now."

"You had your chance. Now it's not going to stop until every fuckin' one of you are fuckin' dead," answered Bernie.

Bernie McLaughlin

With that, Buddy pulled a .38 special handgun from the right front pocket of the Townie jacket and shot Bernie in the forehead. McLaughlin dropped to the sidewalk, dead. McLean fired three more shots into his body. More than one hundred people were eating lunch in the square at the time of the shooting. They absolutely froze, and Buddy loudly proclaimed, "Everybody saw nothing."

McLean walked toward Bobo's car. He scrambled underneath a slow-moving tractor-trailer that was passing through City Square. He made it to his waiting friends and climbed into the passenger seat of the automobile.

"That was a lot of shooting. Was it just you?"

"Yup. Let's go."

Petricone had opened the trunk so that his license plate could not be read. He followed Buddy. Nicholson had the car in gear. As he closed the door, Buddy calmly told Russ, "Don't drive crazy. Go over the bridge, and we'll double back into Somerville through Chelsea and Everett."

Russ hit the gas and they took off down the street. As they climbed and reached the midpoint of the Tobin Bridge, Buddy tossed the pistol out the window, over the railing, and into Boston Harbor.

"Is he dead?" asked Russ.

"Yes, he's gone."

The men were quiet for the rest of the ride. Within fifteen minutes they were back in Somerville and parked behind a bakery on Winter Hill. As they were driving, Buddy was thinking, *This is only the beginning. Things are going to get bad.*

Boston police, on the lookout for the getaway car, spotted the sedan driving through Sullivan Square and into Somerville. They radioed ahead, and within thirty minutes Buddy and his friends were tracked down inside the back of the Capitol Bar and placed

Buddy and Bobo Petricone, arrested

Buddy's mugshots

in custody. Apparently, a waitress inside the Morning Glory, who also was nightclub singer, identified Buddy McLean as the shooter. He was arrested for the murder of Bernie McLaughlin.

# Sentenced

Petricone was released. Nicholson was not charged. Buddy was held at the Boston Police Station in City Square, Charlestown. The Townie cops tried to scare Buddy into making a confession.

"Punchy's outside with the Hughes brothers. They want to get back here and kill you. Tell us what you did so we can get you out of here."

"I didn't do anything, but you can send them in. I'll fight every one of them right now," replied Buddy.

"He really is a tough bastard, isn't he?" muttered one cop to the other as they walked away.

"I wouldn't want to fight him," replied the other.

Through Arthur O'Rourke, Jean hired a young hotshot lawyer reputed to be outstanding at defense representation. He came highly recommended by Buddy's Teamster friends at Local 25. The attorney, F. Lee Bailey, had Buddy released and home within twenty-four hours.

The next day, over drinks at the Capitol Bar, Russ Nicholson and Bobo Petricone discussed Buddy's quick exit from lockup.

"How the hell did he get out so fast?" asked Petricone.

"It was a couple of things, from what I heard."

"What was it?"

"He has a fantastic lawyer, plus, they didn't find a gun, and the witness recanted her story."

"Someone probably convinced her."

"Tommy and John. They broke into her place and tore it apart."

"Good. That fuckin' bitch. She better keep her fuckin' piehole shut now."

"Yeah, I heard Tommy wanted to make sure, so he shredded her wardrobe."

"Did he use the hook?"

"No, I think he used a fuckin' meat cleaver."

The two of them roared with laughter.

After many continuances, Buddy's lawyer was able to lump the two assault charges along with the murder charge into one sentencing.

The murder charge was dropped because of a lack of witnesses and the inability to find a weapon. However, Buddy was given a two-year sentence for the two previous Somerville assault charges. The judge in Buddy's trials gave him the maximum amount of jail time for the two charges.

When the judge imposed his sentence, he announced, "Mr. McLean, I realize the evidence against you here is not very strong. You seem to be a likeable young family man. However, we all know that you are no angel, sir. And that there are people on the streets of Boston who are looking to do you harm."

"Your Honor, I can handle my own problems."

"I'm sure you are very capable, Mr. McLean. However, for your safety, and the safety of others, I believe it is best for you to be incarcerated for a while to let things cool off."

"Your Honor, I have to look after my family."

"In my opinion, sir, they will be safer with you off the street."

The McLaughlin gang was livid. They wanted McLean released so they could kill him. Punchy vowed to his cohorts, "We'll get him. He's a fuckin' dead man. He'll have to sleep with both eyes open 'cause we're coming after him, sure as shit."

*May 14, 1962*

A week later, Buddy began serving his time at Walpole State Prison. Petricone was given probation for the assault he and Buddy were charged with at the Mystic Avenue sandwich shop. Nicholson was not indicted, but he was being investigated.

Buddy entering prison, 1962

Nicholson decided to retire from the MDC Police before they could fire him. He lobbied to attain a pension. It was never settled. He did not live to see it happen.

Buddy urged Petricone, "Get as far away from Somerville as you possibly can."

Alex "Bobo" Petricone

Bobo relocated to Hollywood, California. He dropped sixty pounds and took acting lessons. He changed his name to Alex Rocco and started winning small parts in minor motion pictures. His big break came in the early 1970s when he was cast as Moe Green in *The Godfather*.

Back in Massachusetts, and with all the confusion surrounding him, Buddy never realized that he most likely had killed the wrong McLaughlin brother. Although it was Bernie who spoke to Buddy about evening the score, it was Eddie who ordered the dynamite.

When he was apprised of the situation, Joe McDonald felt terrible: *If I hadn't gotten him involved in the first place, he wouldn't be going through all this shit right now. I've got to help him out somehow and, at the same time, not get pinched myself. Poor guy, that nice young family—it's not right. I have got to help him.*

# The Gang War

With Buddy in jail, his friends tried to keep things in order. They met in the VFW hall.

Howie began the meeting with, "Fellas, we need to solidify ourselves as one unit and stay organized. We have to conduct our day-to-day business without getting killed."

"That's going to be difficult," spoke up Billy Winn. "Not only are the McLaughlins out to kill Buddy, they want to wipe out the rest of us, too. And they outnumber us by a lot."

"Yeah, that's true," replied Howie. "But I have good news, Joe Mac is going to help us." Everyone sat up as Howie continued, "He's getting us a shitload of guns."

"Is he coming back?" asked Tommy Ballou.

"If he does, it'll be low-key. He won't be in the open, but we all know he's the best. When the McLaughlins find out Joe's with us, they'll be scared shitless."

"Yeah, but that won't stop them," piped in John Hurley. "They're coming, sure as shit. What else can Joe do for us?"

"He has a safe house we can use in Medford. We're going to be moving around a lot, so they can't pin us down. We won't be going home much either. Joe has plenty of room, and nobody is going to bother us. He has a couple cars we can use, too. He said to travel at least in pairs and more whenever we can. Always be on the lookout—don't let them sneak up on us. We have to be

311

packin' at all times, and we have to practice shooting. Also, no more going out to collect debts. From now on, the bettors come to us and pay up-front. If they win, they come back and we pay them. We'll operate out of Pal Joey's. We're going to hire a few guys to watch the door and the streets. Buddy said to bring in Paul Raymond. He's a good fighter."

"Not with Buddy he wasn't," exclaimed Tommy.

The men chuckled.

"What else, Howie?"

"Buddy's cop friends are going to be keeping an eye on us. Joe said that's good because it will make it hard for the McLaughlins to pull any shit. But at the same time, we've got to be smart. Don't do anything stupid. Don't get drunk. Go out of your way to be nice to the cops—you know, wave, buy them a coffee. Just do what Buddy would do."

On the same day, in a Charlestown apartment, Eddie McLaughlin confidently told his men, "They're going to be weak without McLean around to lead them. We're going to surround them, and we're going to mow them down. And we're gonna get McLean, too."

It did not take long for the feud to get started.

*July 7, 1962*

George "Ox" Joynt

George "Ox" Joynt was a Somerville resident who worked for the McLaughlin group. He provided muscle and enforcement for the Charlestown debt-collecting business. One afternoon in the Capitol Bar, he made it known to Buddy's friends that, "You fuckin' guys are in way over your heads. You're all going to be dead within a year. None of you will live, even McLean. You guys don't stand a fuckin' chance."

Russ Nicholson walked behind Ox and quietly told him, "Shut your fuckin' mouth right now or you're going to end up like Bernie."

"You don't fuckin' talk to me like that. I don't take orders from you, you fuckhead. You better fuckin' back off or I'll have twenty Townies in here in five minutes."

Tommy Ballou closed in on Ox. He pressed a gun into his rib cage and told him, "It's time to go, big boy."

John Hurley and Russ had Ox surrounded.

"All right, all right. I'll leave."

"Too late, Ox," responded Russ. "You just told us you're with the McLaughlins. They're the enemy, and so are you. You're taking a ride with us."

Ox panicked. He tried to push through the Somerville men but was unsuccessful. Then he screamed, "Somebody call the cops."

Tommy smashed a straight right punch to one side of his jaw, and Hurley hit him with a left hook to the other side. The Ox went down in a heap. Lights out.

A man with an Irish brogue stepped up from the crowd and said, "Put the Tom McCann's to him (stomp on him). He's got no friends in here."

"No," replied Russ, "we're takin' him outta here."

Buddy's friends loaded the Ox into his car and drove him to a remote area off Route 16 in nearby Medford. When he came to, Russ handed Ox a shovel and told him, "Start digging."

"No fuckin' way. That's not happening. I'm not digging a fuckin' hole for you fucks to put me in."

Russ told him, "You will, or we'll kill your fuckin' family after we kill you, you fuckin' rat, fat piece of shit."

Ox sobbed tears as he dug his grave. He begged for his life. "I'll move out of state. I'll take my whole family with me. You'll never see me again. Please. One chance. I promise, I'll never give you guys any more problems. Just let me go."

Hurley looked at Nicholson standing behind Ox. "What do you think, Russ?"

Russ pulled a pistol from his jacket and shot Ox in the back of his head. The big man fell face-first into his grave. He shot Ox twice more in the back.

Tommy had an astonished look on his face as he told Russ, "Wow, Russ. I didn't think you had it in you."

"Yeah, well, now you know. Let's fill it in and get the hell out of here."

*September 8, 1962*

A Townie counterattack occurred when Howie Winter's car was blown to smithereens while it was parked in the Mystic Avenue Housing Projects. It was unknown who set the device, but it was assumed to be the Charlestown men. Fortunately for the Somerville side, no one was hurt.

Bobo Petricone's wife had driven the vehicle during that morning, and another woman borrowed it in the early afternoon. But the car did not explode until it was parked for an hour in a lot near a playground in the projects.

At the same time, in Charlestown, Punchy was meeting with his men. "I want to take out McLean while he's locked up."

"How do you want to do it, Boss?" asked Stevie Hughes.

"See if you can find someone who's locked up with him that could get the job done."

"That's a tall order, Punch," said Hughes.

"Yeah, I know, it might take three or four good men to get it done. But I want you guys to start considering it right away."

"All right, but if we can't find anyone to take on the job, how about a guard or someone else who works there?"

"I'll look into that."

Buddy assumed the McLaughlins would be coming after him and he tried to stay a couple of steps ahead of them. He instinctively knew, *I have to outsmart them. Be ready, all the time.*

# Prison Time

*May 1962*

Buddy was sent to Walpole State Prison, home to the most dangerous inmates in the state of Massachusetts. His reputation as a great street fighter and then killer of the fearsome Bernie McLaughlin had preceded his arrival. There were plenty of hard looks and quiet conversations directed toward McLean as he settled in. Buddy figured, *It's just a matter of time before someone makes a move.*

For his part, Buddy worked out harder than ever, and was ready to attack in the blink of an eye. He constantly reminded himself, *Be ready. Always be ready.*

*September 9, 1962*

A couple of good-sized Charlestown men decided to take on the deed and collect a lucrative bounty from Punchy. While eating lunch in the dining hall on Sunday, the pair discussed their options.

"There's McLean."

"I see him."

"He doesn't look like much."

"Everybody says that. Don't fuckin' fall for it."

"A bunch of us saw him working out in the yard, and in the gym. He's the real deal, all right."

"How are we going to do this then?"

"I'm not sure about the details yet, but I want to find a place or a spot where he is by himself."

"Except for us."

"Right, then while you distract him, I'll kill him."

"Punchy's going to owe us, big time."

"Yeah, because this isn't going to be easy."

"Why are you saying that? What are you worried about? You scared of him?"

"Shut the fuck up and listen. All the guards in here like him. They respect him. They're watching his back all the time. We have to plan this out, make sure it's the right move, and then practice it . . . a lot."

"You make it sound like we're going to kill the fuckin' warden."

"You're a fuckin' idiot, you know that? We're only going to get one shot at this. We can't fuck it up. Do you want to do this or not?"

"Yeah, I'm in. I'll do whatever you want. Fifty-fifty split, right?"

"Yeah, fine."

The Charlestown men discovered that Buddy was granted a second shower each day, alone, after completing his ten-mile run in the yard. When he finished showering, he had to pass through a short, narrow, isolated hallway to make it back to his cell.

It was about an hour before suppertime. Buddy finished his shower, and he put on clean, fresh clothes. He carried his sweaty clothes and towel in a laundry bag, and he had a separate bag for his toiletries. As he left the shower and walked into the small hallway, Buddy instantly sensed danger and readied himself for the attack.

"Hey, McLean. You got some change?" asked one of the Townies, holding an empty glass bottle of Coca Cola while he leaned against the wall. The other Townie stood silently across from the bottle man, his right hand in his front pocket. *Here we go.*

Buddy marched straight toward the two big men. He suddenly threw his bags into the face of the bottle man and immediately attacked the other, who was pulling a blade from his front right pocket. Buddy grabbed the blade man's right wrist and his face simultaneously. He plowed the blade man into the brick wall, fracturing the back of his skull. The other Townie rushed in and smashed the bottle over Buddy's head. Buddy dug his index and middle fingers into the blade man's eyes and kneed him in the groin. Then, Buddy spun his captive, who had dropped the blade, into the bottle man. The bottle man lunged for the blade, but Buddy intercepted him with a thunderous right cross to his left jawline. The blow sat the man down. Buddy proceeded to unload on the Townies.

Sixty seconds into the one-sided bloodbath, two other inmates happened by.

"What the fuck," said one of the inmates.

"Get lost, or you're next," threatened McLean.

The pair retreated. The onslaught continued.

Twenty minutes later, the Townies were taken by ambulance to a nearby hospital. McLean was in his cell, reading the *Boston Record American*. Three guards and the captain entered his cell. Buddy stood quickly, not certain of what was about to happen. The men backed up a step, then the captain asked Buddy, "Are you responsible for that assault outside the shower room."

"They came at me. I was only defending myself."

"Don't you think you went a little too far?"

"They had weapons. What would you have done, Captain?"

"We have the blade and the broken bottle. Does either one belong to you?"

"Is either one of them stabbed or slashed?"

"What about the bottle?"

"Do you want to feel the lump on the back of my head?"

The captain shook his head, and he and the guards left Buddy alone. A couple of days later, he was transferred to Norfolk State Prison.

Norfolk also had a hard-core, dangerous population, though it was considered a step below Walpole in that category. There was, however, some good news waiting for Buddy.

McLean found out he had a few friends who were also locked up at Norfolk, including the recently incarcerated Joe McDonald and his brother, Leo.

"What the hell are you two doing in here?"

"Same as you," responded Leo. "Passing the time."

Joe smiled at Buddy. "Leo and a few of his pals had the bright idea of robbing the dairy plant over in Stoneham. I wasn't even there, but where they covered their faces, everybody assumed I was one of them. They gave me ten years, just like that. Probably to catch up for a lot of the stuff I got away with."

The men had a good laugh. Buddy smiled at Joe for a moment.

Joe asked his friend, "What are you grinning at, you convict?"

"I can't believe you got caught. Are you slipping in your autumn years?"

"Don't be a wiseass. I came home to see my family. There were a few things I had to tend to. Next thing I know, the cops had the house surrounded. It was like they were waiting for me to show up. Jesus Christ! They've nothing better to do?"

They both had a good laugh and sat quietly for a while. Buddy looked over at his friend, knowing that Joe would never admit to it, but he probably let himself get caught so he could be in here with him.

When Buddy arrived at Norfolk, there were many inmates, as well as guards, who welcomed him. However, there were a few convicts who doubted Buddy's reputation. On his first day in the yard, the trouble started.

A group of men from Springfield began to size him up.

"He don't look like much."

"You're right, Ace. Why don't you go over there and belt him in the face?"

"Fuck you. You go do it."

Both men were suddenly slapped hard on their heads. "He's mine, you fuckin' little girls." The men fell silent.

Rico Sacramone with future Massachusetts
politician, Joe DeNucci

An Everett middleweight boxer, Rico Sacramone, sneered at the Springfield group as he walked past them. He was a talented fighter doing a bit for armed robbery. He walked up to Buddy and the McDonald brothers in the prison yard and asked Buddy, "You supposed to be some kind of hard-ass, McLean?"

The short-tempered McLean countered, "You want to find out?"

"Yeah, I do. When?" asked Rico.

"Right now," answered Buddy.

"All right," smiled Rico as he raised his fists.

*Bang!* Buddy smashed a right fist into Sacramone's mouth, knocking him flat on his back.

"What the fuck? Did you see that? One punch, Sacramone goes down," exclaimed Ace as he and the others headed toward McLean.

After he fell, Sacramone rolled up to his feet. His mouth was pouring blood, and although Rico was a little unsteady, he muttered, "That was no big deal. Come on, tough guy."

Joe Mac stepped between them to prevent intervention from prison officials. "Let's go in the gym and have a boxing match instead." Buddy and Rico agreed.

They moved to the gymnasium and tied on gloves. A good-sized crowd of inmates, including Ace and his Springfield friends, as well as a few guards, assembled for the chance to see Buddy McLean do what he was famous for.

Sacramone possessed tremendous hand speed and was very light and quick on his feet. McLean kept pressing forward, popping his jab off Rico's head. Sacramone was spinning and slipping away from Buddy's constant attack. A few times, Rico countered with a quick flurry of punches. Buddy seemed unfazed by Sacramone's combinations and delivered his signature walloping body shots. The thunderous blows slowed Sacramone enough for the Somerville man to close in and zap a hard one-two square on Sacramone's face. Rico's head snapped back, and, when it returned, Buddy's left hook cracked his jaw. Rico's eyes rolled up into his skull, and he was unconscious before he hit the floor, though Buddy caught him with a lightning bolt right cross on the chin as Rico began leaning to his left.

With his adrenaline exploding, Buddy circled the laid out Sacramone. He began pounding his gloves together. "I'm just getting warmed up. Who wants to go next?"

Ace and his friends remained stone quiet. There were no other takers. Joe Mac walked up to his friend and convinced Buddy, "Come on. Let's go eat. There's nobody in here for you."

"All right," responded Buddy. He scanned the room for another fighter, then pulled off his gloves. The Somerville men headed toward the dining hall. The audience remained mute until McLean left the gymnasium.

Later, one of the guards reported to his coworkers, "The population had the common sense to not play with fire. A single word to an angry Buddy McLean might spark an inferno. He is un-fuckin'-believable."

That same evening, the swollen-jawed Rico Sacramone stopped by Buddy McLean's cell. Buddy was sitting on his bunk, reading a newspaper.

"What do you want?" demanded McLean.

"I just want to say, good fight," responded Sacramone.

"How's your jaw?"

"Broken."

"Maybe I'll feel bad about that in a few days."

"No hurry."

They laughed together.

As time went by and they got to know each other, Buddy and Rico became friends and occasionally worked out together. Buddy was to be released from prison before Rico. "When you get out, come look me up."

"I will," Rico promised.

After his release from prison, Sacramone went straight to Winter Hill, looking to join Buddy's group. He was welcomed in and became a loyal soldier to the Somerville gang leader.

During Buddy's time in Norfolk, Jean made weekly trips with their children to visit him. She kept Buddy and his friends supplied with quality meats, fresh vegetables, and fruit. Jimmy and Michael helped Jean carry in the groceries. Buddy included a few prison guards when it was time to eat. Buddy turned his correctional facility environment into a more social atmosphere with his close-knit friends having sit-down dinners in a private area.

## August 12, 1962

Sunday afternoon, Jean showed up with all the kids. They all sat at a table waiting. Buddy walked into the room, and a big smile appeared on his face. He was wearing a white T-shirt and beige khaki pants. He was the picture of perfect health. "Hi, everybody!"

"Daddy's here," yelled Lea as she ran and jumped into his arms.

Jean gazed at her husband—tanned, muscular—and thought, *What a handsome man.*

The family sat together and talked as they ate sub sandwiches from Leone's. After lunch, Jimmy and Michael did push-ups for their father. Lea climbed up on Buddy's lap next to Kellie and said, "Daddy. Look, my tooth is loose."

Buddy said, "Let's have a look."

He reached in with his thumb and index finger and wiggled the tooth. He gave it a little tug, and out it came.

At the end of the visit, Buddy kissed and hugged his family. Then he promised them, "I'll be home real soon."

# Planning Ahead

During each day in prison, Buddy spent several hours with Joe McDonald. They worked out, took long walks around the yard, and had long, detailed conversations. Most their talks centered on future confrontations with the McLaughlin brothers. "There's going to be a lot more bloodshed," stated Buddy.

"That's a guarantee," answered Joe Mac.

"And I'm going to see to it that my family and friends don't get hurt."

"How are you going to do that?"

"As soon as I get out, I'm going to kill every one of them, starting with Punchy."

"Not alone. There's a shitload of them, and they're spread out. And listen, these guys are professional killers. You can't underestimate them."

"I'm not afraid of them," he told Joe.

"I know you're not," Joe responded.

"I know how these guys are. They'll come after everyone who is important to me, and they won't stop."

"That is true, but you can't take them on by yourself."

"Why not? I'll move my family out of state, and then I'll come back and start picking them off, one at a time."

"Buddy, they will kill anyone you like. You can't move everyone out."

324

"Joe, this is my fight. I'm going to kill every one of those bastards."

"Listen, they're sneaky, conniving fucks. They'll get someone you know and trust to set you up for a hit. They'll have a fuckin' cop pull you over on a routine stop, and the motherfucker will walk up to your car and shoot you in the face. They'll grab your kids off the street and hold them for ransom. When you show up to pay them off, they'll take your money and kill you and your kids. These guys get together and they scheme. They're smart and they're vicious. There's dozens of guys they'll pay to fuckin' hunt you down. They'll bring in pros from New York, people you've never seen before. The shooter could be dressed as a fuckin' priest and pop you when you're in church, or he might be the choir boy, for Chrissake. They're going to surround you, and then they're going to fuckin' close in."

"I'll take the fight to them, starting with Punchy. Then I'll work my way down the list."

"There's too many of them, plus, they probably have spies hanging around in Somerville. You won't know who to trust. They might even try to turn some of your friends against you."

Buddy thought for a moment, then asked, "All right, then what do you think I should do?"

"There'll be a lot of men who want to help you. Let them. Just be smart, get organized, and make damn sure you can trust them. Don't tell too many of them your plans for the McLaughlins. Only your close friends need to know what's going to happen. Change your routine. Don't be out in public. Don't drive the same car. Always carry at least one pistol all the time. I'd have at least four on me, if I was you."

"Where do you carry them?"

"One in each front pocket and one on each ankle."

"Jesus, if I had you with me, I wouldn't need anyone else."

"That's probably true, but you don't have me right now, so if you want to come out of this alive, you better listen real good. If you nail the fat fuck, you're right. The roof will cave in on the rest of them. But that's not going to be easy because Punchy's already made himself scarce. Plus, he knows your face, and he'll have some of his boys with him. That fuckin' Hannon is an evil little prick. He kills for enjoyment. He's slick, too. You'll have to outmaneuver him."

"How should I get Punchy?"

"You don't. You get someone else to kill him. Someone he doesn't know or someone wearing a good disguise. And they must be good at it. No amateurs."

# New Associates

Another man Buddy met in prison was Tony "Blue" D'Agostino. Tony worked in the kitchen, and Buddy liked how Tony could add flavor to the normally bland meals. "You should open a restaurant when you get out. You'd be rich in no time."

Tony "Blue" D'Agostino

After his release, Tony became a loyal friend to Buddy. He was also the first man to volunteer to become one of Buddy's bodyguards against the Townies.

A huge addition for Buddy was uniting with the infamous Boston Mafia hit man, Joe "The Animal" Barboza, and a few of his friends. Buddy and Joe Mac met Barboza in Norfolk. Barboza's reputation was that of a methodical, psychopathic killer who acquired a real taste for his trade. A Norfolk inmate from Lynn, Massachusetts, told Buddy that Barboza once bit a man to death over a delinquent payment. This murder supposedly took place on a pool table inside a cleared-out barroom at Revere Beach.

Another story had Barboza killing his partner in a truck hijacking of fur coats destined to be delivered to a downtown Boston department store. After he murdered his friend, Barboza attended the man's wake and funeral, where he walked up to the widow, handed her an envelope with cash and promised her he would, "find the people responsible for this and make them suffer."

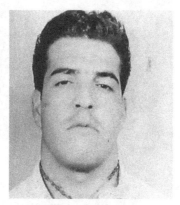

Joe Barboza

Although they were not pleased with Barboza's past antics, Buddy and Joe discussed having Barboza join them. "He's very good at committing murder, and he wants to be with us," stated Buddy.

"Yeah, plus the McLaughlins are not aware of this."

"He's not with the Angiulos anymore, and he hates the McLaughlins."

Joe Mac felt that, "As long as we hire him for professional hits, on specific targets, he could be valuable."

Buddy agreed, "It would be better to have him with us than against us."

Barboza took an instant liking to Buddy and Joe Mac. He did not have a lot of friends, nor did he trust many people. After spending time with Buddy and Joe Mac, Barboza felt a sense of belonging, protection, and relief. The Somerville pals were quiet and reserved among the prison population. Yet everyone knew not to inconvenience them. Barboza liked the reputation they enjoyed and yearned to have the same for himself.

As Buddy and Joe Mac became better acquainted with Barboza, they began to ease him into their social gathering of inmates.

The three conversed in Joe Mac's cell one afternoon.

"What are you going to do when you get out?" asked Joe Mac.

"I have a little crew of good, solid guys. I might look to expand with them. Why?"

"Well, maybe, you might consider working with us."

"Absolutely! Sure. You guys just say the word. I'd love to be with you guys," replied Barboza.

"What about the North End? Will they be angry about that?" asked Buddy.

"Fuck them. I have no future with them. They're the reason I'm in here to begin with."

"And you won't get nutty and go on any fuckin' killing rampages, will you?" asked Joe Mac.

"And you need to promise us that you won't eat anyone," added Buddy.

"Ha! No. Whatever you guys want, I'll do it. All professional."

Buddy and Joe looked at each other and nodded in agreement.

"Fine," said Joe. "You come see us when you get out."

"Great. You won't be disappointed."

Barboza had boxing experience and top-notch street-fighting skills. He was especially adept in the use of a knife. He was average height, five feet ten inches, and weighed around one hundred eighty pounds. He was an avid fitness enthusiast, though he was also a heavy cigarette smoker and a big boozer.

Barboza had an extremely large head, but women found him attractive. He dressed neatly and had an outgoing personality. He was charming to all females and fascinating to the youth of his Maverick Square, East Boston, neighborhood. To the men in East Boston and surrounding areas who knew or knew of him, Joe Barboza was an intimidating bully, loan-shark enforcer, and killer who operated his affairs by keeping men in constant fear. Barboza was also a quiet admirer of Buddy McLean.

After concluding conversations and agreeing to the terms set forth by Joe McDonald and Buddy McLean, Joe Barboza became an associate of the Somerville gang.

An inestimable force was coming to Winter Hill.

As Buddy was about to gain his freedom, he reflected that his time in prison had been somewhat productive: *I picked up some good men. This part is over. Now I've got to get organized and be ready. I'm going to kill every last one of them.*

Buddy leaving prison, 1963

# Back on Winter Hill

*May 23, 1963*

As soon as Buddy returned home to Somerville, Punchy went on the offensive. He began sending his men up to Winter Hill to see if they could get a drive-by shot at McLean. Punchy's brother, George, reported back, "He's up there all right, standing right out there in plain sight. But he's got a lot of people around him, and I'm sure every one of them is packin'."

"You can't get a shot at him?"

"From the car, I could, but, like I said, there's a shitload of people hanging around. I might hit the wrong guy. Plus, there's cops up and down Broadway. It's like they're waiting for us to make a move."

Punchy thought for a moment. "They probably are waiting for us. He might be setting a trap. That fuckin' McDonald could have a sniper on a roof. Tell the men to stop going up there."

"All right."

Punchy picked up the phone and dialed Steve Hughes Sr.

"Steve, it's Ed. I want to put a hit on McLean, and it has to be someone from out of state, and he has to be top-notch. Do you know of anyone?"

"Yeah, there's a guy down in New York. He was trained by Trigger Burke. They say he's as good as Burke. I'll see what I can do."

Elmer "Trigger" Burke was a famous hit man from New York City. In the mid-1950s, he began training a young man from Hell's Kitchen. After Burke went to prison in the late fifties, the protégé took over for Trigger. Only a few people knew who the young man was or what he looked like. One of those in the know was Joe McDonald. Always a few steps ahead of everyone else, Joe Mac put a call in to a Navy friend of his from Brooklyn. Joe's friend knew Burke's protégé, and he met with the young assassin in a Manhattan barroom.

"Listen, pal. You don't want to get involved with that shit up in Boston."

"Why not?"

"It's not your fight, and you'll only end up having those guys up your ass till they tear it apart. Besides that, it's a very dangerous friend of mine who told me about all this, and he knows who you are. He told me to tell you, 'Stay the fuck out of Boston.' I would heed that warning."

"It's a one-man contract. I'd be in and out in no time."

"Yeah, the guy you're going to hit has a lot of friends, including my friend Joe, and he won't let it go if you take the job. He already knows all about you. He knew about you before you were even offered the contract. That's why I'm sitting here with you right now. You don't need this shit."

He paused a moment, then the protégé replied, "All right. I'll call and cancel out."

*June 4, 1963*

On a bright, Tuesday afternoon, Buddy was standing with a few friends in front of their newly purchased auto-repair garage on Marshall Street. Besides being a legitimate business, the garage also served as a meeting place for the Winter Hill men. The McLaughlin Gang was quiet. No one had seen or heard from them.

Buddy's son Jimmy and his best friend, Kevin McInnis, came walking along from Northeast Junior High School, a few blocks down the street. "Hi, Dad," Jimmy called out.

"Hey, Jim. How's it goin'?"

"Good. What are you guys doing?"

"We're watching the little honeys walk by," piped in Tommy Ballou.

"Aren't they a little young for you, Tommy?" asked Jimmy.

"Never too early to plan for the future."

"Come on, fellas, I'll give you a ride home," said Buddy while rolling his eyes and shaking his head at Tommy's remark.

Jimmy asked, "Dad, can I drive?"

"Are you crazy? They'll lock me up again."

"No, they won't. All the cops love you."

"Come on, Buddy, give him a shot," piped in Tommy Ballou. "Besides, he's taller than you."

"Who asked for your opinion?"

"Okay, don't go by me. I'm only in charge of having fun," responded Tommy.

Buddy turned and tossed the keys to Jimmy and said, "Let's go."

Buddy and the boys slid into his brand-new Chevy Impala parked at the corner of Broadway and Marshall Street. Jimmy shifted into drive, and the youngster cruised down Broadway for about one block before making a gentle U-turn. They started back up Winter Hill before turning right onto Temple Street. Jimmy was doing a commendable job of driving the car when they came upon a woman who was waiting to cross Temple Street.

"Hold on. Let her cross," instructed the senior McLean.

"Why, Dad? She's ugly," countered Jimmy as he began to press on the brake pedal.

333

Kevin McInnis began cackling laughter in the back seat.

"What did you say," asked Buddy with an irate look on his face.

"Dad, that woman is so ugly, she'd have to sneak up on a glass of water."

Kevin gasped from the back seat when he saw Buddy's big left hand swing back. Thinking he was about to catch a backhand in the mouth, Kevin flinched. Instead, Buddy's hand swung forward and slapped the back of Jimmy's head. The boys went mute as the woman crossed Temple Street in front of them.

Then Buddy warned the boys, "Never call a woman ugly. It's disrespectful, and there's no such thing as an ugly woman anyway. Some women are better looking than others, and that's all there is to it. Never forget that."

Buddy turned around to Kevin and asked, "You got that?"

Kevin politely answered, "Yes, sir."

A week later, Buddy received a phone call at the 318 Club concerning his new friend Joe Barboza, who had been released from prison. A group of young men from the Beachmont section of Revere were having a problem with Barboza. Buddy invited them up to Winter Hill. The next day, Buddy sat with three rugged athletes in the back room of the 318. The young men were patted down for weapons before being allowed to meet with McLean.

"What can I do for you boys?"

Fred Riley, a top-notch football player and boxer, was the spokesman for the group. "Mr. McLean."

"Call me Buddy."

"Buddy, Joe Barboza said he is going to kill a friend of ours."

"How come?"

"Our friend had a beef with one of his friends down at Revere Beach over a girl. Our friend beat the shit out of his friend, and now Barboza says he's going to kill our friend. We're not going to let that happen. The bartender down at Sammy's Patio knows we're out to get Barboza. He told us Barboza is a friend of yours, and that we should talk to you first."

Buddy paused for a moment, then replied, "He is a friend of mine. I'll talk to Joe, and we'll see what he has to say. In the meantime, you guys try to avoid him and don't go after him. You understand?"

"What if he's out looking for our friend right now, then what?"

"Tell the kid to take a vacation for a few days. Go up to Maine. It's nice up there. He could bring that little chickie with him."

Everyone at the table laughed. Then Buddy finished with, "I'll call you guys after I talk with Joe."

"Okay, Buddy. Thanks for letting us come up here and for meeting with us."

Buddy called Fred Riley the next day and told him, "Everything is going to be fine, and the problem has been taken care of."

"Wow, that's great, Buddy. What do we owe you?"

"Nothing. You're all set. But it's probably a good idea to stay away from him, and I told Joe the same thing."

"Will do. Thank you, Buddy, and if we ever see you at one of the spots on the beach, everything is on us."

"All right, kid. See ya."

After he hung up the phone, Fred Riley thought, *That McLean, he is something. He took the time to help us out when he has all that shit going on with the McLaughlins. He has that big reputation as a great street fighter, and though none of us have seen him fight, he has to be legit. There are too many tough people backing the claim for him to be just that good. I like him. I hope he makes it out of that shit alive.*

335

# Fearless

## June 10, 1963

Buddy returned to work at the Charlestown docks and to driving for the Teamsters. The two work sites were right in the middle of enemy territory. He left his car at home each morning and walked or grabbed a ride from a passerby to the docks or the Local 25 union hall in Sullivan Square. After putting in a full day's work, Buddy would head for home. Several friends provided him transportation.

But there were a few times when he walked back to Snow Terrace.

Connie Hughes reported to Punchy, "I couldn't fuckin' believe it, McLean was walking through Sullivan Square this afternoon, by himself."

"Are you shitting me?"

"No, Stevie was with me. Ask him. It was McLean."

"Why the fuck didn't you shoot him if it was McLean?"

"We only had thirty-eights; we would have had to get up close. Plus, we weren't sure if he wasn't setting us up."

"What do you mean?"

"Maybe he was packing a few guns himself, or he might have had some of his boys following, out of sight."

Punchy sighed, "Or maybe both."

The McLaughlins were not alone in wondering about McLean's daring move. The Somerville police chief received a call from the Boston police chief. "What the fuck is your boy McLean doing walking around in Charlestown? Does he want to get his head blown off?"

"Yeah, we heard all about it. What the fuck you want us to do?"

"Keep him the fuck out of here."

"He goes to work down there. We can't stop him from doing that."

"Yeah, well, be on the lookout for some trouble, because it sure seems to find him."

No one considered that Buddy was not afraid of the McLaughlins and that he relished the thought of taking them on by himself: *Come on boys. Show your faces.*

## June 15, 1963

On Saturday afternoon, George McLaughlin attempted to take a drive-by shot at Buddy as he walked up Broadway in Somerville. The shot missed badly, making Buddy wonder aloud to his friends, "I couldn't tell if he was shooting at me."

Tommy Ballou responded, "Ray Charles can shoot better than him."

Howie Winter advised Buddy, "You've got to have bodyguards with you, all the time. Those bastards are not going to quit."

"Then my friends become targets, too."

"We're all in this together. Remember what Joe Mac told us, never travel alone."

Although Buddy knew he was more capable than his friends, he agreed to the suggestion, thinking, *It will reassure Jean that my back is being watched and our family is protected.*

Buddy instructed Jean, "If we're out in public together and someone starts shooting, hit the ground fast and lay flat on your stomach until the shooting is over."

Jean replied, "You're crazy! I'm not going to throw myself down on the sidewalk."

"You will if you don't want to get your head blown off."

"If anybody tries to shoot me, I'm going to shoot them. I want a gun."

"No. I don't want any guns near the kids, and I don't want them to know about any of this shit. The last thing I want to see is our kids living in fear."

"You're right. They'll be scared to death if they find out. You have to protect us from all this."

"I will. Just remember what I said—you hear a gunshot, you hit the ground fast and lay flat."

"Maybe I'll just stop hanging around with you."

"Yeah, you could, but then you'd miss the opportunity of my company."

"Oh, and I'm going to lose sleep over that?"

"Wow."

\* \* \*

Months went by without any word from the Charlestown men. Buddy was sure they were planning something, but he could not figure out what they were up to: *I know they're trying to turn people I'm friendly with against me. Most of them are intimidated now and afraid for their lives. I can't trust them now. They might try setting me up for those bastards. Be alert. Be smart. Be careful. Keep them off balance. Scare the shit out of the ones on the fence, so they mind their own business.*

# "Stay neutral"

*April 3, 1964*

On Friday afternoon after work, Buddy spoke to a group of longshoremen in Charlestown and another group of Somerville men he was suspicious of, plus several individuals who had contact with the McLaughlins. The message was the same for everybody: "This problem I have with the McLaughlins is none of your business. I know they have been talking to you. You may have told them you want to stay out of it, and that would be the right thing to do. But I have no way of knowing where you really stand. I'm not looking for you to help me with this. I just want you to keep out of it. So, starting right now, you are to stay away from me, my family, and my friends. If I find out that you have been talking to the McLaughlins or you are planning on helping them in any way at all, then I'm coming after you. Be smart. Your families still need you. Stay neutral."

Less than a month later, the McLaughlins struck. A Boston criminal named Frank Benjamin drunkenly stated, "McLean is going to wipe out the entire McLaughlin Gang. They don't stand a chance in hell against him. He's going to be running Charlestown pretty soon. I think McLean will be looking to put some men to work down there. I'm going to ask him for a job."

He did not realize a man from Roxbury who was working for the McLaughlins was also in the bar drinking and overheard the statement. Thinking that Benjamin was a member of Buddy's gang, the Roxbury man quietly walked up to Benjamin and shot him in the back of his head. The shooter then proceeded to call Punchy McLaughlin.

When McLaughlin arrived and observed the body surrounded in blood, he asked, "Where's the gun?"

He handed the pistol to his boss, who asked, "Is this a cop's gun?"

"Yeah, it is, a detective in Dorchester. He was drunk in here one night and I grabbed it. Why?"

"When they take the bullet out of his head, they can trace it back to that gun."

"What should I do?"

"Cut his head off and bury it in the woods somewhere. Then, get rid of the gun. Throw it in the ocean, way offshore. And one more thing . . . listen real good. This bar is closed for good, starting right now. Burn it to the ground tonight. You hear me?"

"Yeah, Boss."

# Oh, No!

The Charlestown gang caught Russ Nicholson off guard. He was meeting with a partner to collect his share on a scam they were running. The pair were extorting money from older, rich Boston area men who were cheating on their wives with beautiful prostitutes in Florida. When he exited his car on an East Boston street, he was surrounded by a half dozen armed McLaughlins.

"Hi, Russ. Your partner just sold you to us," stated Willie Delaney.

"What the fuck are you talking about?"

"Let's take a ride, Russ," suggested Stevie Hughes.

"I'm not going anywhere with you assholes."

"You'd rather die right here? Take a ride, and you might talk us out of it."

"Where are we going?"

"You'll find out. Get in."

"I'm going to regret this."

Hughes smiled at the tall Somerville man as he was handcuffed and ushered into the car. The Charlestown gang, in two vehicles, drove Russ out to a remote dirt road in Wilmington, Massachusetts. Punchy and Georgie were waiting for them. When Russ took a few steps from the car, Punchy came up behind him and shot a bullet into the back of Big Nic's head. He fell into a ditch next to the road. George took the gun from Punchy and shot a second bullet into Nicholson. "That's for Bernie."

Russ was found later in the day. When news of the murder got back to Buddy, he was shocked and in denial.

"No! ... Aww, God damn it! There's no way. I just saw him last night. Are you sure about this?"

"We're sure, Buddy. John Canty told us, and he's been looking to tell you himself. He's over at Russ's house right now," replied John Hurley in front of Howie Winter and Tommy Ballou. Buddy slowly shook his head and began to cry.

He got into his car and drove over to Russ's house to be with his family.

Later, after they mourned the loss, the Somerville men organized a fundraiser for Big Nic's family. After raising their glasses in a toast for their friend, Buddy vowed to his pals, "We're going to send every last one of them to hell."

The men nodded in agreement.

*June 7, 1964*

The McLaughlins, however, felt that momentum was on their side, and they became brasher. Not even a month after Russ's murder, they moved again. This time, they went for the kingpin.

It was a bright, warm Sunday morning. Buddy finished a workout at the Somerville YMCA on Highland Avenue. He was jogging home. He had a .38 caliber Smith and Wesson revolver cupped in his right hand while he trotted along the streets of Somerville. He made a quick stop at Joe McDonald's house on Marshall Street. Joe was napping, so Buddy dropped off a roll of cash to Joe's wife and continued on his way. Joe had recently escaped from a minimum-security prison facility with the help of his good friend Buddy McLean, and he had been hiding out in several locations in Greater Boston.

Buddy walked from Joe's house on Marshall Street up past the Marshall Motors' garage near the corner of Broadway. It was closed for the weekend. He was by himself. He was wearing a white T-shirt with the sleeves cut off, a pair of black and white plaid shorts and black high-top canvas sneakers. He had put the gun in his right front pocket. He was heading home to take a shower.

Maxie Shackelford

As he turned left onto Broadway, Buddy came face-to-face with a Charlestown ambush. They were parked in front of the 318 Club. Their windows were rolled down. Harold Hannon was ready with a loaded pistol. When Buddy came around the corner, Hannon pulled up the weapon, extended it out the window, and fired.

"Damn!" At the last second, Buddy spotted the barrel of the gun protruding from the open window. He dropped to a crouch and scampered back around the corner as the bullet whizzed over his head. Buddy pulled his pistol from the front right pocket of his shorts as he ran to the side door of the 318 Club on Marshall Street. He pulled on the door handle. It was locked. "Shit!"

Maxie Shackelford, the Charlestown driver, came roaring around the corner with Hannon leaning out the window, his pistol held ready with two hands. Another man in the back seat was not ready to shoot. He was tossed to the driver's side as the car made the hard turn. Buddy crouched a bit and sprinted right past them, heading back toward Broadway. McLean fired three shots on his way by. One of the bullets clipped Hannon's left shoulder. Hannon still managed to squeeze off three more shots. None of them were successful. Buddy did not break stride as he took a tight left turn around the corner of the building and raced up to the unlocked front door of the 318.

He rushed to the back of the bar and vaulted over the slab of oak. *It better be here.* From under the bar, McLean pulled a box of ammunition and a second pistol, which he placed on the bar. He reloaded his gun and checked the other. It was loaded. There were a half dozen patrons sitting at the bar. The bartender did not move from his spot at the sink. Nobody else moved or said a word. Buddy sprinted out the side door to Marshall Street with a pistol in each hand. *Come on, you bastards.* His adrenaline was maxed out. He wanted nothing more than a chance to take on the three Townies. They were long gone.

The furious McLean marched directly into the midday Broadway traffic with the purposeful stride of a man impervious to fear. *Those motherfuckers!* The automobiles screeched to a halt as McLean crossed Broadway and entered the Capitol Bar, guns stuffed in each of his front pockets.

The saloon had a loud, sizeable crowd, oblivious to what just happened across the street. Several greeted Buddy as he made his way toward the back. Buddy passed by a table of four men, one of them his brother in-law Bobby Kelley. Bobby hollered, "There he is, the King of Somerville."

"Not now, Bobby," replied Buddy.

"Hey, say hi to my friends."

Buddy looked over at Bobby's pals and continued walking.

One of Bobby's friends interjected loudly, "Bobby, that's the toughest guy in Boston? Look at them pants."

McLean stopped and turned on a dime as he pulled the pistols, pointed and fired over the man's shoulders and into a refrigerator. *BaBoom!* "Not. Now!"

The place became deathly silent as Buddy walked up to the bar, set the guns down in front of him, and sat on the stool that was always reserved for him. The bartender came right over, and Buddy told him, "Whiskey, and make sure those guys stay away from me."

The bartender poured and served Buddy's drink in a flash. Then he went over to Bobby's table and told them, "If you know what's good for you, you'll stay the fuck away from him right now." Bobby Kelley started to get up.

McLean yelled at him, "Sit the fuck down, and shut the fuck up!"

Buddy had swigged his drink by the time the bartender was back, and Buddy pointed for another. "Give me the phone, too." He quickly downed his second shot as he dialed the number. Joe McDonald picked up on the first ring.

"I have to talk to you, right now."

"What's the matter?"

"Come down to the Capitol."

"I'll be there in five minutes."

He made it in two.

# Joe McDonald

Joe McDonald

Joe McDonald was pretty much a one-man army. Born in 1917 in Nova Scotia, the McDonald family moved to Somerville when Joe was a young boy. He was small for his age, as was his older brother Leo. To help themselves stand up against East Somerville's tough neighborhood bullies, the McDonald boys took the initiative and learned how to box. They became ambidextrous with their fists, and the bullying came to an end. Joe was quiet but had a chip on his shoulder from the tormenting he had endured when he first came to Somerville. He developed a sharp temper and could become infuriated to the point of violence in an instant. He kept mainly to himself. He was smart and very handy. He could fix anything around the house and could rebuild all types of engines. Joe started committing crimes in his teen years. He usually worked by himself but would sometimes bring along his brother Leo to act as a lookout.

When he became more experienced and confident, Joe Mac started robbing banks. Never pulling a stickup close to home, McDonald made sure to learn the fine details of the bank he was targeting. He studied the routines of the people working in the bank for a couple of weeks. He knew when the bank would have a large amount of cash. He knew who to see about emptying the vault. He was always in and out in a few minutes to his waiting stolen vehicle with a powerful engine for a clean getaway.

In 1940, Joe Mac decided he needed to have a purpose in life. He joined the United States Navy with his younger brother Jackie. They were assigned to the USS *Quincy*.

At first, they patrolled the Atlantic seaboard. After the attack on Pearl Harbor, the *Quincy* was assigned to the South Pacific, specifically, Guadalcanal harbor.

In the early morning hours of August 9, 1942, the *Quincy* was surrounded and attacked by Japanese warships. Relentless bombing and fires doomed the ship. The *Quincy* went down in less than an hour, four miles from Savo Island.

Though wounded, Joe saved as many of his shipmates as he could in a short amount of time. He would later receive several commendations for his bravery. Of the 800 men on board, 147 were wounded and 389 died. Joe's brother Jackie did not survive.

One of the last men to abandon the *Quincy* was Joe McDonald. Only when he was helped over the railing of a rescue ship did Joe collapse and break down at the loss of his brother and shipmates.

When he returned to Somerville a reluctant, decorated hero, Joe was a changed man. He kept to himself and refused to talk about what happened in the Pacific. He sat in his father's kitchen and drank alcohol for days at a time. Then he would dry himself out and start going to the YMCA to struggle through grueling workouts as though he was training for a title fight. This cycle repeated itself for several years until he met a young Buddy McLean training at the Y to accomplish his goal.

Helping Buddy jumpstart his fitness and punching ability gave Joe a positive outlook and raised his spirits. Buddy was forever grateful, and a friendship was bonded for life.

# Helping His Friend

Joe Mac walked into the crowded yet subdued Capitol Bar, where a path was instantly made for him. When Buddy finished relating the story, Joe Mac paused for a second, then told Buddy what had to happen next.

"You can't live at home anymore. You have to have guys with you all the time. We have to get better organized and eliminate every fuckin' one of them. We need another safe house. Get someone to look after your family. Give them plenty of money. No more booking or working on the docks for you. Stay out of Charlestown. You have to disappear. We'll get Howie to run the business. I'm going to talk to Sal, too. He'll help us keep things under control. Hurley and Old Man Raymond will get us everything we need, and they'll keep everybody informed. We're going to need more help. It's time to put Barboza to work. Let him bring in some new faces that the McLaughlins don't know. It will be expensive. But you know what? We're going to kill every last one of them motherfuckers."

Buddy was silent, but he nodded in agreement. Then he got up from his stool, shook Joe's hand, then hugged him. "You're right, Joe. We'll get them all. But you have to lay low now. The FBI is looking for you."

"Now how the fuck do you know that?"

"I've got friends in high places, too, you know. They said you should take off."

"I hate to leave you with all this shit."

"Don't worry, we'll stay in touch. Just leave messages here. We'll work it out."

The quick talk with Joe inspired Buddy to reorganize his men. *I've been lucky so far. This won't last. I've got to get ready for a war.*

# Getting Even

*August 1, 1964*

FBI agent Paul Rico called Buddy. "I have information on Harold Hannon and Punchy McLaughlin."

"What is it?"

"Hannon pays regular visits to a woman in South Boston. She's a pro. I have her address."

"What about Punchy?"

"He's been bouncing around at different locations down the Cape and on the south shore. He has a few men with him, but not all the time. He has a lady friend who lives in Canton, but she's going to be moving. I'll let you know where, when I find out."

"Okay, thanks."

Then Buddy called Joe McDonald.

Harold Hannon

"I have an address where Hannon goes to get laid."

"All right, we'll get her to help us set him up. Get one more guy to come with us for backup."

Buddy called Tommy Ballou.

"Tommy, we're going to get Hannon. I want you to come with us."

"I'll be glad to. I hate that motherfucker. Remember, he killed my friend Tommy Sullivan, and, of course, he almost got you. Who knows how many others he's killed. The world will be a better place without him in it."

"That's right. Just be ready to go."

*December 17, 1957*

Tommy Sullivan was a tough Charlestown boxer/longshoreman. Buddy and Tommy Ballou worked with Sullivan on the Charlestown docks. Sullivan stood up for a friend who was being bullied by Punchy in a Townie barroom. McLaughlin hit Sullivan on the head with a steel pipe. Sullivan turned and wrestled the pipe from Punchy. Then he proceeded to pound McLaughlin. After he was done, Sullivan warned Punchy, "You better let this go, McLaughlin, or the next time I won't stop."

*December 24, 1957*

A week later, Harold Hannon and Punchy McLaughlin were waiting in a car parked outside Tommy's mother's home in Charlestown. They knew he was going to be leaving for work at any moment. As Tommy exited the multi-family dwelling on Bunker Hill, McLaughlin walked up to him. Hannon flanked him.

"Hey, Tommy!"

"What the fuck do you want?"

"Say your prayers, Tommy," Punchy told him.

Hannon began shooting Tommy in the back at twenty feet, and he closed in as he continued firing. Tommy died on the sidewalk.

More than six years passed, and the early evening murder was not solved.

## August 4, 1964

Buddy was standing by the window inside the woman's South Boston apartment. He was looking down at the street below when he saw Hannon pull up in his vehicle.

"He's got someone with him."

Tommy peeked out. "That's Willie Delaney. He's a collector. We'll get a two-for-one here."

Will Delaney

"He's a young kid," exclaimed Buddy.

"Yeah, but he'll kill you if he has the chance," replied Tommy.

"Hi, honey," said the prostitute to Hannon as she opened the door. "Come out to the kitchen for a minute. Bring your friend, too."

"You gonna feed us, doll?"

"It's a surprise."

Hannon and Delaney walked into the kitchen, only to see Joe McDonald sitting at the table with a gun in his hand. "What the fuck is this?" demanded Hannon.

Delaney started to run, only to get pushed back into the kitchen by Tommy. Buddy appeared through a side door. "Sit down."

The men were patted down, disarmed, and their wallets were taken. Hannon was handcuffed. Delaney was tied with an extension cord. Buddy gave the prostitute Hannon's cash and told her, "Go do some shopping."

"I'm going to get you for this," Hannon told the woman.

"I doubt that," she replied.

"You fuckin' cunt!"

Buddy hit Hannon on his ear with a thunderous slap, knocking Hannon to the floor. Then he pulled Hannon back up and onto his seat.

"You killed Tommy Sullivan. Why would you do that? He was a good man. He never bothered you."

The dazed and sore Hannon stuttered, "I d-d-don't know w-w-what the fuck you're t-t-talking about, and I don't know n-n-no fuckin' Tommy . . ."

Buddy stared at Hannon for a long moment. *This motherfucker tried to shoot me.* He grabbed Hannon's face and shook him. Hannon sat up straight.

"What's going on in Charlestown?" asked McLean.

"Nothing," replied Hannon.

"Where can I find the Hughes brothers?"

"How the fuck should I know?"

"What about Punchy?"

"I don't know where he is either."

"Who's running the show over there?"

"Nobody. They all took off. What's with all these fuckin' questions?"

"These questions need answers. You better start talking to me right now."

"I don't fuckin' take fuckin' orders from you, you motherfucker. I'm fuckin' done talking."

"We'll see."

Hannon sat on the chair, his eyes fixed straight ahead.

"How about you? Do you want to tell me something?" Buddy asked Delaney.

"Yeah, you fuckin' guys can fuckin' kiss my Irish ass," answered Delaney.

Buddy smiled and nodded to him.

Delaney looked over to Hannon for approval. He got none.

Tommy Ballou piped in, "I think I'd rather kiss your sister's ass instead of yours, if you don't mind, which I believe is going to be pretty soon."

"You shut the fuck up, Ballou, you fuckin' traitor."

"All this disrespectful talk toward my friend here, not a smart move on your part," responded Tommy.

Buddy asked, "Hannon, did you kill my friend Russ Nicholson?"

"No. I wasn't even there. Why are you asking me all this? I don't know what the fuck you're talking about."

"You tried to kill me. I figured you might have had something to do with a few more."

"Fuck you. If I was gunning for you, we wouldn't be talking right now. You'd be fuckin' dead in the ground. Now let us out of here, right fuckin' now."

"Gee, Hannon, I don't think you're in a position to give orders right now."

"Give him what he wants, Hal," encouraged Delaney.

"He's not getting shit from me."

With that, McLean nodded, smiled, walked to a closet, opened the door, and brought out a blowtorch. Delaney became

355

frantic. He urged Hannon to, "Tell him what he wants to know, now! He's going to fuckin' set us on fire!"

Hannon told Delaney, "Keep your fuckin' mouth shut."

Buddy lit the blowtorch and said, "Last chance."

"Fuck you, McLean."

Buddy fired the flames straight into Hannon's genitals. Hannon screamed. Buddy pulled the torch away and Tommy Ballou put out the fire with a bucket of water. Buddy asked Hannon, "You got something to say now?"

Hannon told McLean, "Y-y-yeah, they meet every Monday morning at different locations, usually in front of police stations where they feel it's safe."

"Where, and what time is the next Monday meeting?"

"I'm not sure," answered Hannon.

Buddy asked, "Is that all you have?"

Hannon replied, "Yeah, that's it. Now let us fuckin' go."

"You think you're going to walk out of here?"

"Fuckin' right, or you're a fuckin' dead man."

"You had your chance, Harold. Remember? This is what happens when you failed to kill me."

"Hold on a minute, I got money in a safe. You can have it all if you let us go."

Buddy smiled at Hannon and told him, "We already knew about the safe. My friend Joe here sent a few of our friends over to your places in Everett and Dorchester. They cleaned you out."

"What?"

"Yeah. Just so you know, we're going to give the money in the safe to the families of Tommy Sullivan and Russ Nicholson."

"No, no fuckin' way. That's a lie."

"Yeah, and thanks for all those guns and ammo. We'll make good use of that, too."

356

Hannon sat stunned and defeated. He did not say another word. Delaney was shaking in his seat. His eyes were bulging as he watched Buddy.

Buddy looked at Joe Mac for a second. Joe gave Buddy a silent nod. Buddy walked behind Hannon, looped a piano wire around his throat and garroted him with the cut off shaft of a hockey stick. He died in seconds. Delaney began crying and vomited on his shirt as he witnessed the murder.

McLean told Delaney, "Listen, I really don't want to, but I have to kill you, too."

"No. Wait. I won't tell nobody. I promise. I'll leave town today. Please."

Buddy looked at Joe Mac, who shook his head no and walked out of the room. Buddy turned his attention back to Delaney and said, "I can't take that chance, kid. You have to go."

"Wait. Wait. I'll tell you anything you want to know. Just give me a minute."

"What can you tell me?"

"Harold wasn't lying. They meet in front of a police station every Monday morning. But they never say where until that morning. I can call you when I find out where the next meeting is going to be."

"Anything else?"

"They've got a spy in Somerville, someone you trust. He knows a lot."

"Who is it?"

"I don't know. Only Punchy and George know the name. You have to believe me, I don't know his name. Can I go now?"

McDonald returned from another room. He had a jar of sleeping pills in one hand and a bottle of Jack Daniels Whiskey in the other. He ordered Delaney, "Shut up and take the fuckin' pills, then wash them down with this."

"No. Wait, Buddy. I helped you. Can you let me go?"

"Sorry, kid."

Delaney cried as he swallowed a half dozen sleeping pills and drank a good amount of whiskey. He soon slipped into a coma. Buddy slapped Delaney in the face a couple of times to make sure he was asleep. He walked behind the unconscious Delaney and untied him. *God, please forgive me for this.* He lifted Delaney and threw him over his shoulder. McLean and his friends loaded the dead Hannon and unconscious Delaney into the trunk of Hannon's car. They drove to a nearby dock and threw Harold Hannon and Willie Delaney into Boston Harbor. Delaney eventually drowned.

# Loud and Clear

They did not bother weighting down the bodies. Joe Mac believed that when the dead gangsters were discovered floating in the harbor, it would send a strong message to Charlestown. He was more than right. The double murder shot fear throughout Greater Boston. When Jerry Angiulo received the news, he told his men, "Stay the fuck away from Somerville. Don't give them any reason to get pissed at us. Those motherfuckers are not to be fucked with."

Jerry Angiulo

After reports of the brutal double homicide reached Charlestown, a few low-level Townie comrades sent word to Somerville that they no longer wanted to be involved in the feud. McLean sent word to meet with him on Winter Hill. Three Townies walked into the Capitol Bar, unarmed, and into the middle of two dozen of Buddy McLean's friends. The Townies were frisked, then were escorted across Broadway and down Marshall Street to the garage.

They were marched to the back office, where Buddy was waiting for them. "Come in, fellas," Buddy said as he shook hands with each man. "Have a seat. What can I do for you guys?"

"How about you let us come work for you? Maybe you'd like to expand your territory."

"Are we talking about Somerville taking over the Charlestown gambling operation?"

"We're talking about you taking control of everything: gambling, shylocks, the docks, the bridge, everything. Everything the McLaughlins had is now up for grabs, even into Southie. We want to work for you."

"Who's in charge over there right now?" asked Buddy.

"Nobody. Punchy's gone. The Hughes brothers are hiding, too. It's all broken down. It needs to be reorganized. We heard you were a reasonable man. We'd rather work for you instead of the Mafia."

"I might have a few friends who will help you get back on your feet. Then maybe we can work out a deal. I'll talk to my friends and see what they think. Then I'll get back to you fellas soon. Does that sound okay?"

"Yeah, sure, that's fine. Thanks for meeting with us, Buddy."

"Now, you boys are staying out of my fight with your boss. That's right, isn't it?"

"Absolutely! Totally neutral."

"All right, that's what I want to hear. We'll talk soon."

The Townies left the building. Buddy brought Tommy Ballou and John Hurley into the office and told his men, "You were right. They want to team up with us. It could be a nice opportunity for you two guys to run Charlestown someday. But I'm not sure that I should trust them just yet."

"Not while Punchy and the Hughes boys are still breathing," responded Hurley.

"Right. You guys see what you can find out, but don't put yourselves at risk. Stick together when you go down there. Bring Barboza and a few of his pals with you. When everybody sees that Joe is with us, it'll scare off any potential challenges to grab the rackets, and it'll make them think twice about taking a shot at you."

"Is he going to be a part of this?"

"Not yet. Maybe in the future."

# Uncertain

Rumors, threats, and plans for his own murder became daily news for Buddy. He tried to stay cool and organized. However, he began to have doubts about the loyalty of his friends: *McLaughlin has been trying to buy or threaten people to turn against me. I'm not sure who I can trust. Delaney said I have a backstabber in Somerville. It could be someone in my crew. I can't be sure who is really with me. I might have to kill one of my own friends.*

The daily stress of knowing that twenty men who lived five minutes away were out to kill him occupied his thoughts throughout the day. He hardly slept. He ate on the run, and his workouts were cut short. He often practiced shooting his pistols. He became quick and accurate with both hands. Though he showed no signs of fear and never once considered moving, running, or hiding, Jean noticed him alone in their living room one night, pacing back and forth, repeatedly reciting the words, "Lord, I know who my enemies are. Protect me from my friends."

*August 20, 1964*

"I feel so bad for him," Jean told her mother one afternoon over a cup of tea. "He doesn't know which way to turn. He is surrounded by friends who are being offered a lot of money to turn against him. And then, some of his friends are getting threats from the McLaughlins that their families are going to get hurt if they don't turn against Buddy. Those sons of bitches are starting rumors that some of Buddy's friends have already switched sides. The poor bastard doesn't know who to believe."

# The War Rages On

*September 4, 1964*

George McLaughlin dispatched a fresh-out-of-jail, bank-robbing lunatic named Ron Dermody to drive to Somerville, run in to the Capitol Bar, and shoot Buddy McLean. Dermody did as he was told, but he shot the wrong person. After he fired three shots in the crowded and loud barroom, Dermody turned around and ran for his life. The man who got shot was a friend of Buddy's named Charlie Robinson. There really was no resemblance between Buddy and Charlie except that they both had blondish hair. Buddy was not even present when the shooting took place.

Ron Dermody

Charlie Robinson was the carpenter Buddy had hired to build an addition on the rear of the McLean house. Robinson's injuries were not life-threatening, and he would soon return to work and the Capitol Bar.

Buddy Mclean did not take the attack lightly. He was furious that another one of his friends was shot. He gathered his men in the back room of the 318 Club and told them, "Those motherfuckers had the balls to try that in broad daylight, right in our neighborhood."

Tommy Ballou asked Buddy, "What do you want to do about it, Boss?"

"I want you and John to go over to Raymond's and get us lots of firepower right now. We'll pick you up in thirty minutes."

"Tony, I need two boilers (stolen cars). Are they ready?"

"They are, Buddy. Two-way radios, hats, glasses, binoculars, gloves, disguises, first aid, everything we need. I even have grenades, all packed and ready to go."

"All right. You and Rico go get them and pick us up right here. Are the gas tanks full?"

"Yup. We're all set."

"Good. Hurry back."

Twenty minutes later, Buddy slid into the front passenger seat of a black Cadillac. He had Jimmy Sims drive. Tommy and John Hurley rode in the back. Everyone was heavily armed. The second vehicle, a black Ford, had Tony "Blue" driving, with Rico up front and Billy Winn in the back.

Buddy was on the radio, "Let's go."

"Right behind you," answered Rico.

"We're going to go down Main Street to City Square."

"Roger that."

"If you see anyone, let us know."

"Will do."

Five minutes later, Buddy spotted Stevie Hughes stepping out of an apartment building on Main Street, Charlestown. Buddy grabbed the radio. "Pull over, but stay in the cars. I'll take him myself."

Buddy slid out of the Cadillac and came running up the sidewalk behind Hughes, who was unlocking the passenger door of his car. He grabbed Hughes by the back of his collar and rammed the barrel of a .38 Special into his lower back. Buddy quietly told Hughes, "Time for you to take a ride, Stevie."

Then, just behind Buddy, came a voice. "Daddy, who's that?"

Buddy held on and turned as Stevie answered, "This is Buddy, and he's a friend, honey. Go back inside for a minute."

Stevie's daughter went back into the building. Stevie was visibly shaking. Buddy's men were watching every move, waiting. Finally, Buddy sighed a long breath.

"Today is your lucky day, Hughes. Your little girl just saved your life. I'm telling you right now. The next time I catch you, you're a dead man. You and your brother and the rest of your pals should think real hard about quitting this life and moving out of Charlestown."

After a short pause, Stevie responded, "Thank you, Buddy, I'll tell the rest of them what just happened. Thank you."

Buddy let Hughes go and went back to his men. Steve Hughes hurried back into the building. As Buddy closed the car door, Tommy asked, "What happened?"

"I'm not going to kill a man or kidnap him in front of his daughter."

The men were silent. Buddy got back on the radio. "Everybody back to Somerville."

Tommy and John looked at each other and slowly shook their heads.

Finally, John spoke up and said, "I hope we're not going to regret that, Buddy."

Buddy softly replied, "Me, too."

\* \* \*

Later the same day, Ron Dermody reported back to George McLaughlin that he had killed Buddy McLean. The McLaughlins were already aware that McLean was still alive because Steve Hughes reported what had just happened to him.

Georgie told Dermody, "I don't know who you shot, but it definitely wasn't McLean. We can't have men who fuck up like that working for us. You're on your own, Dermody."

Dermody panicked and he called FBI agent Paul Rico to ask if he could meet with him. Rico agreed and set up a time and place for that night. Then Rico promptly phoned Buddy and told him where Dermody was going to be waiting.

Buddy drove by himself to an intersection at the Watertown-Belmont line where Dermody was sitting in his car. It was dark out, and the intersection was not well lit. Buddy pulled in behind Dermody. There was nobody around—the area was silent as death. He double-checked the license plate of Dermody's vehicle and a recent photograph of Dermody. Both items had been supplied by Paul Rico only an hour earlier. He kept his lights on and the engine running. McLean got out of his car and walked quickly up to Dermody. Without saying a word, McLean blasted five thirty-eight-caliber bullets through the driver's side window and into Dermody. Buddy turned and walked back to his car. *Another one gone. I should have killed Hughes, too. I'm probably not going to get that chance again.* He shifted his car into gear and drove away.

Dermody died in his automobile.

# Going after Punchy

*November 25, 1964*

The Winter Hill hit team caught Punchy off guard outside a Boston hospital. While McLaughlin was inside visiting a friend, Joe McDonald sat behind the wheel of a stolen car in the parking lot. Waiting for McLaughlin to exit, Joe reminded his passenger to, "Get up close, and shoot him right in the head." Next to Joe Mac was an assassin disguised as a rabbi.

As Punchy strolled out of the building, the rabbi quickly walked up and shot him in the face. Punchy immediately turned and ran back inside. The shooter fired at the Charlestown boss twice, hitting him in the back as he staggered away. "I need help!" garbled Punchy as he collapsed in the lobby. Security came running. The shooter made his getaway.

McLaughlin was badly wounded and admitted for emergency surgery. Though he lost part of his jaw and had damage to a lung, he survived.

While recuperating in the hospital, Punchy moaned to his visitors, "I'll probably never fuckin' chew food again."

A minute later, his fugitive brother George showed up. "All this because you had to grab a broad."

As soon as he was discharged from the hospital, Punchy went back into hiding.

*December 3, 1964*

John Hurley reported to Buddy, "Georgie McLaughlin is still on the run. Remember, he shot that guy over in Dorchester back in March."

"That wasn't anyone we know."

"No, some young fella named Bill Sheridan."

"Why did he kill him?"

"Well, the way I understand it is, Georgie was at a party, and drunk as usual. He gets into an argument with a different guy at the house. He goes to his car and gets his gun. Then he comes back into the house and shoots the wrong guy."

"Jesus, what an idiot."

"You got that right. I guess we can take Georgie off the hit list now. He's gonna get the death penalty."

"Yeah, well, he still has to go to trial. Let's see how it plays out."

"He's going to death row. There were a dozen witnesses. He's a dead man."

"That's what they were saying about me with Bernie."

"That's true."

Buddy then called Joe Barboza. "Hey, Seagull, how are you doing?"

"I'm doing great! I'm going to get married."

"I hope I get invited to the wedding."

"You're at the top of the list."

"All right. That's good, I'll look forward to it."

"What's up, Buddy? Anything I can do for you?"

"Yeah, see if you can track down Punchy for me. Maybe you can get a few of your friends to pitch in and help. He's been hiding out down at the Cape. But his brother is going to go on trial for murder. That might bring him back to Boston."

"All right, my friend. I'll get right to it. If I find him, do you want me to kill him?"

"If he's right in front of you, yes, go ahead. But don't take any chances of getting caught or hurting anyone else."

"Okay, Buddy. I understand."

Barboza and his men began inquiries at dozens of businesses throughout Charlestown. Most of them had been extorted by the McLaughlin gang at one time or another. At each stop, everybody knew nothing.

Then Barboza started using a different approach with the Townie business owners. "You know, if you help us get rid of that bum, you're going to see better days ahead."

"What do you mean by that?"

"I mean that you're not going to have to pay anyone to be in business anymore. Buddy McLean's not like that. He'll leave you alone, but he's always ready to help if you need him."

"Yeah, I heard that about him. He's a good man. But listen, nobody knows where McLaughlin is. He's done here. We'd tell you if we knew. Everybody hates him. He's gone. That's for sure."

# Another Murder

*March 1, 1965*

The murders continued. Not all of them were directly linked to the McLean-McLaughlin Gang War. Over in the North End, Gennaro Angiulo decided, "This is the perfect time to eliminate some of our enemies and let the blame fall on the Irish. Then, at the same time, we stay neutral and let them eliminate each other. After it's over, we move in and take over everything."

"That's a great move, Boss," stated Illario Zannino.

"I think so. Get ahold of Barboza. I want him to kill that fuckin' Teddy Deegan. He thinks he's going to get away with robbing our card games? Everyone will think we're weak. That little fuck has to go."

"I'm on it, top of my list. I'll call 'The Nigger' (Barboza)."

Barboza and a few of his men killed Deegan, in Chelsea, on March 12.

# Interrogating a Friend

*June 4, 1965*

While Barboza was looking for Punchy, Buddy had something else to think about: *The Hughes brothers are still down there. They were following Hurley. I find those bastards, they're dead. They didn't take my advice to leave. No second chance for them. What were they doing with John? I wonder if Hurley could be the spy. I can't take the chance. I'm going to hate this, but I must do it.*

Buddy called John Hurley to meet him at the Capitol Bar. It was a Friday morning; the place was closed for business. Joe Barboza and Billy Winn were at the bar when Hurley walked in. They looked but did not speak to him.

"Where's Buddy?"

Buddy appeared from a back room. He told John, "Sit down, right there."

Hurley sat at a table near the back of the room. Buddy sat across from him.

"What's up, Buddy? What's goin' on?"

"You tell me."

"What do you mean?"

"Are you with them?"

"How the fuck can you say that to me? After all these years! What the fuck is wrong with you?"

"First, you came up with a story that the Hughes brothers started shooting at you when you were getting off work. You dove into a fuckin' puddle?"

"I did. It was two feet deep, maybe more. Let's go down there. I'll show you."

"And no one else saw that happen?"

"I was the last guy to leave. I had to take a shit."

"Must have been a long fuckin' shit," added Billy.

"Fuck you!"

Buddy interrupted, "Knock it off! Billy, I'll handle this."

"I can't believe you think I'm a traitor."

Buddy stared at his friend with dead eyes. "Then you told Tommy that the next day Stevie chased you onto a trolley heading in town and that you got away by jumping off and hiding in Jordan Marsh."

"Yes, I did."

"You were on that ride for a while. How come neither one of you made a move?"

"I didn't have a gun. It was in my car."

"What about him?"

"He probably thought I was packing, or maybe he thought I had backup. Either way, this shit is done. If you think I'm a fuckin' rat, then let's settle it right now."

Hurley started to get up. Buddy sprung up and pushed him back down. "Shut up and sit there." Hurley stayed put. Buddy walked over to the bar and picked up the phone. He turned his back to John for a few moments, then continued the conversation while looking at John. He gave a little nod as he said, "I'll let you know." Buddy walked back to the table and sat down.

"All right, why didn't you tell me about all this shit when it happened?"

"I fuckin' called you when I was fuckin' hiding in Jordan Marsh. I called you here and at your house. You weren't in either place. Ask Jimmy. He took the call at the house."

"I'll look into that. One more thing, why was your car parked outside Driscoll's the other night when the Hughes brothers were in there?"

"I wasn't in there. I haven't been in there in months. Who fuckin' said I was in there?"

"Joe Mac. That was him on the phone."

"Well, I'm not the only guy in Boston driving a white Buick. He should have written down the license plate."

"It wasn't Joe who spotted the car. Listen, I hope to hell that you are not with them. But, unfortunately, this is how things are going right now. I have to be careful."

"I understand. But let me just say this, and I don't care if you believe me or not." John's eyes began to water, and his voice choked as he said, "You are a brother to me. I love you. I will stop a bullet for you. I'm not a traitor."

Buddy stared hard into John's eyes, then replied, "I feel the same way about you, John. I hate that I did that, but it had to be done."

Hurley nodded. They stood up, shook hands, and hugged each other.

Then Buddy told John, "Meet me back here at five o'clock."

# Defiant

Hurley returned to the bar later that day. Buddy and Tommy Ballou walked up to him and Buddy asked, "Do you have your gun?"

"Yes."

"Good, we're taking a ride to Charlestown."

With the interrogation behind them, the three friends slid into Buddy's automobile and headed down Winter Hill. They pulled up in front of Driscoll's. Buddy told his men, "I just want to see who's in there and ask them a few questions. You guys just be alert. Tommy, give John another pistol."

Tommy reached into the glove box and pulled out a loaded .38 Special. He turned around and handed it to Hurley. The men exited the vehicle.

When they walked in, Buddy looked around, then strolled up to the bar and politely asked, "Can we get a beer?"

Everyone knew who he was. The astonished bartender took a second to comprehend McLean's presence, then quickly brought him three bottles of Michelob and let him know, "McLean, I don't want any trouble in here, and I don't know anything about all the shit that's going on."

"Relax. Everything is fine. I'm just looking for Punchy and the Hughes boys. Can you help me?"

"No, I haven't seen any of them."

"Then who's taking your action?"

"O'Toole and Shackleford. They come by."

"Is that right?"

"Yeah. Sometimes the kid, Delaney, comes in."

*Not anymore.*

Buddy nodded to the bartender, then turned toward the twenty or so leery customers sitting quietly in the room. One finally said to his friend, "Let's get the fuck out of here."

Buddy immediately told them, "No! Sit down! I'm not staying. But if I find out that any of you are with the McLaughlins, or you're helping them, then you become my enemy. If you want to help me get rid of them, then you can leave me a message at the Capitol Bar. Otherwise, stay neutral."

He turned back to the bartender, laid a fifty-dollar bill on the bar and told him to, "Set them up." Then he waved to the group of men and walked out the door. Hurley and Ballou followed him.

When one of the customers received his beer, he stated, "If I didn't see that with my own eyes, I wouldn't fuckin' believe it. He's got huge balls coming in here. He gets right to the point, though, doesn't he?"

"Yeah, he does. Tell you the truth, I think I'd rather have him around here instead of Punchy. Punchy never bought us a round."

The next day he returned to Driscoll's, this time only with Tommy. While Buddy was there, someone called the cops, fearing violence was about to occur. Within a few minutes, two Boston police officers entered the barroom. Tommy was standing next to Buddy, and when he saw the cops come in he slipped his hand under Buddy's jacket and took his gun from inside the belt. He then casually walked to the men's room and locked the door.

Buddy was approached by two police officers, and one asked, "Do you mind if we search you for a weapon?"

"Sure, go ahead," as he raised his arms.

When he was found to be clean, the other cop asked, "McLean, why would you risk your life like that? You shouldn't be in Charlestown at all."

Buddy smiled at them and stated, "With you guys doing your job so well, I've got nothing to worry about."

The cops sighed and slowly shook their heads. "Do us a favor and go back to Somerville."

"Yeah, tell Punchy and his boys that I was asking for them."

The cops looked at him and then each other. Without a word, they walked out the door.

A few minutes later, the Boston Police Department made a call to the Somerville Police Department, "Hey, your boy McLean is hanging around in Charlestown like he doesn't have a care in the world."

"Yeah, that's him. He's nuts. He's not going to listen."

"Well, he might be looking to start more trouble with the McLaughlins, and he'll definitely find it if he keeps this up."

"You're right. I'll let the chief know what's going on. We've been keeping an eye on him and his friends. Maybe we should step it up a little."

"We're going to do the same thing here. Our guys just frisked him, and he was clean. But he's taking a bad chance by coming in here like that. There's only so much we can do."

"I think you're right, but if both sides see more cops around, they're less apt to be shooting at each other."

"Time will tell."

## July 6, 1965

Buddy showed up for work at the Charlestown docks like everything was normal. After putting in a full day of work, he walked home to Somerville. Most of the men working on the

Charlestown docks liked and respected Buddy. They warned him a few times when they saw a McLaughlin associate in the area. Buddy's close pals, John Hurley and Tommy Ballou, worked alongside him and were armed.

Maxie Shackleford reported back to the Townie crew, "He's got his friends with him all day. I'd say they're all packing. And the fuckin' cops are always hanging around, too."

Punchy looked at his men and asked, "How do we fuckin' get him?"

Steve Hughes responded, "We get him when he's not expecting it."

"When the fuck is that?"

"When he's in Somerville. He'll let his guard down. Then we'll get him."

"We fuckin' tried that already. How'd it work out?"

"I wasn't there. Don't blame me."

Maxie Shackleford jumped into the conversation. "What the fuck are you saying?"

"I'm saying you and Harold fucked it up."

"I'll fuckin' kill you, you fuckin' fat fuckin' punk."

"Try it right now, motherfucker."

"Shut the fuck up, everyone," hollered Punchy. After a silent moment, Punchy told Stevie, "You get McLean. That's your job. Have Connie work with you. If you need anything, you let me know. Can you get this done?"

"It's going to take some time, but I'll get it done."

"Yeah, well how fuckin' long will it take?"

"Can't say when, but it'll happen."

"Well let's hope it happens before he fuckin' gets us," stated Punchy, ending the meeting.

As Punchy walked to his car, Joe Barboza studied him from fifty yards down the street. When Punchy pulled away, Barboza followed him. Eventually Barboza lost Punchy on a long winding road in Weston. Barboza phoned Buddy. "I think I'm getting closer to finding Punchy's hideout."

"Okay, let me know when you're sure, and we'll get a crew together and set up a trap."

# Winter Hill Hit Squad

*August 6, 1965*

On an early Friday morning, six heavily armed men lay in wait along a winding road. John Hurley was stationed a mile ahead. He was high up in a tree. He had binoculars and a two-way radio. He had a perfect view of the road below.

At a little after seven, Hurley spotted what looked like Punchy's vehicle driving toward him. Looking through the binoculars, Hurley verified, *that's him.* He got on the radio, "He's coming. Get ready."

As Punchy slowed down to come around a tight bend, the assassins popped up and began firing. Punchy stomped on the gas pedal and took off down the road. "Motherfuckers!" He was hit three times, but he managed to drive for his life.

From his rearview mirror, Punchy saw two cars coming up from behind. They were coming fast. Punchy got out to the main street and gunned it toward Route 128. The Somerville crew was catching up. Punchy was wounded badly: *I can't drive like this. They'll catch me on the highway. What am I going to do?*

Just then he spotted an exit ramp coming off 128. *It's the only chance I've got.* He drove up the exit ramp, onto the highway, straight toward oncoming traffic. Seeing Punchy take the suicide turn, Joe Barboza called off the chase.

Punchy drove himself to the nearest hospital. He ran inside and yelled to the staff, "Call the cops. They're trying to kill me!"

Punchy was immediately attended to. His hand had to be amputated.

# His Little Girl

At a meeting with his men, Buddy informed them, "Punchy's going to get out of the hospital soon."

"It'll be hard to track him," piped in Joe Barboza. "He'll have cops all around him. They'll try and sneak him out at night or through a side door, or they'll disguise him."

Tommy Ballou asked, "We can't go in there and finish him?"

"No," responded Barboza. "Absolutely not. One of my guys checked it out. He's got a cop outside his room at all times."

Everyone looked at Buddy. "We'll have to get him when he gets out. Until then, let's be alert and ready for anything."

Just then a phone call came in for Buddy. "Buddy, it's Charlie, I'm at Somerville Hospital with your daughter. She took a bad fall."

Buddy hung up the phone and sprinted out the front door. Howie Winter ran after him. They were at the hospital in a couple minutes.

Buddy had rehired the fully recovered Charlie Robinson to finish building the addition at the rear of the family home. The job was coming along. Buddy's youngest daughter, Kellie, was watching Charlie work. Charlie was working inside the house on the second floor. Kellie tried to climb onto the banister and sit while she watched Charlie work. The four-year-old lost her balance, slipped back off the rail, and landed headfirst on the iron radiator nine feet below. Charlie picked her up and rushed Kellie to the emergency room at Somerville Hospital.

Buddy rushed into the room, where he found his little girl lying on a bed, a sheet pulled up to her chin, and her head wrapped in a bandage. She was scared and confused. She looked at her father's face and began to cry.

Buddy's eyes filled with tears and he called to the nurse. "I want the best man you've got for my daughter, and I want him in here right now."

The nurse nodded and left the room. He stood next to Kellie with his hand on her shoulder and he said, "It's going to be okay now, pretty girl."

Howie told Buddy, "I'll see what I can do. Charlie, you stay with Buddy until I get back."

Buddy and Charlie nodded. Kellie sobbed and said, "Don't leave me, Daddy."

He said, "I'm not going anywhere. I'm staying right here with you."

He held her hand the whole time she was there. The tears were streaming down his face.

# Sadness for the Canty Family

*December 1964 to August 1965*

While Buddy was feuding with the McLaughlins, John Canty was dealing with a problem no parent deserved to face. His oldest son, Mark, was diagnosed with brain cancer. Mark was the same age as Buddy's son Jimmy. Mark had several inoperable tumors growing in his head. The Canty family rallied around the young teenager. It was a grim and unhappy time for John and his family. Relatives and friends pitched in to help.

Buddy showed up at the house. "John, I want to help. Let me give you some money."

John felt bad, but replied, "You know I appreciate your offer, Buddy. And it's not because of your situation or the people you associate with. It's just the way I am. I know that you have more than your share of problems to deal with right now. The McLaughlins are on the run, but they're not going away. They want you dead, and that's never going to change. You have your own family to take care of right now. You and I will always be friends, but right now, I have to find a treatment, or a medicine, or a miracle, to save my son."

Buddy replied, "I understand, John. If you change your mind and you need me for anything, just call the house."

"Thanks, Buddy, I will."

"And I'll check in every so often."

"Fine."

## April 3, 1965

The Cantys tried getting help for Mark through the Boston Red Sox-sponsored cancer research program, the Jimmy Fund. The research was to find a cure, mainly for children. The Cantys were willing to have Mark try any new experiments or treatments that might improve his chances for survival. Without much explanation, the Jimmy Fund turned them down. The Canty family was sent home with no other suggestions for Mark.

## April 11, 1965

Apprised of the lad's status, Buddy drove over to the Canty home in the Ten Hills neighborhood of Somerville. The two friends sat alone in the kitchen drinking beer and talking about life in general.

At one point John stated, "Not even a year ago, everything was great. My son was a healthy, strapping young man. Now look, he's almost gone."

"I'm sorry, John. It's not supposed to go this way," said Buddy.

"It's killing me that I can't help him." The tears began to well.

"You've done everything you can for Mark. Now, God is going to take over. If you believe and have faith in that, it's going to make you feel a little better. It's like knowing that, someday, you'll be together again. And I believe that with all my heart."

Canty sat silently staring hard into the eyes of Buddy McLean. After a long moment, John slid back his chair, stood up, and walked around the table. As he was doing so, the big cop motioned Buddy to do the same. Buddy stood, and John wrapped his arms around him and squeezed like a bear. The two men began to cry.

Finally, John let go of his friend, took a deep breath, and asked Buddy, "How about another beer?"

"Sure," answered Buddy.

*May 2, 1965*

Buddy continued stopping by the Canty residence, usually on Sundays. He often brought along beer, and pizza from Leone's. On this Sunday morning, as they were leaving church, John's son Sean asked, "Dad, is Buddy coming over today?"

"I don't know, why?"

"I like it when he comes over. He's fun. And I think he makes you feel better, for a little while."

"Yeah, he is fun, and it is nice when he visits."

"Buddy is like part of the family, Dad, don't you think?"

"He's a really good friend, Sean, and if you think he should be a part of our family, that's okay with me."

"I do, but you're still my favorite guy, Dad. When I grow up, I want to be just like you."

"Thanks, Sean, it's nice to hear that. And I want you to do better than me. If I can help you make that happen, then I did my job. Let's get home to your brother."

"Okay, Dad. Maybe Buddy will be there with some pizzas."

*The little guy is right. It's nice when Buddy stops by. It does us both good. But, I fear there is much dread that lies ahead for him, too.*

*March 10, 2012*

Sean Canty eventually became a Somerville cop. Early in his career, Sean suffered a life-threatening, on-the-job injury. He never fully recovered and was forced to retire at a young age.

One afternoon he was having lunch in the Mount Vernon Restaurant in Somerville with a couple of his friends. "My father is the greatest man I ever met. He was my best friend and my absolute hero. But he took my brother's sickness the worst of all of us. Watching my brother suffer took a lot out of my dad. He was always sad, except when Buddy McLean came by the house. Buddy had a way about him that made you feel good. He was like part of the family. It was that smile or the cheerful attitude. He got us to think about other things in life for a while, and he was great with my brother."

One of Sean's friends added, "Toughest guy there ever was, and nicest, too."

"That's right," replied Sean. "A unique individual."

"What do you mean?"

"Everything he did, everything he said, seemed important."

"Really?"

"Yeah, little things were important. I remember the first time I shook hands with Buddy. He said, 'That's not how men shake hands. You look him in the eye, and with a strong grip you give him a firm shake. Now, let's do it again.' We did. Then he said, 'Good. That's how it's done. Always remember that.'"

Sean's friends smiled and nodded their heads.

## August 16, 1965

Mark Canty died of brain cancer. He was fifteen years old. It was a sad time in Somerville, not only for the Canty family, but also for the thousands of Somerville residents who knew, respected, and loved John Canty.

The morning after Mark passed, Buddy McLean, Howie Winter, and Sal Sperlinga showed up early at the Canty home. The men simply nodded to John Canty and proceeded to unload the trunk and back seat, filled with groceries. When they were finished, Buddy asked John, "What else can we do for you?"

"Nothing," replied the big cop. "You guys have already done more than anyone else, and I'll never forget that. You guys have your own problems to handle. I wish I could help you."

"John, we see cops hanging around all the time. We figured you had something to do with that."

"Well, most of the cops around here happen to think pretty highly of you. It wasn't hard to get them to be more visible in your neighborhood."

# Better Days

*August 25, 1965*

Buddy received a phone call from Joe McDonald. "Hi, Buddy. How's it going there?"

"You heard about John Canty's son?"

"Yeah, my wife told me. Sad news. Young fella. I feel bad for Canty. Send my condolences, will you?"

"I will."

"How's everything else?"

"Pretty good right now. Are you on the road?"

"Yup."

"Do you need anything?"

"Nope, I'm just calling for an update."

"Howie is taking care of all the books. It's rolling along. He's got some good men helping him. I got some nice tips from the Teamsters for a couple shipments we're going to grab. We're doing fine."

"That's good. What about you? Are you being careful?"

"Yeah, I took your advice. Tommy and John are with me during the day. When they're not, they keep an eye on what goes on in Charlestown. Tony D'Agostino and Rico Sacramone are with me at night. During the day, they work in other areas, along with Billy Winn and Jimmy Simms. Barboza is out there. He has his own crew. They haven't found Punchy or the Hughes."

"That fuckin' Punchy's got nine lives. Okay, well, we know they're not going to quit. I'll call you next week."

"All right, Joe. Thanks for the call."

The next day, Buddy set up a highly profitable truck hijacking of color television sets. Buddy's crew worked with Jerry Angiulo and Raymond Patriarca. It was professional perfection. And everyone made a nice week's pay.

Buddy had Tommy Ballou, Rico Sacramone, and a Teamster truck driver deliver the television sets to Baltimore. They returned to Somerville a few days later for a meeting at the Capitol Bar. The crew was seated at a table toward the back of the bar. Buddy was at the table with Howie Winter, Joe Barboza, Tony "Blue" D'Agostino, John Hurley, Raymond Grande, Billy Winn, Jimmy Flynn, and Jimmy Simms. Tommy and Rico pulled up a couple of chairs to join the group. Buddy ordered a fresh round of drinks. He was in a more relaxed and cheerful frame of mind. Buddy asked Tommy, "How'd it go?"

"Everything went good except for one thing on the way back."

The men at the table listened intently and Buddy asked, "What?"

Even Tommy's riding partner, Rico, had a surprised look on his face, not knowing what Tommy was going to talk about.

Tommy continued, "We stopped at a strip bar in New Jersey and had a few drinks, you know, to take the edge off. After we left the bar, we pulled into a motel down the street. Afterward, there weren't any girls around, so I went to sleep. I was dreaming that I was making love to a beautiful dancer from the club. I was about to shoot my load when I woke up, looked down, and there's Rico, sucking on my dick! No shit!"

An explosion of laughter, then Rico countered, "Tell the truth, Tommy. I was takin' a shit on your face!"

Gut-busting fits of yells, hollers, hiccups, and table pounding preceded Tommy's final blow. "Yeah, when the stripper danced up in front of Rico and took her top off, he started cryin'! Wah! Wah! Wah!"

Even Buddy had tears of laughter streaming down his face as the Somerville lads temporarily set their troubles aside.

That same night, the men went out to Blinstrub's, a Boston nightclub. A great time was had by all.

Winter Hill Pals at Blinstrubs. Left: Howie Winter, Ernie "The Greek", Aniello Squillante, Bob Martini, Carlo Gianelli, Eddie Coleman. Right: "Tony Blue" D'Agostino, Younger McDonald, unknown, Sal Sperlinga, Dick McGinlly, Raymond Grande.

# A Young McLaughlin

*August 31, 1965*

The next day, and almost four years after his father, Bernie, was gunned down by Buddy McLean, eighteen-year-old Charlie McLaughlin was having lunch in the jam-packed longshoreman's diner at the Charlestown docks. He was sitting at the counter enjoying his meal when the door to the diner opened. Buddy McLean walked in. The lively, loud diner became stone-cold silent. Charlie spotted his father's killer approaching from the corner of his left eye. As McLean walked down the aisle, Charlie swiveled his stool around to face him. The sudden movement caught McLean's attention. Charlie spit on the floor just in front of Buddy and said, "Fuck you, McLean." Buddy stopped on a dime, stared long and hard at young McLaughlin, but did not say a word. He proceeded forward to speak with the people he came to see. On his way out, the Winter Hill boss passed by Charlie McLaughlin a second time. They glared at each other again. Not a word was spoken or a breath taken until McLean closed the door behind him. In unison, the midday crowd expelled a sigh of relief.

The next day, Tommy Ballou walked up to Charlie at the docks and told him he heard what happened. Although he was a friend to McLean, Ballou lived in Charlestown and was lifelong friends with the McLaughlin and Hughes brothers. Ballou

392

encouraged Charlie, "You better kill McLean before he kills you. He wants all you McLaughlins dead, and he won't stop until every single one of you are in the ground. And that means your whole family, too."

"My uncle ordered me to stay out of this."

"Yeah, well, it looks like it's too late now. McLean thinks you might be dangerous, and he's planning on killing you."

"What should I do?"

"You've got to kill him first. I'll help you set him up. He trusts me."

"Should I do this myself?"

"You can bring your uncle or any of his guys if you want. But if that happens, I'm going to want a nice reward for helping you guys."

"I'll think about it."

"Yeah, well, don't think about it too long, 'cause I guarantee, McLean has already made up his mind."

The same night, Charlie received a phone call from his uncle Eddie (Punchy). He asked Charlie what Tommy Ballou had said to him. When Charlie relayed Ballou's plan to Eddie, the uncle warned his nephew, "Stay away from Ballou because he's setting you and the rest of us up for a hit by McLean. Ballou was friends with us for a long time, but now he's with McLean, a hundred percent."

# Tough Times for Punchy

The word traveled back to Somerville that Punchy McLaughlin was scared to death of Buddy and his friends. Several months before, he had moved out of Charlestown. His criminal empire began to crumble. He attempted to run his operation by phone, but it was not effective. People who owed money to the McLaughlin gang were not paying.

One time, Punchy's men, Maxie Shackleford and Jimmy "Spike" O'Toole, were sent to a South Boston tavern to collect on an outstanding debt. Three Somerville men were there, ready and waiting to trap them. As the two Townies entered the building, one Somerville man made his presence known too soon, allowing the Charlestown men to barely escape. Punchy also concluded that McLean had guys placing large bets with them, and they had no intention of paying if they lost.

Buddy did the same thing with Punchy's loan-shark business. Teamsters and longshoremen were not paying back on the loans they received from the McLaughlins. "Yeah, let them try and get their money."

The McLaughlin collectors became reluctant to perform their duties for fear of being ensnared by a Somerville hit squad. Punchy ordered his men, "Shut everything down."

Back on Winter Hill there was an air of confidence brewing. Buddy's men felt that victory was within reach. Tony "Blue" boasted to the crew, "The McLaughlins are done, and everything they have will soon belong to us."

McLean had different feelings. He told his men, "Fellas, this isn't over. Not by a long stretch. We haven't won anything. Those guys are still out there, and they're not quitting. This won't be over until they're all in the ground."

Buddy's men nodded in agreement, but they remained self-assured.

# Hanging with His Pals

*Labor Day Weekend, 1965*

On Sunday afternoon, Buddy walked from his home to the Capitol Bar. He had finished his morning workout, gone to church, and decided to have a few beers with his friends before Jean served up Sunday dinner. His men were drinking at a table toward the back of the establishment. Buddy sat down in the seat that was reserved for him, against the back wall facing the front and back exits.

After taking a long swig from his beer mug, Tommy Ballou slowly shook his head as he casually mentioned, "Punchy's gotta be sweating worse than a jig writin' a check."

The roaring laughter started. Then Rico Sacramone said, "Don't call them that, Tommy, I got a lot of black friends."

Tommy replied, "Yeah, that's good." Then he asked Buddy, "Hey, what's black and white and rolls around the sidewalk at Kelly's?"

"What?"

"Rico and a j-boo, wrestling over a fuckin' French fry."

The walls were shaking from the wailing laughter. Then Tony D'Agostino, slowly shaking his head, took a stab at defending Rico.

"Yeah, Tommy. At least Rico and I get more ass than you'll ever dream of."

"Yeah, you two guys get them and do what with them?"

"Anything we want, right, Rico?"

"Right, T. Maybe we could let Tommy watch us so he could learn a few things," Rico chimed in.

Tommy raised his eyebrows and nodded to the others at the table. Then he responded, "Why would I want to watch you two guys embarrass yourselves and the rest of us? Two dagos are going to teach me how to treat a lady? Both your brains together weigh less than a sailor's wallet on a Monday."

The last statement brought down the house. The flabbergasted D'Agostino and Sacramone were speechless. A few minutes later, Tommy went to their table with a couple of ice-cold mugs of beer. He placed the mugs in front of his associates and told them, "When I rib you, I like you. Don't take nothing personal, boys." Then he clapped them on the back and said, "Sometime I'll take you boys in town with me and we'll have a good time."

When Tommy walked away, Tony sarcastically muttered to Rico, "I can't fuckin' wait."

A few minutes later, Buddy received a phone call from home. It was Jean letting him know that, "Dinner is just about ready. Come home and get it while it's hot."

"I'll be there in a couple of minutes, and I might be bringing some of the boys with me."

"Yeah, what else is new?"

He hung up the phone, walked over to his friends, and asked, "Who's hungry?"

Jean was used to this routine: Buddy bringing home unannounced guests for dinner. Thus, she always made sure to have plenty of food cooked when she was ready to serve.

Buddy arrived home with five of his friends, all eager to dig in to one of Jean's home-cooked meals. Buddy entered the front door followed by Tony, Rico, John Hurley, and Billy

Winn. Tommy Ballou brought up the rear. The first four men, plus Buddy, were quiet. They were not sure if they were going to be welcomed when Jean realized how many men Buddy had brought home with him. Just then, Tommy offered his customary greeting to Jean, "My good woman, how nice of you to have us over for Sunday dinner." Then he handed her a dozen red roses.

"Where did he get the fuckin' flowers?" Rico quietly asked Tony.

"He probably grabbed them out of someone's trash on the way over," answered Tony.

Tommy made himself at home in the living room while Jean was making accommodations for her unexpected company. He sat in a big cushioned chair as he chatted with Buddy's sons Jimmy and Michael, who were sitting on the couch watching television. Just then, Buddy's daughter Lea walked into the room and greeted Tommy.

"Hey, pretty girl!" He grabbed her and tossed her straight up and caught her as she came down. Lea thought it was great and laughed hysterically as he did it two more times.

Then Jean called out, "Dinner's ready. Come on in."

Tommy sprung out of the chair and headed out. Michael followed Tommy. Lea stepped onto the chair Tommy was sitting in and started bouncing up and down. She bounced from the cushioned chair to the couch where Jimmy was still sitting. Jimmy was getting annoyed and decided to head out to the dinner table. As he was passing by Lea, she bounced back to the cushioned chair, at which point a handgun toppled onto the floor.

Jimmy picked up the weapon and brought it out to Buddy.

"Hey, Dad, whose is this?" said Jimmy as he held up the pistol.

Buddy looked up and instantly jumped out of his chair and rushed over to Jimmy to take the gun. Jean saw this and exploded, "Jesus Christ! What the hell is that doing in my house? I told you bastards I don't want any guns around my kids. Now this? You nuts are going to hurt someone."

Tommy immediately knew it was his gun. "Awe shit! I'm sorry, folks. It must have fell out of my pocket when I was playing with Lea."

With an angry look, Buddy handed the gun to Tommy. Everyone began eating their meal. The normally talkative dinner table was silent for a while until Jean cooled off. Then she asked, "Do you want some more mashed potatoes, Mr. Dillinger?"

Buddy and Jimmy looked at Jean, not sure of who she was talking to. Jimmy asked her, "Who are you talking to, Ma?"

"Or maybe it's Wild Bill Ballou," as she began to smile at Tommy.

"Oh sure! Absolutely! This meal is delicious! Ain't that right, fellas."

"You bet!" "Outstanding!" "Best I ever had!" came the compliments from the men.

Buddy just sat there looking at his men while slowly shaking his head.

Jean told them to, "Knock it off and eat your dinner, or you're not getting dessert."

Outside on Jaques Street, a Somerville police cruiser drove slowly past Snow Terrace. "Everything is quiet."

"Roger that. Keep an eye on him," replied John Canty.

"Ten-four."

Canty had recently suggested to the chief of police, "A heavy police presence around McLean will make the McLaughlins think twice before trying more shit."

"That's a good idea, John," replied the chief. "See to it."

# A Near Miss

*Labor Day, 1965*

Normally on Sunday mornings after church, Buddy and several friends played softball. The site for these games was Trum Field, Somerville's beautiful diamond-gem ballpark located off the Sperlinga side of Winter Hill, on Broadway, between Magoun Square and Ball Square. This weekend the game was scheduled for Monday.

The McLean team regularly squared off against a group of talented younger men from Somerville. A few of them sold football betting cards for Sal Sperlinga. Sal played with Buddy, as did Sal's brother Bobby, plus the members of Buddy's inner circle. The games were well played and highly spirited. A Somerville patrol car was parked on Broadway next to the park.

A few of the younger players wondered about the consistent police presence. They approached Buddy. "Hey, Buddy. How come the cops are always hanging around during our games?"

"They're probably checking to see if any of you young whippersnappers have any arrest warrants."

"Ha! Right. You sure they're not here for you?"

"They might be. I never ask."

"Hmm."

"If you want to be nosey, go up there and ask him. Or do you want to play ball?"

"Let's play."

In Buddy's mind, he figured *they're not being a pain in the ass, and it's probably keeping the Charlestown boys from pulling any shit.*

Both teams were getting ready to warm up when Bobby Sperlinga pulled up to the sidewalk next to the park. His car had a half dozen bullet holes in it. His brother Sal asked, "What the hell happened?"

"The Hughes brothers were getting some target practice in last night. I pulled up next to them on the parkway in Everett, by accident. They thought I was you," responded Bobby.

"How do you know that?"

"One of them said, "Hey, Sal. Want to bet you don't fuckin' make it home tonight?"

"Then what happened?" asked Sal.

"I gunned it and they started shooting."

Sal and Buddy looked at each other for a moment. Buddy announced, "No game today, boys. Sal, can you come up to the bar?"

"I'll be right there."

Buddy ordered his men to meet up at the Capitol Bar right away. Sal told his guys and his brother to go home, and then he drove up Winter Hill to meet with Buddy.

The young ballplayers were just getting ready to leave when a friend of theirs, Ronnie Flynn, showed up. He was an extremely tough and talented Somerville boxer who was quickly making a name for himself. The twenty-two-year-old middleweight had recently bashed two monsters from Somerville's Union Square. The first victim was the enormous Ron Phelan, who went down after a three-punch flurry. The second was Big Joe Bruno, who Flynn knocked out with one punch. Ronnie Flynn had nothing to do with the ongoing gang war, but he thirsted for an opportunity.

"Where's Buddy McLean?" asked Flynn.

"He's up at the Capitol. Why?" asked one of his friends.

"I want to fight him."

"No, you don't. Don't be fuckin' stupid. He'll fuckin' kill you, plus he's in a bad mood. Stay the fuck away from him," warned Bobby Sperlinga.

"I'm going up there," said Flynn. He jumped back into his car and sped up Broadway. His friends hurried behind him.

Flynn and eight young Somerville softball players parked their cars and walked toward the Capitol. Every step of the way they tried to change his mind, but to no avail. Flynn stormed into the crowded bar and loudly demanded, "Where's Buddy McLean?"

"What do you want?" asked Big John Devine, who was making sure nobody interrupted Buddy's meeting.

"I want to fight McLean."

"What happened? Someone dropped you on your head when you were born? Is that it?"

"There's nothing wrong with me. I want to fight him."

"All right, enough of this shit. All you boys have to leave right now."

"I'm not leaving until I fight him," exclaimed Flynn to his friends and a few others in the barroom.

Sal got up from Buddy's table and told Devine, "I'll take care of this."

He walked over to the young men and said, "You guys better leave right now, or, I promise, you won't be walking out of here."

"I want to fight him, Sal," responded Flynn as he loosened his neck and shoulders.

Sal stood in front of Flynn, looked him in the eye, and said, "I know you can fight. But you're not as good as me. Do you agree with that?"

"Yeah," Flynn reluctantly agreed.

"And I'm not even in the same league as him. Nobody is. So why the fuck would you want to fight him?"

"I don't know. If you want to be the best, you have to fight the best, right?"

"Not if you don't want to have your fuckin' face messed up for the rest of your life, you don't."

"I'm not afraid of him, Sal."

"Well you should be." Sal then turned to Ronnie's friend. "Hank, you get him and all the rest of the boys out of here right now. Or, I promise you, it's not going to end well."

Hank turned to Ronnie Flynn, "Let's get out of here. You heard what Sal said. You can't see it right now, but he's doing us a huge favor. Everything about this is a bad idea. So far you haven't done anything that's going to get us killed. Let's get out while we can."

"You can go if you want."

"Listen, I know you're tough, but I'm not leaving without you, and these guys are the last people you want to piss off. Let's just go."

Ronnie Flynn's eyes began to burn. He looked hard toward Buddy McLean, sitting with his friends at a table at the back of the room. Buddy was not aware of what was happening at the front door. After a long moment, Flynn turned and walked out the front door. Hank breathed a sigh of relief and followed him out.

*Friday September 10, 1965*

After hearing about the attempt on Bobby Sperlinga, Buddy was enraged through the rest of the week. Everyone knew to give him space. Tommy Ballou mentioned to John Hurley, "I pity the fool who picks a fight with him this week."

Buddy was sitting by himself at the back of the Capitol Bar. It was just around midnight. He had been drinking for a couple hours. Everyone stayed clear of him. Tommy and John entered the bar and walked up to their boss.

"What's up?" asked Buddy.

"Ray Collins is over at the 318," answered John.

"Yeah, so?"

"He's over there drinking, and he says doesn't have the money he owes us."

"How much does he owe?"

"Seven hundred."

Buddy slid his chair back, stood up, grabbed his pistol off the table and slipped it inside his belt. "Let's go."

The three men walked across the street to the 318. Buddy pulled open the door. There were about fifty people in the bar. Buddy headed straight to the table where Ray Collins was seated with a few others. Collins was a middle-aged Boston man who enjoyed associating with crime figures. Previously, he was a regular bettor with the McLaughlin brothers.

"Hey, Buddy, how are ya?"

"You owe me seven hundred dollars. I want it, right now."

"I don't have it on me, but I can—"

Buddy did not wait for the man to finish. He lifted Ray Collins and his chair onto the table. The room went quiet.

"Buddy I—"

"Shut the fuck up," Buddy ordered, then loudly warned the rest of the people in the bar, "Anyone who doesn't want to see this better get the fuck out, right now!" He pulled his pistol and pointed it at Collins's head. Half the bar quickly emptied.

Collins was visibly shaking in his seat. Buddy told him, "You don't come up here to our bar, acting like a big shot, buying drinks, then telling my friends you don't have the money. You must think we're stupid or that we're gonna let you slide. Which one is it?"

"None of that, Buddy, I was going to pay you tomorrow, no lie, on my mother's soul."

"You do think I'm stupid," as he cocked the pistol. The bar was silent.

"Please, Buddy, wait, I'll get it for you right now. I'll go home and get the seven hundred. It'll only take me an hour."

Buddy looked at him for a long moment, then nodded. "Is that your Cadillac out front?"

"Uh, yeah, it is."

"Give me the keys."

"What?"

"You don't understand English, Ray? Hand them over."

Collins reached into his pocket, then gave Buddy the keys.

Buddy told him, "This is just in case you decide to not come back with our money."

"But how am I going to get home now?"

"Ask one of your friends or take a cab. You said one hour, you better hurry."

Ray Collins slid out of his chair and off the table. Another man agreed to give him a ride. They hurried out the door.

Buddy turned to his men and handed John the keys. "When he gives you the money, give him back his keys."

Hurley nodded.

Before he left, Buddy walked up to the bartender and handed him a one-hundred-dollar bill. "Set up the house and keep the rest for yourself. And I think that guy pissed himself over there."

The bartender nervously laughed, then responded, "Okay, Buddy, I'll take care of it. Thanks, Buddy."

After Buddy walked out and the door closed, the clientele, in unison, loosed a long sigh of relief.

405

# A Chance to Reminisce

*September 12, 1965*

Buddy and a three of his friends were walking up Sydney Street in Somerville when they happened upon a dozen young boys playing two-hand touch football in the street. Buddy stopped to watch the game.

"Does that remind you of us?" asked John Hurley.

"It sure does."

"The good old days," chimed in Howie Winter.

"That's right, pal," responded Buddy.

"It's seems like only yesterday," added Hurley.

"I miss that. I wish we could go back," responded Buddy.

Just then a young boy, no more than seven years old, smashed into a parked car while he was making a fine, over-the-head, fingertip catch. The kid held onto the ball as he went down on the pavement, gasping for the breath that was knocked out of him. Buddy walked up to the youngster and said, "Nice catch, Champ. The Patriots could use a guy like you. Why don't you get back in there?"

The little football player looked up to see a sharp blue-eyed man with broad shoulders and a big smile. He pulled himself up and returned to the game. As the game continued, the little boy looked over more than once toward the man who had encouraged him to keep playing. The man was talking with his friends as they continued to watch the game. But, one time, the boy caught the man's eye. He nodded his head, smiled again, and said, "That's it, keep playing."

A few minutes later, the game ended as the boys were called into their houses for supper. As the young lad headed toward his house, Buddy called to him, "Hey, Champ. You could be real good, but you need to get bigger and stronger. You should start doing push-ups and pull-ups every day."

The boy looked at the solidly built McLean, nodded, and started to walk again.

"Hey, eat everything on that plate. And drink lots of milk."

He smiled at Buddy, nodded again, and waved. As he reached the top step of the front porch, the boy's uncle walked up and asked him, "What did Buddy McLean just say to you?"

The boy turned quickly to see Buddy walking away with his friends toward Temple Street. Buddy overheard the boy say to his uncle, "Wow! That's Buddy McLean? The toughest guy there ever was!"

# Going After Punchy

A few days later, at the Marshall Street garage, FBI agent Paul Rico criticized Barboza and his men, "That was sloppy work, Joe, very unprofessional."

Barboza explained, "We don't know where he's living. That makes it difficult to track him."

Rico nodded and walked away. The very next day at the garage, Rico handed Barboza a slip of paper with an address written on it.

"What's this?" asked Barboza.

"It's where McLaughlin's girlfriend lives. That's where he's been hiding out," replied Rico.

Barboza gave the information to Buddy, who in return told Barboza, "Punchy has been going to his brother Georgie's murder trial in Boston. He's riding a bus each morning from West Roxbury to the courthouse."

"Wow, how'd you find that out?"

"Joe Mac called me. He knows someone at the courthouse."

"All right. How do you want to do this?"

"We'll meet with Joe today and come up with a plan. He's going to want to drive out to that bus stop and check things out."

"Yup. Good idea."

"Then we'll practice a few times. Do you have a shooter?"

"Yeah, a young guy from Roxbury, served in the military. Nobody knows him."

"We're going to want to meet him. He has to get up close. I want the job finished this time. And without hitting any innocent bystanders."

"Don't worry, Buddy. This kid is good. You'll like him. He'll get the job done."

"What's his name?"

"Steve Flemmi."

The next day, Buddy, Barboza, and Joe McDonald put together a plan to ambush Punchy. Buddy had the hit squad practice a few dry runs at the bus stop. When he was satisfied, Buddy told them, "You guys are ready. He won't get away this time."

## October 10, 1965

On a Sunday afternoon, a chubby Somerville police officer named Younger MacDonald, one of Buddy's favorites, strolled into the Capitol Bar. He was carrying a brown paper grocery bag that had nothing in it except for a huge bunch of carrots. Buddy and his crew were sitting at their table in the back of the bar. The cop stopped at the bar for a glass of Scotch, then ambled over to Buddy's table.

Tommy Ballou mused to the detective, "Is your wife putting you on a diet?"

The detective looked at the carrots and responded, "Oh, these are not for me. They're for you fellas. They'll improve your eyesight so maybe you can shoot straight."

An eruption of laughter, and then Tommy's counter, "When was the last time you caught a crook?"

"That was the night you pushed that guy out the window at Whalen's."

"I was never charged for that."

"Yeah, only 'cause Buddy took care of it."

The cop placed the bag of carrots in front of Ballou and smirked as he said, "Tommy, they're all for you. From what I heard, you can't hit the water from the top of a bridge."

# Punchy's Last Day

*October 21, 1965*

Punchy McLaughlin was standing at the West Roxbury bus stop. He was on his way to the courthouse in downtown Boston. As he stepped up to board the bus, Barboza's man came up behind and shot the Charlestown boss twice from point-blank range. Punchy turned to face his assassin and stepped off the bus. The assassin kept shooting. As he started to go down, Punchy handed a shocked female bystander a brown paper bag and told her to, "Hold this."

Punchy McLaughlin

Then he died on the sidewalk, like his brother Bernie had four years earlier. Inside the brown paper bag was a loaded pistol.

Buddy was parked diagonally across the street with Jimmy Sims, Joe McDonald, and Tommy Ballou. One of Barboza's associates was parked around the corner from the bus stop, waiting for the assassin. The shooter was Steve Flemmi from Roxbury. He was an up-and-coming gangster looking to make a name for himself.

Steve Flemmi

The assassination went like clockwork, along with a clean getaway. The men drove back to Somerville with plans to celebrate the death of a once-feared Charlestown crime boss. All except Buddy: *I don't get it. Kill a guy, then have a party. They act like it's a hunting trip. This is a matter of survival. These guys think it's over; it's not. Shackelford, O'Toole, and the Hughes brothers. Four more, plus some we might not even know about.*

At the Capitol Bar he told his men, "We have to keep looking for them. They're still out there. Don't let up. It's not over yet. Barboza was good today. Let's get him to help us finish off the rest."

The day after Punchy's murder, Stevie Hughes sent a message to Winter Hill that the brothers wanted a truce. Buddy considered their plea: *How can I know if they really mean it? I gave them a chance to leave, but they're still down there. I have to call Joe. He'll know what to do.*

Buddy called Joe Mac's wife and told her to have Joe call him. Buddy received the call the same night.

"The Hughes brothers want a truce," started Buddy.

"Do you trust them?" asked Joe.

"No, I don't."

"And you have to remember, their old man would be tear-assed if he found out they laid down. They're gonna listen to him. You should not trust anything they say."

Buddy sent a message back to Charlestown: "No truce." The brothers vanished.

# Reflecting

*October 27, 1965*

A week after the McLaughlin hit, Buddy was standing outside Raymond Grande's pizza shop talking to a few of his friends.

Bobby DeSimone asked Buddy, "Is it over?"

"No, there's still a few of them out there," replied Buddy.

"You don't think they just skedaddled?"

"Not these guys. Their old man (Steve Hughes Sr.) would never allow that."

"Yeah, but they're outnumbered by a lot now."

"That's true, but they've been in this line of work for a while now. They're good at what they do. They'll recruit some new guys while they lay low. It's the Townie way, them against the world. They never give up. I'll be lucky if I live another year."

"Wow. This wasn't even your fight."

"That's true, too. But what was I going to do? Let them murder my friends?"

"I don't know anyone who would do what you did, Buddy."

"Yeah, well, if you don't stand for something, you'll fall for anything. You know what I mean?"

"Yes, sir, I do," replied DeSimone with a thoughtful look on his face.

Buddy's words hit the bull's-eye. DeSimone never forgot what his famous neighbor told him, and he would repeat the line many times to many people. The saying snowballed and became a favorite line used by men to their sons throughout Greater Boston and, eventually, across America. As years went by, the line: "If you don't stand for something, you'll fall for anything," became words to live by for millions of Americans. However, most of them never knew who first said it or the story behind the expression.

# A Fateful Night

*October 31, 1965*

On Halloween night in Somerville, each home could expect an average of five hundred kids trick or treating. The sea of costumes parading the streets of Winter Hill this year was typical.

Jean McLean escorted her daughters through the neighborhood. Michael went out with his friends. Jimmy stayed home and handed out the candy. Buddy was home with Jimmy for a while. When the family returned, the girls got ready for bed and Buddy tucked them in. He kissed his wife and left the house with Rico Sacramone and Tony D'Agostino, his bodyguards.

They stopped briefly at a few places collecting debts. Then the three drove up Broadway in Buddy's new automobile and parked in front of the closed-down Capitol Theater, across the street from the Winter Hill hotspot, the 318 Club. They met a few more pals inside, and Buddy and his bodyguards decided to stay and have a few drinks. They ended up socializing until closing time. Buddy was in a jovial mood throughout the night. When Somerville patrolman Ed Kelly walked in to clear the patrons out, Buddy walked up to him, smiled, and shined his badge with a napkin. He told Kelly, "That's for good luck."

Before he left the 318, Buddy phoned Jean at home and asked, "Are you hungry?"

"I could eat a little."

"Why don't you call in an order at Bobo's and I'll pick it up. I have Rico and Tony with me."

"Okay, I'll call it in."

Buddy and his bodyguards exited together. The trio began walking across Broadway toward Buddy's vehicle. As they came to the middle of the street, a young Somerville man named Richie Murnane yelled out from the doorway to Regene Pizzaria, "Hey, Buddy, young Raymond has something for you."

The three men veered off course from Buddy's car toward the pizza shop. Once inside, Buddy was handed a roll of cash from Old Man Raymond's betting agency. Young Raymond then asked Buddy, "Are you guys hungry?"

Buddy told him, "I just ordered Chinese."

"How about a drink for the road?"

Buddy accepted. After swigging their shots of whiskey, Buddy and his men said goodnight to their friends and exited the shop.

They walked up the sidewalk together, three across. Somerville police officer John Bavin was standing on the opposite side of Broadway in the doorway of the Winter Hill Grill. He watched as the men approached Buddy's car. Rico stood next to the front passenger door, Tony was by the rear passenger door. Buddy continued up the sidewalk to the front of his vehicle and began to step off the sidewalk in front of his car.

As Buddy made the turn, Stevie Hughes suddenly emerged from the dark shadows in the lobby of the abandoned Capitol Theater.

Steve Hughes

He was armed with a pump-action shotgun aimed at Buddy from twenty feet. McLean never saw it coming. He was hit in the side of his head and was slammed back onto the hood of his automobile. Sacramone's head was scalped, and he fell to the sidewalk and into the gutter. D'Agostino froze for a second, not comprehending what just happened. He was hit by the second shot in the shoulder and elbow. Buddy remained conscious long enough to pull himself upright and step toward Stevie Hughes. Hughes pumped and fired his third shot, hitting Buddy in the chest. Buddy dropped to his knees in front of his car, then slowly lay down. Hughes fired another round at the Winter Hill men, then ran back into the lobby and through the rubble behind it.

At the time of the gunfire, Richard Murnane was standing inside the Regene Pizzeria, just down the hill from the ambush. He shouted to the owner's son, young Raymond Grande, "They just got shot!"

Murnane sprinted out the door and up the street toward Buddy and his friends. He placed his leather jacket over Buddy's shoulders and back.

Bavin witnessed the attack from directly across Broadway. He radioed for help after Buddy and his men went down. During the shooting, Bavin stood frozen, less than one hundred feet from the sight. He made no attempt to chase the Charlestown man, letting him run away to a waiting vehicle on Sewall Street, which runs parallel to Broadway.

John Canty was working the midnight shift with Jimmy Reardon. They were driving John's son, Sean, home from Somerville Hospital after he received treatment for a bad strep throat. The paddy wagon they were driving was traveling up School Street toward Broadway when they heard the gunshots from about a third of a mile away. John lit the blue lights and siren, then stepped on the gas pedal. Canty turned right onto Broadway and drove down Winter Hill one block to the scene of the shooting on his left. He made a wide circular left U-turn and pulled up twenty feet away from the man lying on the street, belly down, arms folded in front, head resting on arms, legs crossed, resting, peaceful.

Sean was ordered to stay in the vehicle. The two cops jumped out and ran up.

"Oh no! It's Buddy," Canty exclaimed.

Canty checked Buddy for breathing and a pulse. He found both. Buddy was losing blood fast from his head and chest. Canty wrapped Buddy's head with a sweater. He told Reardon, "Drive him straight to Mass General. It's the only chance he has." He told his son, "Sean, get out and stand on the sidewalk."

The youngster watched as the cops loaded Buddy into the back of the paddy wagon. Before closing the back doors, Canty removed Buddy's gun from his belt. He also pulled roughly two thousand dollars in rolled cash from Buddy's pockets along with his wallet. Then he told Reardon to go. He ordered a Somerville man named Freddie Carr, who had just arrived, to drive Sean home.

Before Sean left, he asked his father, "Is Buddy going to be all right?"

"I don't know. You go home right now, and say a prayer for him."

"All right, Dad."

Sacramone and D'Agostino were taken by ambulance to Somerville Hospital. Their injuries were bad, but not life-threatening. While Reardon was driving to Boston, Canty called ahead to the hospital, alerting the emergency room to a gunshot victim who had been wounded to the head and chest. Buddy was wheeled into an emergency operating room where doctors were waiting to do whatever they could.

When she received the phone call from Arthur O'Rourke, it took a moment for Jean to grasp what happened.

"Arthur, what the hell are you talking about, I just talked to him. He's picking up Chinese food. He'll be walking in the front door any minute."

"Listen very closely, Jean. Buddy was shot when he came out of the bar. They took him to Mass General."

"Oh my god, how bad is it?"

"I think it's real bad. I'm coming over right now to drive you there. You need to get someone to watch the kids. Do you understand?"

"Yes, I'll call my mother. Hurry over." She began to cry.

Jean hollered upstairs to her oldest son, "Jimmy! Get up! Your father's been shot!"

Her voice woke all the children, but they did not comprehend what was going on until they came down the stairs and into the kitchen. They listened to their mother talking with their grandmother on the telephone.

"Ma, you have to come over to the house right now. Buddy's been shot. Hurry!"

She hung up the phone and turned to see the concerned looks from her children. Jean was crying as she pulled them all into her arms. "Nana is coming over. I have to go to the hospital. Say prayers for your father."

The children began to cry.

Jean's family swarmed the McLean house. Her mother, brothers, and sisters arrived within minutes. Jean and her sister Mary were going to ride into Boston with Arthur O'Rourke.

As Jean was about to walk out the door, her mother assured her, "Don't worry about the kids. We'll take care of them. You get to your husband."

During the ride, Jean asked, "What the hell happened?"

Arthur answered, "Someone shot Buddy and two of his men as they were getting into his car. Rico and Tony were the other two guys who got shot. Someone told Howie, and Howie called me to call you. He's going to meet us in there."

The three rushed into the emergency room and saw that Howie was already there. He hugged Jean and walked everyone into the waiting room, where they stayed waiting for an update on Buddy's condition. All of them were crying. While the doctors worked on Buddy, Somerville police officer Jimmy Reardon stood guard at the door of the operating room.

Back at the crime scene, Canty made sure that Sacramone and D'Agostino were safely loaded and shipped off to Somerville Hospital. Then he began questioning potential witnesses. One of the cops informed Canty that John Bavin had witnessed the entire shooting. Canty and a few other cops crossed Broadway to question Bavin, who had not moved from his spot.

Bavin told Canty he got a good look at the shooter, who was wearing a long, dark trench coat. "I'm almost positive it was Stevie Hughes."

"You were standing right here," Canty confirmed.

"That's right. I got a good look at him," responded Bavin.

"Then why the hell didn't you try to help them?"

"Are you crazy? Why would I want to risk my life helping those fuckin' hoodlums?"

"You cowardly, son of a bitch," Canty yelled as he lunged at Bavin and rammed him against the wall of the building. As he was about to start thundering punches into Bavin's face, the other cops jumped in and pulled Canty away.

As livid as he was with Bavin, Canty reasoned, *He's not worth it. I must get to Buddy.* He had one of the patrol cars drive him into Boston. Canty arrived at the hospital thirty minutes after the shooting. He found Jean in the waiting room. He hugged Jean and handed her Buddy's wallet and the two rolls of cash. She placed it in her pocketbook. Canty held onto Buddy's pistol. He found Jimmy Reardon in the emergency ward. The two cops stayed at the hospital and discussed the events they had just responded to. An hour later, Somerville police officer John Donovan arrived and took over guard duty outside Buddy's room. Many of Buddy's friends arrived at the hospital with prayers and hopes of survival and recovery.

As daylight rose, the Somerville police were still at the scene of the ambush. They recovered five brand-new shotgun casings from in front of the Capitol Theater. Buddy's car was still parked in the same spot. The windshield was cracked, and the hood had bloodstains on it. The sidewalk and the street around the car also had large pools of dried blood.

At Mass General Hospital, and after many hours of surgery, it was determined that Buddy had suffered irreparable brain damage. A long deprivation of oxygen was reported as the cause. The gunshot pellets caused a large amount of blood loss.

Despite having been shot in the chest, just below the heart, Buddy continued to cling to life. Doctors attributed that to his finely tuned body. After more than thirty hours, Buddy McLean succumbed.

# Reaction

Loss and chaos overwhelmed Jean McLean. Her mother and sisters gathered at Snow Terrace to care for Jean and her children. Jean's brothers, Bobby and Tommy, soon followed. A tight-knit, strong-willed Somerville family came together to mourn. The man of the house was never coming home, they all lamented.

Beyond the relatives, many neighbors and friends appeared at the house to lend a hand. The children were sent to other homes to let Jean prepare herself for the next few days, all except for Jimmy. He stayed at home to help and support his mother.

The fifteen-year-old elder son was trying to keep his composure and stay strong, knowing that is what his father would want from him. The sadness was too much to bare. He began to withdraw from the people who came to the house. He locked himself in his room or walked out of the house when company arrived.

Jimmy was always close to his uncle, Tommy Kelley, and when Tommy asked Jimmy if he could do anything for him, Jimmy replied, "Yeah, bring my friend Kevin over."

The morning after Buddy was killed, Tommy appeared at the McInnis home and conferred with Kevin's parents. They allowed Kevin to skip school that day and go with Tommy. Upon arrival at the McLean home, Kevin walked up the stairs and entered the front door alone. All the lights were off, and the shades were drawn.

"Jimmy," Kevin called.

"In here," Jimmy responded.

Kevin walked into the darkened living room, where he saw Jimmy seated in his father's chair. Jimmy McLean stood up and asked his best friend, "Do you believe what those bastards did to my father?"

The two pals met in the middle of the floor, embraced each other, and began to cry. Buddy McLean was not only worshipped by his own children; he was adored and idolized by most of the kids in Somerville.

More than two thousand people attended Buddy's wake. The line outside Kelleher's Funeral Home in Somerville went on for blocks. His family was devastated. As were his friends.

The funeral was held at a capacity-filled St. Polycarps Church in Somerville. The pallbearers were Howie Winter, Tommy Kelley, Bobby Kelley, Billy Winn, Harold Earl, "Old Man" Raymond Grande, Bobby Mahoney, Charles George, and John Hurley.

Fifty uniformed and plainclothes Somerville police officers were positioned inside and outside the church to prevent the Charlestown men from having another opportunity to kill any of Buddy's friends or associates. Nothing happened with the Townies, but as she was leaving the church, several Boston newspaper reporters and photographers came at Jean and her son Jimmy. She raised her fist and told them, "You better leave us alone or you're going to be sorry."

Buddy was buried at Holy Cross Cemetery in Malden. He was laid to rest with Mary Rapoza, the woman who raised him. Buddy's death made headlines in all the Boston newspapers and was carried on television and the radio for weeks. *Life Magazine* and *Time* did articles on the Irish gang war.

Buddy was thirty-five years old and still in tremendous physical condition on his final night.

# Revenge

Sacramone and D'Agostino survived. Sacramone would be murdered years later. It took almost a year, but the Winter Hill Gang avenged Buddy McLean's death. Joe McDonald, Joe Barboza, and another man shot and killed Connie Hughes driving north on US 1 in Revere. A few months later, Stevie Hughes and another man not connected with the McLaughlins met the same fate on Route 114 in Middleton. Joe Mac and Barboza handled this one as well. It ended Boston's Irish Gang War.

# Aftermath

## Jean McLean

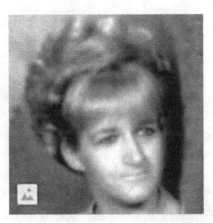

There were many hard years for Buddy's family after his passing. He did not have life insurance, except for a small amount provided by the Teamsters and the ILA. His friends set up a fundraiser for Jean and the kids. Bobby Mahoney, Sal Sperlinga, Joe McDonald, Howie Winter, and a few other friends sent cash envelopes to Jean for a few years. But eventually the help diminished.

Jean endured the years that followed with a mental toughness. She managed to raise the children, maintain the house, pay all the bills, and keep everyone together.

Sitting in her kitchen one Friday afternoon in August of 2013, Jean fondly summed up her twenty-one years with Buddy. As she sipped on a cup of tea, Jean reminisced, "He was a handsome bastard and the hardest working man I ever met. I never wanted for anything. He always made sure we were well provided for. We had our share of fights, and one time I kicked him out of the house. He was fooling around with a waitress down at Coleman's. We got married very young, and he had women coming up to him all the time. I'm sure he didn't ignore all of them. He moved in with his father for a while, but the money never stopped coming to the house. I never told him, but I think I loved him the moment I met him. He's been gone a long time, and I still love him."

Jean McLean passed away on August 7, 2017.

\* \* \*

## Jimmy McLean

After Buddy died, Jimmy shut himself off from the rest of the world. He stayed in his room reading books all day, even though he had quit high school. Not even a year after Buddy died, Jimmy, at sixteen, suddenly left home and moved to California with his best friend, Kevin McInnis. He stayed there for a little over a year before returning to Somerville, where he finished his high school education at Newman Preparatory School on Newbury Street in Boston, then he enrolled at Northeastern University.

Jimmy continued to earn high grades (straight As) in college, as he did as a youngster. Throughout those years, he was in the top one percent in grade point average for the electrical engineering program. When he graduated from Northeastern, Jimmy's cumulative average was a perfect 4.0. After college, Jimmy spent most of his days reading books in his room.

One day, in 1973, Jimmy made a phone call to Washington, DC, in hopes of speaking with President Richard M. Nixon. He managed to talk his way through the red tape, eventually getting Vice President Spiro Agnew on the phone. Their conversation began respectful and calm but soon escalated to a heated discussion as Jimmy began criticizing Agnew's and Nixon's performance in leading the country. The FBI took it as a threat and came by Snow Terrace to speak with Jimmy. When the agents showed up at the door, Jean let them in the house, but Jimmy refused to come downstairs. The three agents went up to Jimmy's room and spent an hour talking to him. After they finished the interrogation/interview and were getting ready to leave, Jean appeared at the bottom of the stairs and asked, "How'd it go?"

One of the agents replied, "Ma'am, your son is the smartest person I've ever talked to. He should be working for us. We could use a guy like him. He educated us on issues about our government and country that the Bureau never taught us. We just warned him to calm down a little and not to threaten anybody anymore. It was actually a pleasure talking to him."

In 1979, however, horrible adversity struck again. The McLeans had to grieve another heartbreaking tragedy. A week before Kellie was set to graduate from Somerville High School, the family received word that Jimmy had passed away in his apartment in Winthrop, near Revere Beach. His death brought the family back to the same state of sorrow they had felt fourteen years earlier when Buddy died.

\* \* \*

## Michael McLean

Michael took Buddy's death very hard. "When my dad died, I lost my best friend. I didn't know which way to turn. My brother took off, and I had bigger, older kids wanting to fight me every day. It was like everyone wanted to fight Buddy McLean's kid now that the 'Kingpin' was gone."

With his brother, Jimmy, on the West Coast, eleven-year-old Michael had to fend for himself. He was forced to become very tough, very fast. After the death of his father, Michael's childhood ended.

There were friends of Buddy's who would occasionally offer Michael advice. Sal Sperlinga once told Michael, "Your father was the greatest man I ever met. Be like him, and you'll do all right for yourself and your family."

Michael inherited Buddy's longshoreman's union card. He works in South Boston and lives in Winthrop with his wife, Maria. Michael is a fitness enthusiast like his Dad. He lifts weights and runs or swims every day. His daughter, Kristi, also has her ILA card, and the two have been employed together for years on the South Boston docks. Kristi is married and has a son, making Michael a grandfather.

\* \* \*

## Lea McLean

Lea was nine years old when she lost her dad. At the time, she was very sad and cried a lot. Her mother's sisters were at the house all the time, and they were very helpful, as was her grandmother. They kept the children busy with chores around the house or playing games, or just taking them out for rides to visit people. One thing that really hurt Lea was that, after her father died, some of the parents of her girlfriends would not allow their daughters to play with her.

"These were some of the same people my father used to bail out when they suffered hard times. They came to my father looking for favors or money, which they never paid back. He used to pay their rent if they fell behind or help them find work. All that was forgotten."

Lea is married to Bobby Caggiano and they have two children, Robert and Tayla. Bobby and Lea own and operate a successful business near Somerville. They live in Medford, which borders Somerville. Their kids were both excellent students and athletes in school. Lea stated several times that she sees her father's trait for working hard in her children. She claims it was their work ethic and self-discipline that led to the success they have had in school and sports.

\* \* \*

## Kellie McLean

Kellie was four when Buddy died. She remembered that her aunts and grandmother came by the house and stayed for days at a time to support Jean and the kids. Kellie spoke of her brother, Jimmy, stepping up to fill their father's role as man of the house. "When he came back from California, Jimmy graduated from high school and enrolled at Northeastern. He pushed the rest of us to stay in school and study hard."

Kellie works with her sister and brother-in-law in the family business. She lives in an apartment building in Somerville. Kellie has a handsome, hardworking son named Derek, who is a roofer living in Milford, Massachusetts. Kellie used to work out at the very same Somerville YMCA that her dad did. It is a short walk from her home. She said that, some days, she found it hard to get the workout done. "I tried to push myself on the treadmill."

The treadmill that Kellie used faced out the front window of the YMCA on Highland Avenue. Across the street, in front of someone's home, is a religious statue of the Virgin Mary. "When I felt like I couldn't go any further, I looked at that statue and, in my mind, I would talk to my father and my brother Jimmy and ask them to help me keep going and finish. And wouldn't you know, they'd come through for me every time."

Kellie went on to say, "After my father died, Jimmy and Michael argued and fought a lot. Michael didn't want Jimmy telling him what to do because he felt that Jimmy had abandoned us when he went to California. They had some terrible fistfights. My poor mother was stuck in the middle of all that."

\* \* \*

## John Canty

The big Somerville cop remained friendly with Buddy's family. He often looked in on them.

During a fight between Jimmy and Michael, a neighbor on Snow Terrace called the cops. John Canty pulled up to the house and saw Jimmy standing in the terrace with a long kitchen knife in his hand. He was arguing and pointing the knife at two Somerville patrolmen, who had both drawn their guns.

Canty immediately called to the officers, "Fellas, back away, I'll handle it."

The patrolmen complied. Canty walked slowly toward Jimmy, who was beginning to shake, and said, "Jimmy, your dad wouldn't want this. It's not the McLean way," as he held out his hand toward Jimmy.

Jimmy looked at him and said, "You're right," and handed the knife over.

As he looked Canty in the eye, Jimmy began to cry. John hugged him and said, "Let's go inside and talk for a while."

John finished his career as one of Somerville's most respected and beloved police officers. He moved his family to the oceanside town of Nahant. In retirement, he enjoyed spending time with his family and friends.

Every so often, someone would ask him a question about Buddy McLean. John would smile and proceed to share a nice story about his friend.

John Canty passed away in 2007.

\* \* \*

## The Winter Hill Gang

Under new leadership, the Winter Hill Gang went on to become more powerful and very wealthy. It was due to the foundation Buddy McLean had built almost a decade earlier. But new members came along, and they were not satisfied with Buddy's methods. They became greedy. The gang branched out and began associating with drug dealers. They also got involved in fixing horse races and extorting other gangsters. Most people who knew Buddy agree that he would have disapproved of such risky ventures, especially the drug dealing.

Fred Riley, the tough kid from Revere who sought Buddy's help in dealing with Joe Barboza, made an interesting observation. Riley, who went on to become a successful lawyer, stated, "After McLean died, Somerville and the rest of Greater Boston slowly started to crumble. It was due to the infiltration of street drugs. This was something I don't think McLean would have tolerated. I don't know if he could have stopped it, but the bad guys knew to stay away from him. He was very much respected and feared. If McLean had survived that war, Whitey Bulger and Stevie Flemmi would not have been as prominent as they became. Not with McLean around. I never knew of anyone like him, before, or since."

\* \* \*

## Howie Winter

Howie stepped up and took the reins after Buddy died. He led them through the end of the gang war. He went on to meet, help, trust, and partner up with Whitey Bulger and Steve Flemmi. This led to his demise. Howie ended up serving more than fifteen years in prison, while Bulger and Flemmi remained free and eventually took over the gang. After he served his time, Howie moved to Millbury, Massachusetts, and into semiretirement.

\* \* \*

## John Hurley

John Hurley remained a longshoreman and went back to work full-time on the docks. On the side he worked for Howie. However, when Howie went to jail, Hurley began to distance himself from the gang. Through the years, John stayed friendly with Michael McLean. When Michael inherited Buddy's ILA card, they began riding to work together.

John Hurley died in May of 2002.

\* \* \*

## Tommy Ballou

Ballou objected to the direction the gang took He did not care for the new members of the gang, nor the activities they were getting

434

into. He began to separate himself from the Somerville group and became close again with his old friends in Charlestown. The new Winter Hill men looked at Tommy as a traitor. He was shot and killed in Charlestown in 1970. The executioner was South Boston's David Glennon. Glennon was then murdered in turn.

# The Bulger Years

Eventually, memories of Buddy McLean began to fade. Newcomers Whitey Bulger and Steve Flemmi, who reportedly also doubled as FBI informants, supplanted Buddy's replacement, Howie Winter and the rest of the original crew. Bulger and Flemmi not only ratted on their associates, they also helped eradicate Jerry Angiulo and his North End group.

\* \* \*

## Joe McDonald

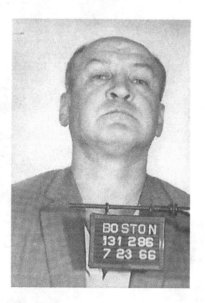

McDonald had been hiding for several years. However, during the 1970s he thought about reestablishing himself on Winter Hill. Worried that Joe Mac might try to take over the gang, Bulger helped the FBI build a case to put Joe back in prison, where he went for five more years. When he was released, Joe Mac was still unaware of Bulger's betrayal. Nonetheless, Joe Mac did not like nor trust Bulger and Flemmi. He decided to retire. But first, Joe wanted to collect all the money that was owed to him while he was locked up.

One afternoon, Joe walked into the Rotary Liquors, in South Boston. Bulger, Flemmi, and a few of their underlings were sitting at a table in the back of the establishment. The two bosses welcomed their former Winter Hill partner with exuberant greetings. Joe Mac's distaste for the underhanded pair made for little patience with them. He got right down to business.

"I came for my money," stated Joe.

"What money?" Bulger asked arrogantly.

"Shut up and listen. If you don't have my money, tomorrow, every penny, I will kill everyone in here."

Nobody at the table said a word until Joe Mac left. One of Bulger's young ruffians spoke first and said, "He can't come in here and talk that shit. Who the fuck does he think he is? Let me kill him. I'll fuckin' kill him right now."

Flemmi spoke next. "You are not going to kill Joe McDonald. He will capture you and torture you until you die. When Joe McDonald says he's going to do something, he will. I say we pay him and be done with it."

The young soldier replied, "That little old fuck isn't gonna—"

"You shut the fuck up, right now," interrupted Bulger. He looked at Stevie, nodded in agreement, and said, "Pay him."

The DEA (Drug Enforcement Agency) had been secretly recording the conversation.

The next day, Steve Flemmi knocked at Joe Mac's front door. He had two suitcases with him. Joe opened the door.

He looked at the suitcases, then said to Flemmi, "If it's right, you won't be hearing from me."

"Don't worry, Joe. It's right," promised Flemmi.

Joe did not acknowledge him. He grabbed the bags from Flemmi. Then, without another word, the "Real Boss" of Winter Hill closed the door.

Joe Mac went into semiretirement. He had more money than he would ever need. He maintained some small dealings, real estate investments, small businesses, and personal loans.

Buddy's longtime friend Jackie Mansfield aided the seventy-year-old Joe Mac by watching his back in case the Bulger group decided to sneak up on "Uncle Joe."

"It never happened," said Jackie, "and it's a good thing for them, because we were always ready. That was Joe, ready and waiting for them. He liked to take long walks. We'd leave his house on Marshall Street and head over to the Ten Hills and walk along the Mystic River. He never said much. It was small talk, like the weather, sports, and sometimes current events. He loved boxing and he liked to talk about the current and old-time boxers. He never talked about his past or too much about his family. He never mentioned Bulger or Flemmi, and I knew enough about Joe to not bring it up. If Joe wanted to tell me something about those guys, or any others, I would just listen and not ask questions. That's the way he was, and there was no changing him.

"Most of the time, Joe would sit with friends or relatives and listen to their stories while twiddling his thumbs. When he wanted to tell you something, he'd grab your arm and squeeze real hard. Then he'd look you in the eye and convey his advice, which may last only ten seconds. But it was a message you weren't going to forget. Whenever Buddy McLean's name came up, Joe's eyes would redden and water. He loved Buddy. He never said much about him, but he always made one statement. 'Buddy McLean was the best friend I ever had and the greatest man I ever met.'"

A few years later, Joe McDonald took a bad fall as he was climbing the front steps of his house. After being rushed to Somerville Hospital for emergency treatment, he was admitted to the Edith Nourse Rogers Memorial Veterans Hospital, in Bedford, Massachusetts. Joe slipped in and out of consciousness for months. When he finally regained semiconscious, Joe Mac was still unable to leave the hospital due to extreme brain damage.

Five years of low-quality life followed, most of it spent in the rest home. Conversations with the boss of Winter Hill were sparse and without emotion, except when the name Buddy McLean was brought up. A sad smile would appear and a slow shake of his head. Then a few words were slowly mentioned in a soft voice, "My best friend in this world."

Buddy McLean's best friend and mentor died in the Bedford hospital.

* * *

## Sal Sperlinga

About seven years after Buddy died, Sal found out that Lea was going to marry a young Somerville man named Bobby Caggiano. Sal stopped by the McLean house and asked Jean if the Winter Hill Gang was going to pay for the wedding.

"I'm not sure."

"I'll look into it."

Sal drove over to Marshall Motors, the headquarters for the Winter Hill Gang. Howie Winter then owned the Marshall

Street building diagonally across from the side entrance to Pal Joey's Lounge, which used to be called the 318 Club and just a couple of doors down the street from Joe McDonald's house. Sal walked into the repair shop and through the garage to the back office, where the new boss and a few others were sitting around a table dividing up thousands of dollars in stacks of cash.

After saying hello to everyone, Sal got right to the point for his visit. "Buddy McLean is the reason you guys have all this money. His daughter is getting married soon, and they need your help. Anybody have a problem with that?"

Newcomers Whitey Bulger and Stevie Flemmi did not speak. Howie replied gently, "You're absolutely right, Sal. Go ahead."

Sal proceeded to collect an equal amount from each man's stack and place it in a brown paper bag that he found in the office. As he was getting ready to leave, Sal reminded the crew, "Let's not forget him. He would've done the same thing for you."

Howie saw to it that the wedding was paid for.

Shortly after he had started dating Lea, Sal gave Bobby Caggiano a bit of advice. As he was walking along a Somerville street one afternoon, Sal pulled up in his car next to Bobby.

"Cag," hollered Sal. "Hold on. I want to talk to you."

Bobby had known Sal for many years. He was aware of Sal's reputation as an exceptionally strong and tough individual. He acknowledged Sal to be a man of honor and loyalty. Sal was also a very serious man who did not beat around the bush. Bobby tried being friendly.

"What's up, Sal? How are you doing?"

Sal did not answer. He got out of his car, marched up to Bobby, grabbed him by the arm, and continued forward down a tight alley between two buildings.

With only inches separating their faces, Sal began, "That girl you're seeing, do you know who her father was?"

"Yeah, of course I do."

"Do you think I'm a man?"

"What?"

"Do you think I am a MAN?"

"Yes, of course I do, Sal."

As his eyes watered, Sal told Bobby, "Yeah, well I'm not one-tenth the man that her father was. You better treat her right. You got that?"

"Yes, Sal. Absolutely."

A few years later, in Magoun Square, Sal saw a young Somerville man dealing drugs on the sidewalk, just outside the shop where he had his football betting cards printed. Sal walked up to the dealer, Danny Moran, grabbed him by the collar, and told him, "I don't want any of your shit being sold around here. You got that?"

"Fuck you, Sal. If it's not me, then someone else is going to. So go fuck yourself."

With that, Sal slammed Moran in the face. The drug dealer went down, and Sal fired three more bombs into his face. He still had Moran by the collar. Sal pulled him up to a seated position and said, "If I see you doing this again, I'm gonna fuckin' kill you," and blasted him again, then he walked back inside.

The very next day, Sal was playing cards with some friends in Magoun Square. The front door to the shop opened, and in walked Danny Moran. Sal asked him, "What the fuck do you want?"

Moran did not answer. Instead, he pulled a pistol from his pocket and pointed it at Sal. He squeezed the trigger, but the gun jammed. Sal lifted the table and threw it at Moran. Everyone in the room scattered. Sal ran toward the back, but there was no way out. Moran cleared the gun and shot Sal in the back. He died a few hours later.

\* \* \*

## The Ballad of Buddy McLean

In October 1998, an Irish folk singer named Derek Warfield released a song he wrote and performed called "The Ballad of Buddy McLean." In a smooth Irish brogue, Warfield recalls the life and death of McLean. Though the song never became popular outside of Greater Boston, it tells Buddy's story in a nice melody with lyrics fit for a folk hero

# Author's note

Research for this book began in 2007. Many friends of Buddy had passed away by then. Most of those still alive declined to be interviewed. The folks who did cooperate helped provide a detailed insight of a historic, violent time in the city of Boston.

During my research, I noticed that many of Boston's senior citizens tend to forget or never knew much about the originator of the Winter Hill Gang. It is sad that younger generations never learned about him.

He was a well-built, super-tough Irishman who worked hard his entire life. He broke the law many times, but was generous to a fault. He was smart and very protective of his family, of his friends, and of his reputation as the best street fighter Boston has ever seen. There are more than a few valuable old-school lessons of life that can be learned from Buddy McLean.

# Review Requested:

If you loved this book, would you please provide a review at Amazon.com?

CPSIA information can be obtained
at www.ICGtesting.com
Printed in the USA
BVHW071445090222
628492BV00005B/131